Routledge Revivals

THE SIXTEENTH CENTURY

THE SIXTEENTH CENTURY

by

SIR CHARLES OMAN

K.B.E., H ON . D.C.L. OXON. AND HON . LL.D. CAMBRIDGE AND EDINBURGH,
F.B.A.
FELLOW OF ALL SOULS COLLEGE, OXFORD, GHICHELE
PROFESSOR OF MODERN HISTORY IN
THE UNIVERSITY OF OXFORD

First published in 1936 by Greenwood Press

This edition first published in 2018 by Routledge
2 Park Square, Milton Park, Abingdon, Oxon, OX14 4RN

and by Routledge
711 Third Avenue, New York, NY 10017

Routledge is an imprint of the Taylor & Francis Group, an informa business

© 1936 Taylor & Francis

All rights reserved. No part of this book may be reprinted or reproduced or utilised in any form or by any electronic, mechanical, or other means, now known or hereafter invented, including photocopying and recording, or in any information storage or retrieval system, without permission in writing from the publishers.

Publisher's Note
The publisher has gone to great lengths to ensure the quality of this reprint but points out that some imperfections in the original copies may be apparent.

Disclaimer
The publisher has made every effort to trace copyright holders and welcomes correspondence from those they have been unable to contact.
A Library of Congress record exists under ISBN: 37001801

ISBN 13: 978-1-138-55579-2 (hbk)
ISBN 13: 978-1-138-56731-3 (pbk)
ISBN 13: 978-1-315-12422-3 (ebk)

THE SIXTEENTH CENTURY

THE SIXTEENTH CENTURY

by

SIR CHARLES OMAN

K.B.E., Hon. D.C.L. Oxon. and Hon. LL.D. Cambridge and Edinburgh, F.B.A.

FELLOW OF ALL SOULS COLLEGE, OXFORD, CHICHELE PROFESSOR OF MODERN HISTORY IN THE UNIVERSITY OF OXFORD

GREENWOOD PRESS, PUBLISHERS
WESTPORT, CONNECTICUT

Library of Congress Cataloging in Publication Data

Oman, Charles William Chadwick, Sir, 1860-1946.
  The sixteenth century.

  Reprint of the 1936 ed. published by Methuen,
London.
    1. Europe—History—1517-1648. 2. Europe—History
—1492-1517.
D228.O45 1975   940.2'32   75-25517
ISBN 0-8371-8118-6

All rights reserved

First published in 1936 by Methuen & Co. Ltd., London

Reprinted by arrangement with Methuen & Co. Ltd.

Reprinted in 1975 by Greenwood Press,
a division of Williamhouse-Regency Inc.

Library of Congress Catalog Card Number 75-25517

ISBN 0-8371-8118-6

Printed in the United States of America

PREFACE

WHEN one has been for four years studying the chronicles, autobiographies, diaries, letters, pamphlets and state papers of a period for a given object of a specialistic sort, there remains with one a general impression of the time, over and above the particular items of information for which one has been seeking. I have long been working out the military history of the sixteenth century—a sufficiently broad and interesting topic—and while completing this task have had to read through countless pages in which the military details are inextricably mixed up with non-military matters which cannot be forgotten. Often some one precious detail of war lurks in the middle of a book of the most unlikely description. After turning over tens of thousands of leaves in Latin, French, Italian, German, English, Spanish and Dutch print, one is left with an accumulation of observed phenomena—religious, cultural, literary, psychological—which the mind is forced to co-ordinate into some sort of general conclusions. As I have stated in some of the pages which follow this preface, I am profoundly averse to formulating ' philosophies of history ', and though I feel impelled to put in order the impressions which much reading and pondering have left with me, I do not pretend to link these impressions into any theory of evolution. There are as many ' ifs ' in history as ' therefores '. The phenomena are always interesting, often contradictory, like the strands of thought and behaviour in an individual human being. I set down my conclusions for what they are worth—though perhaps, as the Preacher remarks, ' of making many books there is no end, and much study is a weariness of the flesh '. But the sixteenth century was a wonderful time.

C. OMAN

OXFORD,
   March, 1936.

CONTENTS

CHAP.		PAGE
	PREFACE	v
I	ON LOOKING FORWARD AND LOOKING BACKWARD	1
II	LOST ILLUSIONS: THE PAPACY AND THE HOLY ROMAN EMPIRE	16
III	THE END OF THE FIFTEENTH CENTURY	31
IV	MAN AND THE UNIVERSE IN THE SIXTEENTH CENTURY	41
V	TENDENCIES AND INDIVIDUALS. THE POPES AND THE KINGS OF FRANCE	62
VI	TENDENCIES AND INDIVIDUALS. CHARLES V AND PHILIP II	81
VII	TENDENCIES AND INDIVIDUALS. HENRY VIII OF ENGLAND	98
VIII	TENDENCIES AND INDIVIDUALS. GUSTAVUS VASA AND SCANDINAVIAN PROTESTANTISM	111
IX	THE OPPORTUNISTS GREAT AND SMALL. ELIZABETH AND CATHERINE DE MEDICI AND OTHERS	128
X	THE TURKISH DANGER, 1520–71	142
XI	THE WARS OF THE SIXTEENTH CENTURY: (a) THE ITALIAN WARS, (b) THE 'WARS OF RELIGION'	173
XII	THE OCCULT IN THE SIXTEENTH CENTURY	212
	INDEX	241

CHAPTER I

ON LOOKING FORWARD AND LOOKING BACKWARD

'I AM an Englishman, and cannot generalize.' There is a great deal of truth in this simple declaration of incapacity, used as a defensive counterblast to the facile power of drawing plausible systems of logic or philosophy from masses of heterogeneous facts, which is the pride of our Latin and Teutonic neighbours. We *are* individualists and opportunists both in thought and in action—dislike general propositions and love exceptions, believe in things practical, have no objection to compromises, are content to 'get on somehow', or 'to muddle through', being, as the Frenchman said, 'sans logique mais grands improvisateurs'.

This is as true in the study of history as in other spheres of human activity. It is better to show *how* things happened than to pontificate on why they happened. On causes one may have one's opinions, but it is unwise to declare that the opinions of other people are wholly wrong, inadequate or misguided. What seems to one student of history the main guiding influence of a period, may appear to another as a mere subsidiary impulse of only secondary importance. When one is dealing with vast and complicated phenomena, such as the fall of the Roman Empire, the Crusades, the Renaissance (whatever exactly that word may mean), the Reformation, or the French Revolution and its consequences, or the aftermath of the Great War of 1914-18, the only safe thing is to accumulate evidence, not to start with generalizations, and to ignore the tiresome phenomena which do not fit easily into them. Often one gets an impression that the most important factors of all have been missed by observers, on account of their personal prepossessions, since no man stresses the existence of facts which tell against his own theory. Yet to expatiate on the more obscure tendencies is a dangerous game, and may end in giving them an importance which they did not possess in the period with which the student is dealing. Most perilous of all is it to fall a victim to phrases, and to endeavour to link up all history on catchwords, such as Evolution, Progress, or Democracy.

Whenever I run upon a writer whose work is full of abstract general terms such as Liberty or Anarchy, ' Immutable ideas of Morality ', Natural Man, the State and its rights, Nationalism or Internationalism, Orthodoxy or Free Thought, I know that I have come upon a propagandist, and must go warily in accepting either his premises or his conclusions. Wherefore the popular phrases about the ' Philosophy of History ' leave me very cold. And I know no more wholesome epigram than that which declares that ' the exercise of political prophecy is the most futile of all the activities of the human brain '. I shall long remember a discussion which I held in October 1918 with a Russian and a Yugoslav friend—both most intelligent persons in official positions—as to what would happen after the collapse of the German army, then obviously impending. Every prognostication which we made as to the future of Europe has gone more or less wrong.

Generally, those who indulge in political prophecy have some special hobby of their own, or some ' axe to grind ', and hope to persuade their audience of the inevitability of some coming event, which will justify their interested forecast. For to make others believe that a thing will occur is a useful help to making its occurrence possible. In these matters prophecy founded on historical analogies is the most perilous venture of all. I can remember solemn statements, made when I was very young, that the French Republic of 1870 would end within ten years in a military dictatorship—after the style of Napoleon Bonaparte. And a similar statement as to the inevitable end of the Soviet Republic in Russia had many attractions a few years ago. But analogies are never complete, and things do not happen as they should.

On Looking Forward and Backward 3

The fact is that History is not a tale of logical processes, or necessary evolution, but a series of happenings—some of them so startling as to deserve to be called cataclysms. One studies these happenings with a cautious conviction that they *might* have happened otherwise, and that no word is so dangerous as the word 'inevitable'. This book deals with aspects of the sixteenth century, but Heaven forbid that I should call it an explanation of the Renaissance or the Reformation—those convenient but question-begging names. I disclaim any wish to fit the phenomena of that strange period into any sort of political philosophy, theory of progress, or scheme of evolution. Some of my observations may perhaps be called 'glimpses of the obvious', others may be ruled to deal with side-shows of no permanent importance. Nevertheless, these 'glimpses of the obvious' seem often to have escaped the notice of historians, and these 'side-shows' had their importance in their day, and may (forgotten though they be) have left some interesting traces behind them even down to this twentieth century.

First, as a fundamental proposition—it sounds dangerously like one of those generalizations which I deprecate—we must recognize that we have come in the sixteenth century to a dividing line in human thought, the period at which mankind ceased to be looking back to an imaginary Golden Age in the Past, and began to look forward to an equally imaginary Golden Age in the Future. The fifteenth century saw the dismal end of medieval conceptions of the world; the seventeenth century was essentially modernist, so far as the leading minds were concerned. Between them lies the period of change and transformation. I do not (of course) wish to pin myself down to the crude dates 1500 and 1600—there were plenty of signs of movement before 1500, and plenty of survivals of old conceptions after 1600. But the main statement is indisputable.

There was a change in the historical perspective of the civilized world which falls into this century. One has to look back a thousand years to find any parallel to such a general change. I am not sure that one would be justified in saying that, if one went forward four hundred years from 1500, there has been another fundamental change in the perspective of the civilized world in our own day—still in process, I will not say progress, for that in its usual modern sense is a question-begging word.

To explain what I mean by a change in historical perspective, I must hark back for a moment from the year 1500 to speak of the age when the last great change had taken place. And I shall presently have to look forward from 1600 to speak of the age that was coming after the critical central hundred years had gone by. In 1500 we are not yet quite out of the period in which two great inspiring theories of world-government were still alive. I mean the theories of the Holy Roman Empire and of the Papacy. Historians and statesmen were still viewing the history of the world with more or less reference to these ideals. Only unorthodox thinkers dared to condemn utterly the theory of either, though criticism of their practical working was as common as it was justifiable.

The moment that man begins to think about something more than the passing trifles and troubles of his daily life, and starts consciously or unconsciously to reflect about himself and his neighbours, their ends and their objects, their past and future, he has begun to look at things in perspective. And when he extends his survey so as to draw deductions from what he knows of the past records of his family, his tribe, his nation, or the neighbouring tribes and nations, he is beginning to look at the world in *historical* perspective. It may be that his knowledge extends by oral tradition over no greater space of time than a generation or two—' tales of a grandfather' may be the limit of his reflections. Or, on the other hand, he may think that he knows the whole history of mankind from the Creation—if he ties himself down to the idea of a creation—down to the all-important present day. Such was the happy conviction of Orosius in A.D. 417, when he sat down to write his Christian history of the world, and such is the belief of Mr. H. G. Wells to-day, when he writes his agnostic history of the world, with equal self-confidence to that of Orosius.

On Looking Forward and Backward

But whether his horizon of knowledge be long or short, whether it be founded on Archbishop Ussher's chronology, or extends back for a hundred aeons to the vague first appearance of *homo sapiens*, the man who has started to consider world-history is constructing for himself a historical perspective.

The average intelligent man (not a professional historian) of 1500—whether French, English, Italian or German—had a completely different historical perspective from that of his great-grandson of 1600. But how far was that the result of the complex cultural changes which (for want of a better word) we call the Renaissance, or of the broadening of the world by the discovery of America and the Indies, or of countless discoveries in science, which made an end of the all-dominating geocentric theory of the universe? Or was it, again, mainly the result of that great spiritual outburst which (again for want of a better word) we call the Reformation? I make no general conclusion, but have countless incidental indications to record.

The fundamental conception of the world held by the ordinary educated West European of 1500 had its origins in the last great cataclysm which had affected the civilized world—the conquest of the Roman Empire by Christianity. It was essentially a Christian outlook, and it had settled down of late into a very pessimistic outlook—almost as pessimistic as that of an old Pagan Roman of the period 320–420 who had seen Christianity triumph, refused to accept it, but had little hope for the future. I mean such a person as the unfortunate Emperor Julian the Apostate, who died—as the legend goes—muttering '*Vicisti Galilaee*', conscious that his fight against the tendency of his day had been futile.

Pessimism is a most ancient and universal creed. Impressed by the tales told them by their respected grandparents, most men have been prone to think (with Horace and Hesiod and the authors of the *Good Old English Gentleman* and the Deserted Village) that we are a degenerate race. All over the world, from China to Peru, nations have been content to believe in the 'Golden Age', the 'Good Old

Times', which have ceased owing to the perversity of the younger generations. Our ancestors were divine or semi-divine. They walked the earth thirty feet high like the Moses of the Talmud, they lived three hundred, four hundred or seven hundred years like Methusaleh. They could, like Homer's Hector, hurl a stone which scarce two of the strongest of modern men, straining hard, could tear from the soil. They were descended from the gods—whether Zeus or Odin. And the land on which they lived was a more genial clime than ours, which produced three harvests a year, and flowed with milk and honey. By some ancestral fault—because Pandora had opened the fateful box that let evils loose, or because Adam and Eve had eaten the forbidden apple, or because some ancestor had shown a fatal curiosity, or broken an ancestral taboo, progressive decay has fallen on the human race. Hesiod formalized the conception for the ancient Hellenic world into the scheme of the 'Five Ages' each worse than that which preceded it, till mankind has slipped from the Golden Age, through those of silver and bronze, into the age of iron, in which poor mortals had finally to dwell.

Passed on, I suppose, from Greece to Rome, and by pagan Roman tradition into the Christian 'Dark Ages', the conception was as popular fifteen centuries after the death of Christ as it had been ten centuries before His birth. And the most pessimistic spirits finished it off with the *Septima Aetas Mundi*, which was to see Antichrist's coming, the Last Judgement, and the destruction of the world, all not so very far ahead. For men were growing steadily worse, as austere minds conceived—the days of the saints were long over, and each generation thinks that its own particular sins are so startling that retribution from on high cannot be long delayed. This conception has cropped up at intervals all through Christian times : I can remember myself a very eloquent and popular preacher, Dr. Cumming, who taught that the Victorian age was so sinful that the well-merited destruction of the world was due about 1872, and he discovered in events of the 1860's all the premonitory signs to be found in the Book of Revela-

On Looking Forward and Backward 7

tions. What a chance he would have had to-day ! Lenin and Hitler would have suited his thesis far better than Napoleon III and Pope Pius IX, in whom he vainly fancied that he could detect indications that were to develop into Antichrist and the 'False Prophet' !

This particular form of Christian pessimism started very early—almost as soon as Christianity had conquered the Roman Empire, and had found that by its conquest it had inherited all the problems of a great civilization that was in its decay. Between A.D. 320 and A.D. 420 the whole outlook of the world changed. There was never such a complete alteration of moral and political values in such a short time, before or since—though the phenomena of the sixteenth and the nineteenth centuries were sufficiently startling. But the break between the old Roman pagan culture and the new Christian culture was far more sudden and complete. Imagine Cicero, Horace, or Tacitus faced by the problems of Original Sin, Justification by Faith, or the precise definition of the Doctrine of the Trinity as the all-absorbing intellectual problems of mankind—and incidentally problems having some importance in practical politics—at a moment when the Empire was being assailed from without by a storm of barbarian invasion far more perilous than that which Marius had turned back in the last century of the Republic, or Claudius Gothicus and his successors in the third century of the Empire !

It is hard to realize the cataclysmic change made in mental outlook of an educated citizen of the Roman Empire by the synchronism in one troublous century of the crash of the old religion with the crash of the military defences of the Mediterranean world. Paganism, it is true, had become a hollow façade ; no one but children, as Juvenal cynically remarked, had much belief in the old gods and their shady morality, or felt that the official religion had much connexion with right or wrong. Mars and Jupiter were as dead as Cincinnatus or Cato, or any of the other traditional exponents of the ancient Roman spirit. And absurd as was the old mythology, there was something still more absurd in the formal institution of Caesar-Worship, with which officialdom had tried to bolster up the waning cause of religion. To bow down before the 'Numen Augusti' or the 'Genius Caesaris', and to style the emperor of the day 'Deus et Dominis Noster' in the style of some third-century coins and inscriptions, was a blasphemous farce, when the divine personage was known to be a miserable, licentious degenerate like Elagabalus, or a vulgar, illiterate soldier of mixed breed like Maximinus I. All that hypocrisy had to go—it was completely worn out, and satisfied the moral aspirations of no single man of common honesty. But it was a terrible jar to those reared in the old system to accept the incoming system of Christianity, with its morality which was obviously superior to any conception of the older Roman world, but imposed a new category of virtues and vices, which the man in the street found it difficult to work in with his sordid daily life. 'Blessed are the meek' and 'Blessed are the merciful' sounded strangely to those accustomed to the pompous ostentation of the Imperial system, and the countless statues and reliefs representing the Roman trampling down dying enemies—still more to a generation that still gloated over the bloody sports of the arena, where prisoners were thrown to the beasts, or hirelings paid to kill each other in duel—with copious betting on the event among thousands of interested spectators. It was one of the greatest triumphs of Christianity when that devoted monk Telemachus [A.D. 405] threw himself down into the arena between the contending gladiators, to meet death by brutal violence, but also to give such a shock to public opinion that the Government had to put an end to those horrid exhibitions. It should be remarked that this happened in A.D. 405, long after Christian had superseded pagan emperors upon the throne. Christian morality had taken years to conquer old-established brutality in such an obviously unrighteous practice. No doubt gladiatorial shows were far more exciting to the average carnal man than the horse races, acrobatic displays, and pageantry which remained as the only substitutes.

But the clash of moralities in the fourth century, as I said before, synchronized with the breakdown of the

On Looking Forward and Backward 9

external defences of the empire, and the irruption of the Goth and Hun into the lands of the old civilization. Some of the last pagan philosophers tried to argue that the downfall of the Roman régime was the direct consequence of the spread of Christianity—a religion for slaves and what we should now call 'pacifists'. In this very natural hypothesis they erred, for the empire was already ripe for its fall before Constantine. And the real diseases were bureaucracy, over-taxation, the lack of local patriotism in the provinces, of any decent nucleus of citizens in Rome itself (there was nothing left save a subservient Senate and the cosmopolitan *faex Romuli*), and perhaps, most fatal of all, the gradual supersession of the old national army—the legions—by innumerable new corps of mercenary barbarians. The *Notitia Dignitatum*, the guide-book to the army and civil service at the end of the fourth century, shows the old legions degraded into garrison troops, and dominated by the alien elements. There was no longer a national army, and the numbers of the whole armed force were inadequate for the defence of a frontier reaching from the Northumbrian Wall to the further border of Mesopotamia, when special stress came upon all points simultaneously; when to the Persian and the Pict on the flanks there was added the central thrust of all the migrant Germanic tribes, Saxons, Franks, Alamanni, Vandals, Burgundians and Goths—with the dreadful impelling force of the Hun pushing them on from behind. A pagan empire would have crumbled as inevitably as did the Christian empire under the weak sons of Theodosius and their successors—perhaps even more rapidly.

The enormity of the change in man's outlook on the world which came from the crash of the Roman Empire was felt most acutely at the time. Orosius wrote his immense general history about 417, at the request of St. Augustine, to demonstrate to Christian Romans that every one had misjudged the story of mankind. From the earliest records of the East down to the Gothic invasions of his own day, man had been a sinful being, vexed from time to time by wars and disasters. Empires had crumpled up, nations been exterminated, all down the centuries. Rome was now undergoing the fate of Babylon or Persia—the Roman Empire had only had a longer existence than the old oriental monarchies. Salvation was for the individual soul, not for the race or the state. Sin was the dominating fact in the world, and sin involved chastisement by a just God. Man must look after his own soul—and by the grace of God might preserve it—but there was no guarantee of salvation for a man merely because he was a citizen of the Roman Empire, or even because he was a baptized Christian. Whether salvation was to be gained mainly by faith or mainly by works, or by the fiat of the Divinity unconditioned by mere faith or works, was another problem ; and that problem was to be discussed by the Christian world down to our own day.

For more than a thousand years onward from the days of Orosius and Augustine, Christian Europe had, as a whole, a perspective in which Sin and Grace were the dominating factors. And the salvation of one's own soul and the souls of others was the all-absorbing task of righteous men. The ordained instrument of salvation was the Church, and in comparison with the Church earthly kingdoms, which were usually fleeting and ephemeral, were of comparatively minor importance. The old idea of the 'diuturnity' of the Roman Empire was superseded by the new idea of the diuturnity of the Church. What were kingdoms like those of the Ostrogoths in Italy, the Vandals in Africa, the Visigoths in Spain, the Burgundians, or the Lombards, but things of a few generations or a few centuries, which vanished away ? The Church might be rent by Arian and Trinitarian disputes, by schisms between East and West, by local heresies, but by divine providence it was to continue, as the prop of the universe. Temporal kingdoms were comparatively unimportant.

We, in this broad sketch, are of course concerned only with the Church of the West—Byzantine history is another story. And by the time at which we wish to arrive, the sixteenth century, the history of the Western Church had become a melancholy tale, even sad enough to make pious

On Looking Forward and Backward

men doubt of the fundamentals. I am not thinking of earlier days of sorrow, as when in the seventh and eighth centuries the wave of Mohammedan fanaticism submerged the Christian east and south, left but a remnant of Christians in old citadels of the faith like Syria and Egypt, exterminated the Church of Africa completely, drove Christianity in Spain into the remotest mountains, and swept for a moment to the walls of Constantinople and the centre of France. Nor do I mean the tenth century, when the Viking from the north and the Hungarian from the east made their terrifying but more transient inroads into the main block of Christendom, and when the bishops of Rome became a series of disreputable adventurers from local baronial families.

Rather am I thinking of the profound disillusion that followed in a much later age, the one that immediately preceded that crucial sixteenth century which forms the main subject of our discussion. This state of mind was much more depressing than the terror which had been felt in the Dark Ages, when it had seemed sometimes possible that Christendom might collapse under the attack of external enemies like the Saracen or the Viking. From those perils Christendom had fought itself free, thanks to Charles Martel and Leo the Isaurian, and minor heroes like King Alfred and Otto the Great. Indeed, Christendom had so re-established its predominance that it had been able to re-assume the offensive against the outer enemy, both in the spiritual and in the military sphere. Most of the Iberian peninsula had been won back from the Moor, so had Sicily and Sardinia ; the Byzantine emperors had recovered Crete and Cyprus and Cilicia from the degenerate Caliphate, which had broken up into jarring fragments. But what was more important, the spiritual offensive had been far more effective than the sword. The Scandinavian kingdoms and the intrusive band of Magyars on the Middle-Danube had accepted the faith, and come into the bond of Christendom : so had the slowly coalescing Polish kingdom : all these were the conquests of the devoted missionaries of the Western Church. And, meanwhile, the Eastern Church had made a similar spiritual conquest of the Russians. By the middle of the eleventh century all the old perils of extermination seemed to have come to an end, and the territorial area of Christendom, east and west and north, had been doubled or even tripled. And internal conditions in the Church seemed to be improving : the scandals of the tenth-century bishops of Rome had come to an end, when the series of unsavoury Johns had been succeeded by respectable pontiffs—largely German at first. The lax monasticism of the Dark Ages had been tightened up by rules imposed by enthusiasts who could dominate the minds of their contemporaries. The culmination of this period of hope was in the Crusades—which were essentially a religious movement in their inception, however much motives of a less idealistic kind inspired many of those who went forth upon them. Along with the genuine pilgrims who sallied out to deliver the Holy Sepulchre there were those who, like the citizens of the Italian naval republics and the Normans of Sicily, looked upon the Crusades as a great venture for naval domination and commercial exploitation in the Levant. And there were military adventurers from all over Europe, the cadets and younger sons of all the noble houses of the feudal West, who dreamed of fiefs and castles in the wealthy lands of the Orient, far more than of spiritual profit.

Nevertheless, the Crusades were both originally inspired by, and maintained for centuries on, a religious motive. A cynical commentator has called them ' the foreign policy of the Papacy '. But this is a very partial view of the situation—Popes (no doubt) sometimes preached a Crusade to distract the minds of pious people from topics of a more domestic and purely political kind, and to put their enemies in the odious position of being found ' fighting against God and the Church ' if they refused to favour the venture. It was always a good card to play against recalcitrant emperors. But the crusading motive was genuine all the same ; the Popes believed in the essential righteousness of the keeping of the Holy Places in Christian hands, or of recovering them after they had been lost : and the strength of their appeal to the Western world was that all orthodox people, small and great, were of that same opinion. To excuse oneself from going on a crusade for rather inadequate reasons was mean and selfish. That the Crusades went on for more than three centuries—we cannot say that they ended before Nicopolis (1396) or even Varna (1444)—is a proof of the reality of the essential motive, though individuals who went on purely religious convictions, like St. Louis of France, who sacrificed all political advantages to the ideal, were less numerous than those who had private personal reasons for the venture. To recover Jerusalem remained as an inspiration for an orthodox prince far into the fifteenth century—it hovered about the death-bed of Henry V, and was seriously considered as a motive by the romantic mind of Charles VIII of France, even Francis I, when young, feigned interest in a notion now grown hopeless. That it was hopeless by 1493 is one of the things on which we must lay stress, when we consider the outlook of Christian Europe on the eve of the sixteenth century. Yet the idea lingered on in a few pious minds for many a year longer. In the middle of the awful chaos of the 'Wars of Religion' that worthy Protestant soldier and philosopher, La Noue of the Iron Arm, devoted a chapter of his commentaries to a splendid dream of a joint attack on the Turk by the united forces of a reconciled tolerant Christendom, when a Spanish, French and Venetian fleet should break through the Dardanelles, and a German, Netherland and French army, headed by Henry of Navarre and Alexander of Parma (!), should cross the Danube and advance to the gates of Constantinople. Unfortunately his contemporaries were not prepared to take the scheme seriously. Protestant and Catholic hated each other even more than they hated the Turk.

But the Crusading idea had died out long before its last echo can be found in the commentaries of La Noue. Many things had combined to sap the strength of the Crusading motive. Primarily, no doubt, we have to recognize that the long-continued activity in the Levant had been a failure in the end. Jerusalem had been finally lost in 1244, after having been once recovered in 1229. The long-surviving line of fortresses and commercial ports along the

Syrian coast had fallen one by one into the hands of the Mameluke sultans of Egypt—Antioch and Jaffa in 1268, Tripoli in 1289, Acre, the vital point of all trade, in 1291. Abandoning their last few sea-castles, the Franks gave up the game and retired by sea. Of all the great conquests of the earlier crusades nothing was left but the isle of Cyprus— and that had been won not from the Saracen, but from the unfortunate Christians of the Eastern Church. The episode of the attempt by the Western Church to master the Holy Places had come to a disastrous end.

But no less fatal to the vitality of the Crusading idea was the fact that the name of Crusade, originally attributed to the idealistic end of recovering the Holy Places of Palestine, had been diverted to other less obviously appealing undertakings. Not only had it been used to cover other enterprises against the heathen at large, notably the attempt of the Teutonic knights to annex not only Prussia but the much larger Lithuania, which was but a half success, for Lithuania remained pagan despite of the Crusaders. But the name Crusade had also been misused for enterprises against Christians; it had covered the assault on the Albigenses, who were Christians if heretics, and (a still greater crime) the greedy adventurers of the Fourth Crusade had, in 1204, sacked and annexed Constantinople, the central nucleus of the Eastern Church. The reigning Pope, Innocent III, had at first protested against this misuse of force, but had ended by condoning the offence, because it gave an apparent opportunity for uniting the lands of the Eastern Church to the Western obedience, though the method had been detestable. This dream had faded away—the Greeks reconquered Constantinople in 1261: the Balkan peoples, thanks to the activity of St. Saba and other resolute prelates, held to their old faith, and rejected many overtures for submission to Rome. So did Russia. All that had been achieved by the abominable 'Fourth Crusade' was to destroy the Byzantine Empire—the old barrier of Christendom against the encroaching Mohammedan—to set up some ephemeral and trifling Latin states in Athens and the Peloponnesus, &c., and to give the greedy merchants of

On Looking Forward and Backward

Venice a commercial monopoly in the Levant for a couple of centuries. The ruining of the Byzantine Empire under the hypocritical name of a Crusade was one of the great crimes of history—and its results survive even to this day. But the final degradation of the Crusade-motive was reserved for the fifteenth century, when the Papacy launched cosmopolitan bands of adventurers against the Bohemian kingdom, in the endeavour to crush a nation accused of heresy and schism, but really guilty of nothing more than a repudiation of papal claims and a determination not to be Germanized by the alien kings of the House of Luxemburg. The doctrinal question of the administration of the Sacrament in both kinds was a miserable topic on which to set war raging all over Central Europe. One resents the idea of Cardinal Beaufort and his English Crusaders being launched as raiders against the Utraquists of Prague. And the war to crush the Hussites was not even successful, but ended in a compromise, after Bohemia, Eastern Germany, and Hungary had been ravaged from end to end.

No wonder that the name Crusade had become ineffective—the last Crusaders, those who perished with Cardinal Julian Cesarini at Varna in 1444, were a small and not over-reputable band. And this decay of the old motive—through misuse—came just at the moment when an effort to save Christendom from the Mohammedan invader was becoming necessary, after an interval of a couple of centuries. The Turks were on the Danube, and ever advancing. No effective help to keep the frontier of Christendom intact came from the West. The one contemporary Pope who took that danger seriously, Pius II, preached the Crusade once more. But the slogan failed to attract any longer. Pius sat in vain at Ancona in 1464 waiting for fleets that never came, and when they failed to appear died of a broken heart. He had looked out from his headland over the Adriatic for long weeks, but nothing turned up save ten Venetian galleys—and the Venetians alone might have sent 100 galleys if they had been set earnestly on answering the Crusading cry. From the rest of Europe came nothing. The game was up.

CHAPTER II

LOST ILLUSIONS. THE PAPACY AND THE
HOLY ROMAN EMPIRE

THE death of the crusading-motive was but one of three great convictions of failure which made the end of the fifteenth century one of the most lugubrious epochs of European history. The other two need longer study and more detailed explanation. I mean the definite and well-proved failure of the two great rival institutions on which the political and religious organization of the Middle Ages had been based—the moral supremacy of the Papacy, and the legal supremacy of the Holy Roman Empire. Both had reached their lowest pitch of degradation about the year 1492–93—a date which combines the death of Frederick III, the most helpless and hapless of Holy Roman Emperors, and the election to the Papacy of Rodrigo Borgia, the most infamous wearer of the triple crown in all the annals of the Roman Church—not excepting any of the wretched Johns—the fifteenth-century pirate or the tenth-century degenerates.

The tragedy of the twelfth, thirteenth, and fourteenth centuries had been the clash between two incompatible ideals, the theory of the Papacy as set forth by Hildebrand and his successors, and the theory of the Holy Roman Empire—that of the Ottos and Fredericks, not the vaguer aspiration of Charlemagne. Both were high ideals—unfortunately they were incompatible, as worked out by the individual Popes and Emperors—probably essentially incompatible from the first. The misfortune was that their clash, and the dishonest, violent, controversial methods employed on each side, ended in disgraceful moral anarchy, lasting for generations and leading to complete disillusionment for all sincere Christians.

The ideal of the medieval Papacy was inspiring enough in

The Papacy and the Holy Roman Empire 17

itself. The conception of the spiritual union of Christendom under the Roman Pontificate, the idea of a force making for righteousness, which should be international, greater than all local kings and princes, and should secure just and decent government all round Europe by its supervising moral control, was a grand one. We might well compare it with the modern ideal of the League of Nations—an equally grand conception. But when the problem comes to hand of applying the moral screw to recalcitrant states or individuals difficulties appear.

Medieval Rome did not regard 'sanctions' in the same way as modern Geneva. Universal peace for Christendom was in the Middle Ages a pious aspiration of a few rather unpractical people. 'Pacifism' was not a widespread dominating impulse among statesmen—lay or ecclesiastical. To-day the gap between economic and military action against an offender is enormous in the minds of all thinking men. Geneva applies the lesser sanctions in the devout hope that the more terrible one may thereby be made unnecessary. If the word War is whispered nations will hold back in reasonable affright.

The medieval Papacy went to the other extreme. It not merely inflicted interdicts and excommunications on kings and their subjects who had refused to accept a papal ruling, but it often turned against them an armed force supplied by those who had something to gain by attacking the contemner of ecclesiastical censures. To put things simply, it did not merely inflict a moral boycott, but it employed, as its international police force, bands of interested spoilers and brigands. And, worst of all, it did not only call in the foreign enemy, but it sometimes fostered and inculcated civil war. To call out subjects in arms against their prince was habitual, and to incite an ambitious heir against his father was not unknown. Half the troubles of medieval Germany were caused by rebellions fostered by the Papacy, and the net result was the complete break up of the German national kingdom, as emperors and counter-emperors bought support by granting away the essential rights of the Crown to win partisans. I do not of course ignore the fact that Italy might make out a counter-claim against Germany for having smashed up, at two centuries of interval, two Italian national kingdoms. But Charlemagne made an end of the quite respectable Lombard state at the direct request of a pope, to whom a Lombard kingdom of united Italy was objectionable. And when Otto the Great made the second German conquest of Italy in 951, the unfortunate Berengar and Adalbert whom he crushed were hardly national kings of an organized state.

But of course it would be quite anachronistic to treat the Papacy as a power that might have been the central force in a united Italy. Such an idea as that of 'driving the barbarians beyond the Alps' was first heard from the mouth of a pope in the sixteenth century, when Julius II formulated it. The Papacy was essentially international and not Italian for centuries. It was at a quite late date that the Roman mob surrounded the Lateran, and terrified the Cardinals engaged in an election conclave with the cry, 'We want a Roman for pope, or at least an Italian'. Down to the fifteenth century many popes and sometimes a majority of the cardinals were 'Transalpines'. The 'Great Schism' of 1378 which inflicted such a deadly wound on the authority of the Papacy that it never recovered its old solidarity, was directly due to the fact that there were so many French cardinals at the moment that they could make a bid for placing the tiara on the head of their own candidate, and where the plan proved only partially successful, could at any rate plant their own man at Avignon, as a colourable representative of the orthodox papal succession.

But long before the 'Great Schism' rent the Western Church in two for forty years, there were other grievances, not political and international but matters of practical Church administration, which were sapping the claim of the Papacy to be the tribunal of justice and the power that decided between right and wrong. The sneer that 'Romae omnia sunt venalia' was heard long before the fourteenth century. Kings and parliaments hated appeals to Rome, and legislated against them, not only because of the intolerable waste of time which they necessitated, but

The Papacy and the Holy Roman Empire 19

because experience showed that decisions were arbitrary and unjust. I need not go into the interminable question of the 'Contest about Investitures,' on which much might be said about the unseemliness of lay interference with clerical elections on the one hand, or about the claim of kings to be free from the danger of persons objectionable to them being thrust into the possession of great fiefs and positions of political importance against their will, on the other. The Papacy in many cases had no hesitation in nominating to high preferment in any country persons hateful to its king. Sometimes they were worthy persons —as in the case of Stephen Langton whom King John so much disliked—sometimes they were not. But the principle of nominations from outside to places of national importance was obviously bad in itself. In the late centuries of the Middle Ages the Papacy was the centre of the system of 'provisors' and of 'pluralities'. To interfere by nomination of successors with the regular devolution of clerical offices in a county was intolerable. Still more so was this the case where the nominated persons were aliens and persistent non-residents, often holding in plurality other preferment outside the realm on which they were intruded. A glance at the table of bishops of Worcester will show a record of two successive non-resident Italian bishops, whose tenure lasted for over fifteen years. But this was habitual all over Europe. And pluralities were as great a nuisance as non-residence. They were sometimes purely local affairs jobbed inside a county for the benefit of some *persona grata* (like Cardinal Wolsey), but generally concerned entirely foreign individuals, nominated by the Papacy under the system of 'Provisors' against which English parliaments used to rage occasionally.

I need hardly mention payments to Rome extracted on various pretexts, from *annates*—for which something might possibly be said as contributions to the central funds of Christendom due from all countries equally—to levies for crusades of doubtful authenticity.

But intense irritation in the highest quarters was often caused by the actual working of papal censures, by excommunication or interdict. Sometimes they fell upon kings neither tyrannous nor irreligious, nor hateful to their subjects, for purely political reasons. It is a surprise when we find that the body of the chivalrous James IV of Scotland, who fell at Flodden, could not be buried because he had died under excommunication—for an alliance with France.

To modern minds the way in which marriages 'within the prohibited degrees' were worked by the church courts is one of the most indefensible features of the time. Robert of France and many more drew excommunication on themselves for marrying a first or a second cousin, to the mighty discomfort of their subjects. The system wrought so much on the mind of King Henry I, the son of Robert, that he sent to Russia for his last wife, because there at least he was certain that he had no cousins. But by propitiating the papal courts a king could buy leave to marry not only his first cousin but his niece, his aunt, or his deceased wife's sister.[1] One king most certainly toyed with the idea that he could get leave to marry his bastard son to his legitimate daughter—another (and a pious one) was reported to be intending to wed his own daughter to keep an inheritance together. These were but projects—but the fact that they were conceivable is a testimony to the way in which the buying of permission to marry within the prohibited degrees sapped all natural morality. But we need not expatiate on secondary causes of disillusionment. The primary cause (I suppose) for the decaying authority of the Church had been the 'Great Schism'.

Just as the Papacy seemed to have achieved its victory over the theory of the Holy Roman Empire, it was stricken with the same curse of doubtful legality of election which had ruined its rival. In the Dark Ages anti-popes, claiming under a dubious election, had been not infrequent : but

---

[1] The best remembered case of marrying an uncle comes from Portugal, where Maria I married an uncle Peter III, who was much of her own age. A quite recent case of taking a niece to wife comes from modern Italy, when Amadeo of Savoy, the son of Victor Emmanuel I, bought leave to marry his sister's daughter Letizia Bonaparte in late Victorian days.

they were fleeting phenomena, always disappearing after a short and vain effort. In the twelfth and thirteenth centuries anti-popes, backed by some emperor at strife with the Holy See, had never been taken seriously or endured for long. On the whole the succession of legal popes was undoubted, and the voice of the Roman See was one and indisputable. Even the long exile to Avignon in the fourteenth century did not lead to the election of anti-popes at Rome, as might well have been expected. It was after the return of Gregory XI to Rome in 1377, which ought to have made succession easy and certain for the future, that the fatal trouble broke out. The election of 1378, which followed on his death, was the first case of thoroughly doubtful legality. The conclave of cardinals, terrorized by a Roman mob, elected Urban VI: the French cardinals (fifteen of them, a clear majority of the conclave), pleading that Urban had been chosen while the sacred college was under *force majeure* and constraint, removed themselves to Anagni and elected Robert of Geneva as Clement VII. The obvious solution would have been that on the death of one of the competitors, their partisans should have consented to recognize the other. But this did not happen—each party went on electing successors to its first nominee, and the schism was perpetuated for more than forty years. It split up Europe into two obediences, mainly differentiated by political considerations. For France and the states which were usually allied to France, such as Scotland, Aragon, and Naples, acknowledged the pope of French choice, who had retired to Avignon, while the kings of England, Portugal, and most of the princes of Germany, naturally found it convenient to recognize Urban VI and his successors, who were actually resident at Rome, since this line of popes was notoriously anti-French.

The Roman and the Avignonese popes fought with the most thunderous weapons of ecclesiastical censure, declaring each other to be impostors, simoniacal, blasphemers, successors of Simon Magus, and children of the devil. The one could excommunicate in as sounding terms as the other. The scandal to Christendom was terrible, because so much could be said against the legality of either line of pontiffs. If a prince or an individual felt any qualms as to the validity of the claims of the person whom he had been recognizing, he must realize that if his choice had been wrong, he was under the most severe ecclesiastical censure on the part of the other claimant, and these censures *might* possibly be operative, to his own eternal damnation. The state of doubt must have been unpleasant, but it was observed that as a matter of practical experience, princes or individuals made their decisions not on grounds of conscience but on grounds of convenience. Martyrs to the legality of one obedience, in lands of the other obedience, were rare or non-existent.

But scandalous as was the situation of divided Christendom from 1378 to 1406, with two lines of popes perpetually excommunicating each other, and each intriguing by unscrupulous means to detach princes from the other's cause, things got much worse in the fifteenth century. Every one who was not personally interested in one pope or the other agreed that the scandal must be brought to an end somehow. Hence came the great 'Conciliar Movement', the plan for bringing together general councils of the whole Western Church, which should exercise authority even over popes, and reform all abuses. The Council of Pisa in 1409 declared both Benedict XIII at Avignon and Gregory XII at Rome to be tainted with illegality, decreed their deposition, and elected a third pope, Alexander V, a respected and learned scholar, to supersede both of them. Unfortunately both Benedict and Gregory refused to resign, and for the moment three popes were in existence simultaneously, each declaring the other two to be usurpers and excommunicate. The Council's Pope, Alexander V, unfortunately died less than a year after his election—if we remember this worthy scholar it is but because he was the only pope save the present wearer of the tiara, to study in Oxford— where he took his degree, though he was not an Englishman but an exiled Cretan. On his death the Council made a horrid mistake, choosing as his successor Balthazar Cossa, who took the title of John XXIII. His enemies soon discovered that he had a lurid past—there can have been no proper investigation into his early life—and formulated their accusations—to quote the amusing lines of Gibbon—in the words that 'the more scandalous charges being suppressed, the Vicar of Christ was only accused of piracy, murder, robbery, rape, and gross sexual abnormalities'. There is no doubt of his having been a most abandoned person—worthy to rank with the Johns of the tenth century.

Though the Council of Constance four years later (1415) ultimately succeeded in discrediting all the three popes—John and Gregory were forced into resignation when all their secular supporters had been scared off, Benedict XIII died at Peniscola years after (1442) still thundering unregarded excommunications, and entirely forgotten—yet the wounds of the Church had not been healed. When a generally recognized pope had been chosen at Constance in the person of Martin V, he refused to take in hand the general reform of ecclesiastical abuses—the programme on which he had been elected : the schism was ended, but the scandals remained. The restored Papacy made it its first object to get rid of General Councils—because councils had claimed, and indeed exercised, the right to deal drastically with popes—to make and unmake them. The Council of Basle, the successor of the Council of Constance, committed itself to a complete scheme of altered administration in the Church, substituting conciliar for papal supervision for the whole of Christendom, and came to such fierce conflict with Eugenius IV, the successor of Martin V at Rome, that it went to the extreme length of declaring him deposed, and nominating Amadeus of Savoy, who took the name of Felix V, to succeed him. This was an unpopular move, as it renewed the division of the Papacy which the Council of Constance had ended with so much trouble. It was also a most abnormal one—a sovereign prince had never before been made a pope—though Amadeus laid down his ducal coronet when he took up the tiara. The Council failed to meet with the general support which it hoped to get against an intransigent pope, and finally was dispersed, while its nominee, recognizing that he was after all an anti-pope only, resigned and recognized the succession of Eugenius IV. The restored Roman Papacy had triumphed over the Conciliar movement, after forty years of contest. This was, in effect, a very Pyrrhic victory, for by defeating the party of the councils, which stood for reform from within, the Papacy had committed itself to the policy of non-reformation, and incurred once more the odium which had lain on the whole institution before the councils in 1406 had taken up the cause of the removal of abuses.

The issue was perhaps inevitable—reform had been associated with the idea of government by councils. This was of course an intolerable grievance to popes, who naturally held that a dictatorship is preferable to a kind of parliamentary government—if we may use modern terms. The councils had to be got rid of. And the attempt to produce a general movement for the union of Christendom in Reform failed hopelessly. No one could say with honesty at the end of the fifteenth century that the supremacy of the Papacy was exercised in the cause of justice, reason or morality, either in the internal affairs of the Church, or the international relations of Europe, least of all in the local quarrels of the Italian powers. At the end of the century, despite of the intermittent efforts of some popes of the better sort, like Pius II, the scandals were as obvious as they had been during the days before the 'Great Schism'. Alexander VI, Rodrigo Borgia, was an even more disgraceful figure-head for the Church than John XXIII had been. To the blatant faults of that ignominious predecessor, he added an unctuous and emotional display of hypocrisy, which deceived no one. Hope seemed gone for the cause of righteousness when that abominable pontiff presided over the last years of the fifteenth and the first of the sixteenth century. What can be a more distressing memory than that of the enthusiastic puritan visionary Girolamo Savonarola, burnt at the stake in the Piazza della Signoria at Florence, for heresy (of all things) because he had not only stood in the way of local jealousies, but had chanced to disturb the political schemes of the villainous old wearer of the tiara, by his adherence to the

French alliance, which Alexander at that time was set on breaking up.

The Papacy in the first year of the sixteenth century was odious to all men of decent religious feeling. Its old rival, the ideal of the Holy Roman Empire, was not odious but moribund. The theory of the old imperialist, or Ghibelline, party during the long struggle was the idea of a laic or secular world-state, as opposed to a world-state dominated by the Roman Church and its head. It had not a very sound historical basis, for though it really went back only to Charlemagne, men supposed, letting assertion take the place of fact, that it was a revival of the old Roman Empire founded by Julius Caesar and his greater nephew Augustus, the first genuine Emperor. The head of the institution called himself Caesar, Imperator, and Semper Augustus, not merely the ruler of Germany and Italy, though he might also be king of the Germans and of the Lombards, and of that third 'Middle Realm', which in common parlance men called by the old and misleading name of Burgundy. Probably this conception of a Christendom in which the 'Holy Roman Emperor' was to be the sun of the European solar system, with all minor planets revolving around him, was essentially unsound. For though Charlemagne had once ruled all the central lands of Europe from Barcelona to the Eider, and from Gaeta to Frisia, the Ottos and Henries, under whom the idea of the medieval empire was really systematized, never had their supremacy recognized in France or in Christian Spain—not to speak of Britain or Scandinavia, which Charlemagne had never owned. It only covered Germany, Burgundy, and the northern two-thirds of Italy. Its whole theory rested on the union of two such incompatible partners as Germany and Italy—and it worked out into being a curse to both. But the idea of a Christian world-state was a grand one, though never perfectly realized. It inspired men of the calibre of Dante, an Italian but an imperialist, and it held out a hope of orderly and just rule by an august central sovereign, who ought to be able to keep order, to suppress local wars of greed or dynastic ambition, to enforce peace on all his broad realms, and to guard Christendom against all external foes. The Emperor, if only all his vassals had been loyal and obedient, would have been at the head of a colossal military power—the Papacy had no armies of its own, and could only fight by suborning the subjects of the empire to rise against their overlord by spiritual censures and moral propaganda. Nevertheless, as we all know, the Papacy ultimately won in the conflict. The Holy Roman Empire had too many handicaps. Firstly, a monarchy theoretically elective, though with a practical preference for the last sovereign's heir, is liable to disputed elections, if the heir is a minor, or obviously unsuitable, or not very near of kin to the deceased sovereign. Hence could come trouble such as supervened on the death of Henry VI in 1197, when the electors had to choose between an infant heir, a close kinsman of mature years, and a great feudal prince with more ambition than claim of the hereditary sort, with long results of civil war. When the Hohenzollern line finally died out, a grasp at the crown of Charlemagne was open to any and every candidate, and local particularism or personal ambition led to successive appearances of doubtfully elected emperors and anti-emperors, who were princes of dominions too small to give them a solid base of military force, such as Adolf of Nassau, Gunther of Schwartzburg, and William of Holland. They had no hereditary claim, and were insignificant enough to make other rulers of larger fiefs look upon them with contempt. The most surprising manifestation of the weakness of elective monarchy was when foreign princes put in a candidature, and got support from some quarters out of mere jealousy between native rivals. Such was the case with Richard of Cornwall—whose only merit was his wealth, and who vanished from Germany when his wealth was spent. Even Alfonso of Castile was taken into serious consideration by electors who disliked more obvious native claimants for the crown, and preferred a probable absentee to a well-known enemy on the spot.

The occurrence of an imperial election always gave illimitable opportunities for intrigue to the Papacy, for the

The Papacy and the Holy Roman Empire 27

Pope could give a valuable moral sanction to the candidate whom he backed, with the certainty of extorting all sorts of concessions from him, in return for propagandic help given. It was true that a strong man, when once elected, might repudiate his bargain, as did Frederic II, the Pope's man in his earliest years, but the Pope's bitterest enemy in his middle age. But in such a case the defrauded Papacy had always the opportunity of stirring up factious opposition and open rebellion among the subjects of the oath-breaker, and excommunication was still a powerful weapon in the thirteenth century, before the 'Great Schism' had made excommunication too cheap.

By the beginning of the fourteenth century the contest for an imperial crown which had lost its glamour had resolved into a triangular duel between the three great houses of Wittelsbach, Luxemburg, and Hapsburg, all of whom put emperors upon the throne, but had never any certainty of succession. There was a century of gap between the first two Hapsburg emperors and their next descendant who got general recognition. Both the Hapsburgs and Luxemburgs got more profit by intruding their members into great fiefs which had gone derelict from the failure of male heirs, than from gaining any general authority over the Empire. Rudolf of Hapsburg, originally owner of an insignificant Suabian county, made a grand heritage for his descendants by getting hold of the derelict Austrian lands—if he had not done so the name of Hapsburg would have lapsed out of the main stream of European history for good. And the Luxemburgs, originally like the Hapsburgs owners of a very modest appanage, made their fleeting fortunes by laying hold of Brandenburg on the extinction of the old Margravial line, and of Bohemia by a lucky marriage. Both lines were powerful as local territorial sovereigns of large dominions, not as direct rulers of the whole empire. Indeed, one essential feature of the original Holy Roman Empire had disappeared when the Italian states ceased to be under any sort of imperial control, as they did after the abortive transalpine expedition of Henry of Luxemburg in 1311–12. After that Italian cities might call themselves 'Guelf' or 'Ghibelline'—they continued to do so down to the sixteenth century—but these were names of local antagonism—Ghibelline never wished seriously to bring back the German supremacy into Italy, though occasionally an Italian prince or tyrant liked to buy the title of Vicar-General of the Empire from an obliging emperor—it meant little or nothing for practical purposes.

There remains only to speak of the one busy and volatile Emperor, who having wide if heterogeneous ideals, tried to make the moribund conception of the earlier ages into some sort of reality. Sigismund of Luxemburg was helped by the fact that the worst and most chaotic years of the 'Great Schism' fell into his day, and that the Papacy was at the very bottom of its discredit. He ran all over Europe with the attractive programme of putting an end to spiritual anarchy by the great 'Conciliar Movement' of which we have already spoken, of reforming the Church, and incidentally of restoring something of the old general influence of the Holy Roman Empire. For the patron of General Councils was a personage of pan-European importance such as no emperor had been since Frederic II. That Sigismund, with a unique opportunity, and a wide ambition, failed in his schemes was a testimony not only to his own inconsequence of mind, but to the fact that the imperial ideal was past mending. He succeeded in frightening a good many people—including the English who thought that his propagandic visit to London might mean a claim that they were vassals of the Holy Roman Empire—and all the princes of Germany, not to speak of the rival popes whom his council deposed. But the general result of his activities was wholly disappointing. The restored Papacy proved as tiresome as the last years of the 'Great Schism' —reform was shelved, councils gradually lost authority and finally were depreciated and dissolved. The restoration of the imperial power in Germany was hopeless—largely because Sigismund plunged the empire into a disastrous war, in endeavouring to suppress anti-German nationalism in his own kingdom of Bohemia. The Hussites, whose fury he had provoked by burning at Constance their prophet Huss—lured to the council by a repudiated safe conduct—gave him employment for all the remaining years of his life. His Crusades against these obstinate heretics ended disastrously—they had invented a new system of tactics which outwitted the German chivalry—and he had to witness the disgraceful insult of the bands of Zizka raiding far into Saxony, Thuringia, and Bavaria. At the same time Christendom was beginning to discover with some dismay the danger of an attack from the rear by the Ottoman Turks, who had just shown themselves for the first time on the Danube. Sigismund in his earliest years, before he was Emperor, had led the crusading army which perished at Nicopolis (1396). He might well have deduced from that awful disaster the conclusion that his main duty was to save central Europe from the Mohammedan peril, and to serve as its warden of the marches against the East—was he not King of Hungary as well as *Semper Augustus*? But the temporary cessation of the Turkish peril in the middle years of his life (due to the incursions of Tamerlane) enabled him to turn all his attention to the West, and it was only in his old age that the problem cropped up again, and found him, when well entangled in his Bohemian Crusades, attacked once more by the Ottomans in the rear. The pressing danger here he neglected—having other tasks in hand. And it was left to John Hunniades in the next generation to stem the Moslem flow. Meanwhile the reform of the Church, and the restoration of the empire, became vain dreams, and Sigismund passed away in 1437, leaving little trace of all his activities behind him. Historians cruelly say that he had been 'hunting chimaeras', and the anecdote best remembered of him is the famous Latin speech, in which having confused his subjunctives and his concords, he burst out upon his critics with the delightful reply, ' Ego sum rex Romanus, et super grammaticam '. Sigismund's immediate successor was his son-in-law, Albert of Austria, who survived his election for a very short time, and died of the plague at the end of an unsuccessful campaign against the Turks, who were once more pushing up the Danube. After Albert followed his cousin Frederic III, another Hapsburg, the most luckless and feckless of all the emperors of the Middle Ages, whose enormously long reign (1440–93) marked the lowest point to which the imperial authority had ever sunk. Bankrupt and always beaten in war, he was driven out of his own dominions by the Hungarians, and as he had no authority anywhere else, was forced to spend his later years in exile, wandering around the free cities of Germany as an unwelcome and expensive guest. He only got back to Vienna in 1491, to die in 1493, aged seventy-eight, a monument of feebleness and incapacity.

The Holy Roman Empire, then, was as disunited as the Papacy itself in the last decade of the fifteenth century—and seemed as out of date as the Crusades. There was no inspiration to be got out of its ideals—the theories of Frederic II, '*Stupor Mundi*', seemed as hopelessly antiquated as those of Hildebrand or Innocent III. The Empire could no more give peace and orderly government than the Papacy could give righteous dealing and spiritual inspiration. The unhappy year, August 1492–August 1493, marks the juxtaposition of the worst of the pontiffs—Alexander VI—and the weakest of the emperors—Frederic III. From whence was hope to come? The old ideals were worn out, after four centuries of internecine conflict between the successors of St. Peter and the successors of Charlemagne. From what source were new ideals to be derived?

CHAPTER III

THE END OF THE FIFTEENTH CENTURY

WE have already appreciated the fact that the last decade of the fifteenth century was a time of disillusion and disappointed hopes. The three great ideals of the Reformed Papacy, the Holy Roman Empire, and the Crusades, seemed all to have been tried and found wanting. As I said before, the year 1492-93 links the names of the most wicked Pope and the most forlorn Emperor that were ever seen, and the last Crusade had petered out in 1464 without even having started from Ancona. Perhaps it may be worth remembering that Henry VIII of England was a child of one year old in the dismal year 1492, and that the word 'the Pope' meant to him, till he reached the age of twelve, that very objectionable pontiff Alexander VI, with the general atmosphere of scandal and murder that hung about him, his family, and his court. The impressions of one's youth cling about one's mind for all one's life. Is it to be wondered at that an intelligent boy of twelve could never get rid of the idea that 'the Pope' *might* mean a very objectionable person, by no means deserving of respect, open to all manner of bargains, and capable of any intrigue? The Papacy, disguised under a sacred name, might mean a power without any moral sanction, and indifferent to right or wrong. If Henry in his later years, when he had developed into a selfish autolatrous tyrant, considered that his personal morals were no ban to his claiming supreme religious authority, he could argue that he had ample precedent in the recent history of the popes. He was reared in the old immoral atmosphere—and showed it.

From whence was inspiration to come if the central focus of Christendom was notoriously corrupt, and the recent attempt to reform it by the 'Conciliar Movement' had come to a disastrous end ? Hardly from a renewal of wild fanatic outbursts like those of the Flagellants of the fourteenth century, which confused self-maceration with self-purification. Hardly from the mystics, whose piety was unobtrusive and self-regarding, and had no organization and no propagandist power. Hardly from the Wycliffite leaven in England, whose exponents seemed to have been crushed completely—we should, to read ordinary histories, believe that they had disappeared completely, were it not that occasional burnings and more frequent notices of abjurations and penances can be traced all through the times of Edward IV and Henry VII ; so that there was still fire smouldering below the ashes.[1] The Hussite movement in Bohemia had never any power to spread outside its own country, had no attraction for aliens since it was essentially national and particularist, and it had died down into a compromise, which acknowledged the long-denied supremacy of Rome in return for the promise to use the Utraquist method of celebrating the Eucharist. Sectarian movements, easily to be accused of being heretical, and often with truth, had no general appeal. The outlook for the simple soul who knew something about the state of Christendom at the moment was gloomy in the extreme. And it did not look as if salvation was to come from the intellectual stir against scholastic ignorance, which was beginning to be visible. The revolt against stupid traditionalism, and the worship of authority founded on ignorance, was a destructive not a constructive movement. When scholars like Laurentius a Valla disproved the existence of the forged ' Donation of Constantine ' on which rested so many preposterous papal claims to temporal power, or when the ' False Decretals ' crumpled up under criticism, it was but a negative benefit to religion. Oddly enough the scholars who first attacked these old delusions were clerics, themselves superficially orthodox, who did not see whither their discoveries were leading. The humorist who said that ' Erasmus laid the egg and Luther hatched it ' only saw a very little way into the matter. Scholarship and research were not the real

[1] See Fisher's *History of the Tudor Period*, pp. 137–9.

The End of the Fifteenth Century 33

parents of the Reformation—they were only incidental assisting causes, because they confuted or weakened old doctrinal supports of accepted orthodoxy.

The fifteenth century was a thoroughly demoralized age. I know of no period so poor of good men of mark, and so full of bad ones. The secular historian thinks of it as the age of Louis XI of France and Richard III of England, just as the ecclesiastical historian thinks of it as the age of John XXIII and Alexander VI. It produces hardly a figure of appealing interest save John Huss, Joan of Arc, and Girolamo Savonarola—and it burnt all three, after trials which were a disgrace to spiritual and lay authority in equal measure. I linger for a moment over the pathetic end of Joan of Arc, merely to remark that the wretched king whom she had crowned did nothing to save her—though he, years after, permitted of the whitewashing of her memory. His adviser, the Archbishop of Reims, remarked that Joan's failure made no great difference—he had, as he explained, his eye on a young shepherd of peculiar simplicity and piety, who might be worked up into quite as effective a propagandist. But France rightly worships Joan of Arc to-day. The successor of the canny weakling who allowed Joan to burn was the typical figure of the fifteenth century—the worst of all the kings of France—cruel, mean, treacherous, forsworn ; to read the chronicle of his reign rouses unmitigated disgust. Yet a comparatively decent diplomatist and historian, Philip de Comines, who had known him well in his old age and served him, sums up his record with the astounding remark, ' though I will not say that I never saw a better prince, may God receive his soul, and admit it into the Kingdom of Paradise '. The faculty of moral censure seems dead in Comines, when he writes these words, long after Louis was dead and the nightmare of his reign was over, in days when the throne had passed to his distant cousin of Orleans. The sense of right and wrong seems blurred in an otherwise intelligent person.

One has more or less the same feeling when one looks round other countries of Europe. Italian historians relate the atrocities of Galeazzo Maria Sforza, Alfonso and

Ferrante of Naples or Caesar Borgia with a certain detachment—such doings were just in the usual way of despots, bloody or treacherous but not surprising. And so with the very disgusting proceedings of the degenerate Henry IV of Castile, unbecoming, no doubt, but not provocative of special reprobation from the chroniclers who wrote them down.

Morality is much the same in England: one has but to read the *Paston Letters* to get an impression of a people grown sordid and materialistic, unscrupulous in their dealings with their neighbours, lost to the consciousness of political honesty. The Wars of the Roses seem to have killed the sense of loyalty—men shifted from side to side with perfect equanimity, as the interest of the moment seemed to dictate. There is a fine instance of *bourgeois* placidity in the record of the Corporation of Norwich, who, having to date an important deed during Warwick's last struggle with Edward of York, send a horseman in haste to London ' to find out who is king '. If Edward is up, the document must be dated as *decimo anno regis Edwardi post conquestum quarti*, but if Henry is in possession it must stand *quadragesimo octavo anno regis Henrici post conquestum sexti*. The corporation will make no inquiry who is their rightful master, will risk nothing for him, but are anxious that the deed should not be dated by the year of the king who goes down—in which case it would not only be null and void, but would bring down unpleasant financial consequences from the ministers of the successful candidate. I detect a similar Gallio-like equanimity in the speech of a Vice-Chancellor of Oxford, who, in 1471, announced with pleasure to Congregation that he had discovered that no member of the University had fallen on either side either at Barnet or at Tewkesbury. Compare this state of mind with that of the Oxford of 1643, when the students who had not already joined one side or another were drilling as a corps of pikemen and musketeers in Merton Field. Loyalty meant something in 1643; in 1471 it was apparently a non-existent sentiment.

Edward IV himself was a typical example of the morality of the generation—easy-going and casual on his off-days, but recklessly cruel on occasion; ready to give a superficial

The End of the Fifteenth Century

adherence to orthodoxy by attending the minimum of masses, and burning an occasional Lollard, but a notable breaker of oaths ; a betrayer of his friends and of countless ladies of every social condition ; very skilled in the arts of extracting money from his subjects or his foreign neighbours, and of spending it with ostentation ; a military genius when occasion made it necessary, but not particularly set on military glory for its own sake. More affable and familiar with citizens and aldermen than was pleasing to the old nobility. Altogether an unscrupulous opportunist, who failed to be a complete tyrant because he was neither afflicted with megalomania, nor given to cruelty for cruelty's sake, and loved to take his ease. One recognizes in him many traits, beside his corpulence, which he transmitted to his grandson Henry VIII—from whom he differed as a man of the fifteenth century differs from one of the sixteenth, showing a much less complicated character. He had no taste for letters or theology, was neither a pedant nor a poser, bent on making a perpetual show of his own talents, and on figuring as the mainspring of the international politics of Europe. And he left his subjects alone, save when acute personal interest dictated the use of the axe or the rope, never pretending to act as a spiritual guide or a patron of unnecessary wars.

If the record of Edward IV is merely that of an unscrupulous fifteenth-century king, that of Richard III may serve as a type of the worst men of a bad age. In the abominable story of his usurpation, it is sufficient to read the documents by which he asserted his claim to the throne, full not only of insolent lies, but of vile insinuations against every one of his relatives, including his mother—indirectly accused of unchastity. It is disgusting to read his hypocritical denunciations against 'the laudable customs and liberties of the realm being broken, subverted, and continued' by his brother's rule for the last twenty years—which he was about to transform into consonance 'with the Laws of God's Church, of Nature, and of England'. To find Crookback talking of the Laws of God and Nature is absolutely nauseous. I cannot help feeling that the most degrading thing in this document is that a bishop is brought in to vouch for the illegitimacy of the children of Edward IV, the unhappy princes in the Tower. This was the same Stillington of Bath and Wells who was, a few years later, implicated in the conspiracy of the impostor Lambert Simnel —another dirty business. If we could only trust Philip de Comines on the matter we should find that Richard's inducement to Stillington to discredit the late king's marriage with Elizabeth Woodville was even more disgraceful than the plain story as it stands [1] to the credit of an English political bishop.

It was an evil age, and good men shuddered at the contemplation of its moral deadness. I do not think that I can give a better example of the pessimistic outlook of Christendom in the last years of the fifteenth century than by mentioning the great *Nuremberg Chronicle* of 1493, that marvellous much-illustrated folio which is one of the early triumphs of the printer's art. History is conceived of in the well-known scheme of the ' Seven Ages ' in which each is worse than that which preceded it. The idea was as popular in 1493 as when Hesiod first adumbrated it two thousand years back. The ' sixth age ' was supposed to be drawing somewhat near its close when the book was printed. So at the end of interminable annals, with portraits of Nebuchadnezzar, Julius Caesar, and Charlemagne, we come to 1492, with effigies of the aged Emperor Frederic III and Pope Alexander VI, with an incidental picture of a great *auto-da-fé*, a burning of Jews. Then follows a blank of six pages, left virgin white, for the use of the owner of the volume, who may fill them up in manuscript with the transactions of the last few years that the sinful world has yet to endure. Then comes the ' Seventh Age ', *Septima Aetus Mundi*, consisting of an account of the End of the World

---

[1] I cannot trust Comines, but his story is that Stillington had a much-cherished bastard son, and that Richard offered to give the youth one of King Edward's daughters—now to be duly bastardized also—in marriage, with a great endowment. But the young Stillington was by chance drowned at sea, shipwrecked on the coast of France, almost immediately after Richard's coronation.

from the Book of Revelations. We see the rise of the 'Beast' and the 'False Prophet', and Antichrist himself, with the Martyrdom of the 'Two Witnesses', the pouring out of the Seven Vials, and finally the Last Judgement with Christ seated on His rainbow throne and the parting of the damned and the saved souls. All these happenings are profusely illustrated with the splendid woodcuts in whose composition Michael Wohlgemuth excelled. He revelled in lurid pictures of battle, murder, and sudden death; his devils, scattered liberally through all these last pages of the 'Seventh Age', are particularly horrible and convincing.

One can perfectly understand this pessimistic conception of the approaching fate of the world in the eyes of readers of a moral and orthodox frame of mind when one considers the contemporary state of Christendom, political and religious. The end of the world might well be at hand in consideration of the accumulated sins of mankind. What was there to hope for? Enthusiasms were all worked out, no spiritual initiative was left. Men felt the blankness of the outlook everywhere. The 'Dance of Death' which Dürer drew was a typical expression of the spirit of the age.

But turn on a few years, and from the perspective of the ordinary man we are no longer at the end of a feeble and moribund Christendom, but at the start of a new and vigorous age, full of explosive ideals, moral, cultural, philosophical, social, religious. The change is complete and astounding, and the foundations of the modern ways of thought have been laid, while the 'Seven Ages' in the depressing series have dropped out of men's conception of the universe. A new visualization of the world had begun. Men were no longer looking back to the Golden Age that lay in the distant past, but speculating as to the Golden Age that might possibly lie in the oncoming future. The long pessimistic wave had died down for the present—an optimistic wave was surging up—destined in its time to die down also.

The sixteenth century was to be no Golden Age—it was full of wars and rumours of wars, of cruel religious conflicts which made the Hussite struggle of the late century seem a small matter, of devastations and persecutions, of fundamental changes in the balance of power among the European states, of a sudden enlargement of the bounds of the known world, with widespreading consequences that no one could have foreseen in 1492. It looks at the first view as a chaotic, even a cataclysmic century. But the net result was not to be evil—rather vital energies were let loose whose existence had not been suspected in the Middle Ages, and old bonds of tradition and ignorance were snapped which had bound Christendom for a thousand years. As I have said before, it is far from me to discuss how far the Revival of Learning, the Protestant revolt against the Papacy, the discovery of America and the Cape Route to the Indies, or the various scientific discoveries of which the most important was that which disposed of the old 'geocentric' theory of the universe, each contributed to the general result. It might be possible to make catalogues of many minor contributory causes of the complicated result.

But the summed-up effect of all such phenomena was the conclusion that since the old conception of things spiritual and physical turned out to be founded on erroneous bases, new ones must be established. This might be done merely by correction of errors, or on the other hand by a radical redistribution of values. The one thing that was certain was that the old limits and definitions were hopelessly out of date. The world was not the centre of the universe: there were other continents than Europe, Asia and Africa, the Papacy was not a beneficent institution working for the differentiation between right and wrong among mankind. The all-pervading scholastic philosophy rested on a series of hypotheses which might be contested; customary national law and Roman law might prove equally illogical if compared. A review of all political institutions in every country might lead to the conclusion that they left much to be desired—whether one tested them by the Bible, by Aristotle's categories, or by Platonic ideals. Confronted with the rediscovered beauty of classical art, all medieval canons of architecture, painting, sculpture and decoration might perhaps be rejected as mistaken—though the word 'Gothic' as a term of reproach had not yet been invented. The old definitions of social castes might be found to be as foolish as the technicalities of chivalry, or sumptuary laws about apparel. It was impossible to know whither scientific discovery might lead, but at any rate it must not necessarily be confused with sorcery, or attributed to the devil. There was a great contest on this point—for long generations after 1500 the scientist might be considered as an uncanny person, against whom *prima facie* suspicion of unorthodox practices might be permissible. For this the scientist himself might often be blamed, for he frequently partook of the character of the charlatan, and dabbled for financial reasons in problems like the philosopher's stone or the elixir of youth. The limits between the possible and the impossible, the permissible and the non-permissible, were as hard to define as they are to-day. If Edison or Marconi had lived in the fifteenth century they might probably have been burned as sorcerers: if in the sixteenth they would at least have been subjected to much injurious detraction, which they might best escape by procuring the protection of some 'enlightened' potentate. Above all, the scientist must keep clear of treason—if he trespassed on that dangerous ground he might share the fate of many astrologers and physicians [1] who went to the stake as wizards or to the gallows as conspirators, because they had lent themselves to calculating the death-hour of the King, or to hastening it by some subtle craft or potion.

The scholar had to be wary also—treason might lurk in over-great laudation of ancient Roman republican virtue, or in propagandic writing against the existing administration

---

[1] As for example the astrological friar of Hinton who cast horoscopes for Edward Duke of Buckingham, or Dr. Lopez, or the unlucky servant of Catherine de Medici who was supposed to know too much about poisons—when the Dauphin died (as the evidence clearly shows) by drinking water from a contaminated well—or Roger Bolingbroke in the preceding century.

of either Church or State. Political philosophy had its dangers, as well as over-pungent criticism of ecclesiastical abuses, or appeals to features of primitive Christianity which were distasteful to the orthodoxy of 1500. A few scholars pushed right through all bounds of Christian creeds, and found themselves in the position not merely of heretics but of mere theists, unitarians, or even agnostics. It was one of the ironies of history that Servetus—who was obviously a unitarian—came to his death not at the hands of the Catholics, but at those of the Calvinists—who might have reflected on their own long record of persecution by the Roman Church. But apparently Calvin was delighted to show that he could burn heretics as well as any inquisitor. The fate of Giordano Bruno was less surprising; one only wonders that an avowed pantheist, with a fad about the transmigration of souls, dared to trust himself in Italy. Perhaps he argued, very unwisely, that philosophy might mask any amount of unorthodoxy, and that the Inquisition was primarily set on heresy hunting, not on the suppression of 'free thought' by burning one who was now neither a Lutheran nor a Calvinist, but only an advanced student of the Renaissance peering into the puzzles of the universe.

But of course the very existence of abnormal inquiries proves the prevalence of more normal ones. The *intelligenzia* was on thinking bent—and its speculations wandered over all spheres human and divine, with a large contempt for scholasticism, all old conceptions of the universe and the soul of man, or accepted tradition of any sort. That it could not completely free itself from all preconceived fallacies we shall presently see, but nevertheless the sixteenth century got rid of a good many of them.

CHAPTER IV

MAN AND THE UNIVERSE IN THE SIXTEENTH CENTURY

THE world has grown terribly small of recent years, and the solar system itself occupies but a minor speck in the awful illimitable spaces of which astronomers tell us, where the massed noughts at the end of a computation fail to impress the normal mortal, who is accustomed to deal with mere thousands and millions. It was otherwise in the Middle Ages, when this earth was the centre of the Universe, with the obliging and regular sun and moon circling around it, and the planets (or such of them as were known) working in more puzzling orbits—mainly for the benefit of astrologers casting horoscopes. The geocentric theory (a most barbarous term) was universally accepted, and the first scientists who ventured to suggest that the earth went round the sun, and not the sun around the earth, got into terrible trouble with the authorities, not for astronomical speculation but for heresy. They were teaching a theory which was ruled to be a leaving from some of the more perverse of the ancient classical astronomers, and in blasphemous contradiction to scores of texts in the Bible, primarily (of course) to the first chapter of Genesis, which laid down the ruling that the earth was created before the sun, who began his daily course only after our own terrestrial habitation had already come into existence.

It makes a vast difference not only to our conception of the universe, but to our conception of man and his place in it, if we accept the geocentric theory, as our own ancestors of the Middle Ages and all their predecessors of every race and creed had done. Some part of the difference between the human outlook in 1500 and in 1600 comes from the facts that between these dates the earth had been discovered to be a much larger affair than had been suspected, and on the other hand it had been found that the earth was not the centre of the universe, but merely one of many planets circling round the sun. The former fact had become general knowledge—the latter was still unaccepted by the man in the street, who was no astronomer; but it was known since 1543 to the leaders of thought and science who had read the problem-book of Copernicus, and coloured the conception of the 'intelligenzia' of the day, if we may use that much-abused word. The human individual had become a much smaller object in a much-enlarged world, and an infinitely enlarged universe.

In consequence there had to be a reconstruction of values, which affected not only astronomy and geography but also religious conceptions. For popular cosmogony had penetrated deeply into religious thought. We may find it difficult to conceive of the medieval idea of a very small world, which some simple folks thought to be a flat world, surrounded by a circumambient ocean. But plenty of maps survive to give us an idea of its character. The limits of the world had shrunken in the twelfth century to an area much smaller than that of which Ptolemy or Strabo and the other old Roman geographers had knowledge. Indeed the Christendom of the Crusades knew exactly as much or as little of Asia and Africa as Herodotus had known 1,600 years before. Now, as in the fifth century before Christ, men believed that beyond an India of no great extent there lay nothing but water, and that Africa was a comparatively narrow continent lying inland for some distance along the Mediterranean Sea. One school of geographers, whose conceptions are embodied in the delightful Hereford *Mappa Mundi*, deduced from Ezekiel v. 5 the fact that a circle drawn with Jerusalem as its central point, with a radius calculated by the distance from the Holy City to the extreme west of Portugal—obviously the end of the world—would exactly embrace the whole land of the earth. For was it not written, 'This is Jerusalem—I have set it in the midst of all the nations round about', and again, 'God is King of old, working

Man and the Universe 43

salvation in the middle of the earth'. So map-making was simplified or complicated (opinions may differ on the subject) by making the earth centre precisely round the Holy Sepulchre, to the sad diminution of Asia and Africa, and the complete distortion of outlying peninsulas like Scandinavia or India, which have to bend inward, in order to fit into the exact circumference as drawn by the compass. The Earthly Paradise, believed in by all medieval geographers, is screwed into the map as a circular island, enclosed by a wall, just opposite to the mouth of the Ganges. A little later, when Ceylon had been heard of, the Earthly Paradise had to recede to a continental position somewhere in Eastern China. Was not some memory of old-world readings hovering in the mind of the sleeping Coleridge, when it produced the gorgeous lines beginning

In Xanadu did Kubla Khan a stately Paradise devise.

The travels of Marco Polo and still more those of the several Franciscan friars who penetrated through the Mongol empire to the Chinese shore of the Pacific, had restored to Asia some of its forgotten width before the thirteenth century was over, and by the middle of the fifteenth the long Portuguese voyages down the coast of Africa, inspired by Henry the Navigator, had shown that the 'Black Continent' extended much farther to the south than Christendom had guessed. But the world was still a small affair. Nevertheless it could contain, in popular estimation, things supernatural—heaven and hell were very close. Hell and purgatory were, no doubt, not so very far under men's feet. Not only did countless edifying tales tell of descents into one or the other, but there were actual points of access—one was St. Patrick's Purgatory in Ulster, a recess into which pilgrims daring to take the downward way, after proper spiritual preparation, could hear the groans of those who were being purified by suffering, and even catch a glimpse of them. And few doubted that volcanoes were shafts sending up the flames of hell from the underworld. Had not a pious hermit seen the soul of the Arian King Theodoric thrust into the crater of Stromboli by a posse of evil spirits? Devils, indeed, in every respectable saintly legend come up out of the ground with a sulphurous smell, and, when duly foiled by the victorious saint, disappear by cleaving the ground to return to their central abyss. Probably every one remembers pictures of the sort. I recall particularly the splendid Gaudenzio Ferrari in the Brera at Milan, where a radiant St. Michael thrusts down the evil one into the mouth of the red pit from which he has emerged. The invariable sulphurous stench of fiends is an argument from analogy—derived from the sulphur fumes of the craters of volcanoes. Dante was echoing the universal voice of medieval superstition, when he made his visionary descents into the Inferno and the Purgatorio through gloomy caverns, ever tending downward to the inmost recesses of the earth.

And if hell was fairly close under men's feet, heaven was not so very far above the clouds. Medieval Christendom did not believe, like the ancient Greeks, that the abodes of the gods were on the summits of an earthly Olympus, an idea paralleled by the Indian conception of gods dwelling on the fabled Mount Meru. But blessed souls rapt upward by angels—as in countless pictures—had not so far to go but that they could, when necessary, return, to comfort those who needed their assistance in some subsequent time of crisis—temporal or spiritual. The universe was not so very large—a serious chronicler maintained that earth's highest mountains *almost* touched the orbit of the moon. Heaven, concealed by the clouds of the firmament, was not so hopelessly out of touch, and visitants from it were if not frequent at any rate pleasantly intermittent. In every medieval picture of the trials of a saint, the devil emerging from his subterranean pit is balanced by the angel fluttering down from the sky.

One feature of extreme importance in the psychology of the sixteenth century is the rapid clearing away by exploration of the old supernatural marvels of the world. To the medieval mind anything in the way of the miraculous might be found by the adventurous traveller. He might come on the Earthly Paradise, or the Fountain of Youth, or the land of the griffin and the roc and the fiery serpent, on an authentic mouth of Hell, or the stream dividing the earth in twain which no living man could pass. All these traditionary beliefs had been chased away by the circumnavigators, Magellan and his likes, who had passed round the whole globe and found nothing miraculous in it, if many things marvellous. The succeeding generation had to fall back on the search for more prosaic quests—El Dorado, the golden city, or the North-West Passage—which would be so very convenient if only it existed—across North America to Japan.

Man's mind had to cope for the future with a world divested of religious romance, if full of practical interests appealing to the adventurer in search of wealth. Westward he would no longer look for the Fortunate Isles or the soul-land of St. Brandan, but might exploit Mexico and Peru—a sordid and murderous—if lucrative—task. Eastward he would not find the Earthly Paradise, or the trees of the sun and moon, but might make a handsome profit by developing the spice trade. The sort of aspiration which had once expressed itself in Crusades, now took the form of an urge for exploration—and exploration with a severely practical notion of financial profit at its back. The man who would once have been a Crusader was now a *Conquistador*—in the seventeenth century he was to degenerate still further in many cases into a buccaneer or a slave-trader—both of whose avocations supplied the necessary excitement, profit, and adventure. But in the sixteenth century the old religious motive might still complicate itself in the cases of conscientious men with the idea of turning the benighted Mexican from his bloody human sacrifices to Christian morality, enforced by more or less drastic means. And the expansion of Portuguese trade in the Far East was at least accompanied by the devoted missions of the Jesuits to China and Japan—which not being backed by the sword were on the whole disappointing in their practical results.

Still—while not forgetting the laudable efforts of Las Casas and his followers the 'Apostles of the Indies' in the

West, or of Francis Xavier and his successors in the Far East, one feels that the inspiration of the sixteenth century was in the main not idealist but materialist. For old conceptions in which the 'Wanderlust' took shape, like the duty to go on Crusade, the real substitute was the urge for exploration—and exploration accompanied by profit. This smote all nations—the Portuguese and Spaniards first, then the English, French and Dutch. In the dim future were trade-wars as an exchange for Crusades.

The medieval folk were perhaps the more happy, in some ways, for their limited ideas. Our own map of the world, already adumbrated by the sixteenth-century circumnavigators and explorers, is dreadfully deficient in romance. It is really very hard to feel an eager interest in the completion of the exploration of Central Africa, or of the ice around the South Pole. When it is finished we do not expect to gain any great good from it, or to hear any particularly startling news about those regions. It will be the difficulties that fall upon the explorers, not the importance of their task, that draws attention to them. The discovery of a few more tribes of thoroughly uninteresting negroes, or a few more ice-blocked bays, has nothing in it to stir the heart of mankind. We look for no marvels to be unveiled, no great problems to be solved. The naturalist may indeed be gladdened by the knowledge of a new type of Antarctic gull, or a new species of tropical plants from the Upper Congo. The collector of folk-lore may gloat over some new and original negro ceremonies of sacrifice or funeral. But these things will not prove very interesting to the mass of mankind.

Now in the Middle Ages everything was in an absolutely different position. There was hardly anything conceivable on which the adventurous traveller might not come. There was a glorious uncertainty in the limits of the very imperfectly explored world. One might find not only populous lands and cities rich far beyond the ideas of Christendom —that luck did actually befall the men of the sixteenth century—but one had the delightful additional chance of running into the preternatural. Some travellers were honestly of the belief that they had seen sights for which no natural cause was conceivable. Others of a less trustworthy mentality *said* that they had done so, in order to impress the friends to whom on their return they had to tell their tale. Marco Polo, though otherwise an honest man and an acute observer, did actually believe that he had come into contact with evil spirits in the deadly passes of the Pamirs, where he came near to destruction. The ingenious man from Liège who hid himself under the name of the apocryphal Sir John Maundeville, claimed that he had drunk of the Fountain of Youth, and approached, though he could not enter, the Terrestrial Paradise. Such statements aroused interest in their contemporaries, but drew no contradiction, because they were regarded as eminently possible.

Such ideas were out of date by 1600—when the explorer hoped to find perhaps a new Mexico or Peru, a short cut by water across the American continent, or a practicable sea route round Siberia from Norway to Japan, but did not expect to gain easy connexion with Paradise or Purgatory upon the face of the globe. Superstition was not dead—there still survived a strong belief in witchcraft, astrology, the philosopher's stone, and what not, but the close touch with the supernatural which the men of the Middle Ages had enjoyed had waned. It suffices to compare the legends of the later saints who dwelt in the centuries after 1500, with those of the medieval holy men, to see what a change had taken place. Miracles are trifling or unconvincing—visions are obviously visions and no more. Public opinion, even among hagiologists, was not prepared to accept too startling statements, which ran too contrary to observed experience. In fact a certain glory had passed away from the world; the supernatural in everyday life was, if not disappearing, at least changing its character most completely. Saints no longer raised the dead, or banned visible demons, or preached with profit to the much-impressed birds and fish, or spoke spontaneously in unknown tongues to the heathen. Compare the lives of St. Francis or St. Antonino of Padua with those of St. Carlo Borromeo or St. Francis de Sales, and we see that something has changed in man's conception of the possible, the profitable, and the credible.

The change between 1500 and 1600 in this respect was of course most marked in that half of Europe which turned Protestant. Saint-making ceased, not so much because there was no longer any central power like the Papacy which could officially gazette saints, and put them in the annual Calendar under their proper day, but for deeper reasons. In a way all righteous men might be considered saints—some sects usurped the name for themselves. But firstly the use of the name had been notoriously abused in the Middle Ages—as thought King Henry VIII when he ordered the name of Thomas à Becket to be erased from the service books—the man had been guilty of manifest treason, said the King, zealous for rights of his ancestor Henry II. No Protestant could tolerate the sainthood of the persecutors of his spiritual forbears, like Dominic or Peter Martyr. And not only were some saints personally objectionable, but the spiritual position of the whole class had been grossly abused by the Middle Ages, when they were made patrons and intercessors who might stand between man and his God. Saint-worship and the intercession of saints for their votaries was a wicked invention, intended to block the direct relations between the human soul and the Deity. Good men of the past might be looked upon as ensamples of godly living, and so reverenced, but they had no power to interfere in the daily life of succeeding generations. It may be added that many of the worst trivialities and irreverent practices of the Middle Ages centred around saints, their shrines, their relics, and their festal days. The Protestant had a rooted dislike to wonder-working images, bones that could be touched for their medical virtues, and indulgences that could be got by visits to some officially guaranteed sepulchre. There was a fatal taint in all of them of exploitation of the laity by interested clerical custodians. Long before the sixteenth century the irreverent layman was beginning to have his doubts about wonder-working relics. The genial Chaucer

Man and the Universe 49

had ventured to hint that he feared that some of them were but ' piggies' bones '. To the modern mind there is something particularly repulsive in the idea of pulling the body of a holy man to pieces, and using bits of him as talismans or mascots. The ghastly little collection of scraps of bone, labelled with venerable names, which one sometimes finds still in churches of the ancient rite, are in themselves depressing. Holy men should be buried decently, not dissected. And it was incredible to the modern mind that a saint, even if he did preserve any interest in his own *disjecta membra*, would be able to procure any benefit to the sinner or criminal who adored them, kissed them, or took them about upon his person as amulets against danger. Consider the well-known scandals about the three heads of St. John the Baptist, or the three bodies of St. Baldred, exhibited in rivalry by three neighbouring churches, and one cannot wonder at the craze for relic-destruction which fell upon Protestant zealots. Many of them, the iconoclast said, were obvious impositions, all of them gave occasion to superstitious practices interfering between God and man. Wherefore they had better be all destroyed or burned with fire.

The pity, of course, from the point of the art-lover and the archaeologist, is that shrines were often triumphs of medieval jewellers' work, that relics were enclosed in priceless receptacles, and that statues and windows, never themselves worshipped, but only placed near some famous tomb, went the way of the rest, as monuments of superstition. Thomas Cromwell's aborninable satellites in their reports to the detestable vicar-general take credit, with numbers given, as to the amount of stained-glass windows that they have demolished in each of their turns. Our only marvel is that any have survived. The Scots and the Dutch were even worse than the English in the destruction of art-work, and the French Huguenots, though their opportunities were more limited, put in some considerable contributions to the holocaust of medieval things of beauty. One shudders to think of Theodore Beza, an educated man and a scholar, watching kegs of gunpowder piled under the high-altar of Orleans Cathedral, and sending altar, relics, statues and all sky-high, with a feeling of conscious rectitude. It can hardly be quoted in extenuation that the medieval custodians of holy things had been themselves great enemies of archaic but invaluable original monuments, and ruthlessly recast shrines or reset relics according to the fashion of their own day, having a considerable contempt for the 'rusticity' of their predecessors and appreciation for their own taste.

This tendency, we may remark incidentally, went on long after the Reformation. While the Protestants were wrecking artistic monuments in the North with iconoclastic fervour, as tainted with idolatry, in the South wealthy cardinals and bishops of the sixteenth and seventeenth centuries were habitually replacing original medieval work with pseudo-classical triglyphs and pediments, Corinthian columns, and marble sarcophagi. *Quod non fecerunt Barbari, fecerunt Barbarini* was an epigram that might be applied, with the proper change of personal names, to half the shrines of Italy. It is distressing to see faded corners of fourteenth- or fifteenth-century frescoes peeping out from behind immense baroque altar-pieces in coloured marbles, plastered on top of them by some prelate whose inscriptions proclaim pompously his malfeasance. But this, though criminal in itself in our eyes, is no excuse for the Protestant wreckers of the North.

But we must not wander too far into side issues, being in search of the major differences in men's outlook on the world that had happened between the fifteenth and the seventeenth centuries. One most notable change—we may ascribe most of it to those vague cataclysms which we call the Renaissance and the Reformation in such different proportions as we please—is the growth of the importance of the layman-specialist in all spheres of life. If we put aside merchants and bankers, who often, not in Italy alone, had achieved importance, the only professional careers of distinction which were not in the hands of ecclesiastics were those of the soldier, the lawyer and the physician. This was specially notable in the line of diplomacy and administration. Chancellors and ambassadors were generally highly placed ecclesiastics. Originally this had come from the plain fact that even the upper stratum of the laity was illiterate, and unfit to discharge functions in which a high education was necessary for competent work. This was gradually ceasing to be the case as the Middle Ages drew toward their end, and the ecclesiastical monopoly of high office was beginning to grow less universal. But, to take an English example, though the first lay chancellor can be discovered in the reign of Edward III, this great office was held by thrice as many bishops as lay magnates right down to the time of Henry VIII. Wolsey was not quite the last episcopal chancellor—Gardiner was destined to hold the office under Queen Mary. And embassies of any importance for international negotiation continued to have bishops at their head far into the sixteenth century.[1] Bishops or archbishops also were for many years Presidents of the Council of the North.[2] The same was the case in France, where the first minister of state was frequently an ecclesiastic not only down to the times of Richelieu and Mazarin, but even so late as Cardinal Fleury in the eighteenth century.

As to embassies, a change commenced when ecclesiastical and lay envoys were frequently sent together on a mission—one remembers the famous Holbein of the two French ambassadors, where the feathered nobleman is balanced by the capped and cassocked ecclesiastic. Presently the ecclesiastic dropped out—in England in the latter days of Henry VIII, who could not trust his bishops of the conservative sort, and did not think his tame prelates of 'the King's religion' quite distinguished enough for the job. But the same tendency was to be seen in France—clerical ambassadors began to grow rare about the same time,

[1] The last case, I believe, of a bishop being employed as a diplomatist in England, was that of Robinson of Bristol, who was one of the signatories of the Peace of Utrecht in 1713. This was wholly abnormal by that date.

[2] Ecclesiastical presidents of this very important administrative body are to be found even in the days of Elizabeth, when she had got together an Episcopate that she could trust.

largely no doubt because the French Government would not send Catholic prelates on political missions to Protestant countries, but also because educated and competent laymen were growing common. The French envoys in London in the days of Edward VI and Elizabeth were always *noblesse* of good abilities—as capable of the necessary evasions and intrigues as could be desired. Philip II, always a little behind the times, tried an ecclesiastical ambassador to the English court in the early days of Elizabeth : but though bishop De Quadra of Simancas sent him a most delightful synopsis of scandals and rumours, he did not turn out to be a prosperous negotiator, and was ultimately replaced by the layman Don Guerau de Spes.

The whole administrative system of Elizabeth was run by laymen—Burleigh, succeeded by his son Robert Cecil, Walsingham, Hatton, Leicester, Buckhurst, Raleigh, &c. Not an ecclesiastic had any notable part in foreign or domestic bureaucratic affairs—Elizabeth's archbishops were restricted to the not always very easy task of dealing with their clergy, whose conservative or progressive (i.e. Catholic or Puritan) tendencies had to be closely watched and shepherded. It was not till the unlucky days of Charles I that a king tried to give importance once more to a clerical element on the Council Board—the Laudian experiment was disastrous, as might have been foreseen from the first.

But it was not in high political spheres alone that the layman won an enhanced position in the sixteenth century. Professional specialists outside the classes of lawyers and physicians had held a very low rank in the Middle Ages. Architects, painters, sculptors, engineers, skilled craftsmen of every sort, musicians, schoolmasters, were little esteemed and commanded very low salaries. No one knows the names of the architects who built our cathedrals and abbeys—it was not the ecclesiastics who did the designing (as has been recently demonstrated) but professionals, whose remuneration was only that of a very superior master mason. No one knows who composed the music of the Middle Ages, and hardly the names of a few gold and silver workers have been preserved. The artist was considered much of the same rank as the house-painter and glazier, and paid on a scale not much more liberal. The schoolmaster got much less allowances than the bailiff on the neighbouring manor. All were held to be more or less parasites on society; they were useful, perhaps even necessary, but not considered to have any social status. Two unlucky kings in this island have it recorded among the many causes of their unpopularity that they loved to consort with musicians, skilled craftsmen and architects, rather than to go a-hunting or to figure at tournaments. I do not know that the artistic minions of Edward II came to any special disaster when their patron was dethroned. But the Scottish nobles gave vent to their disapproval of the tastes of James III by hanging his architect Cochrane, and his musician Rogers, over the arches of Lauder Bridge, along with several other minor professionals, whose company they considered discreditable to their monarch. And public opinion in the governing classes endorsed this drastic protest of Archibald Bell-the-Cat against degenerate and ungentlemanly habits.

The sixteenth century saw an extraordinary change in the position of the artistic specialists. We have only to think of well-known incidents such as the famous politeness of Charles V when he picked up the paint-brush of the aged Titian, or of Francis I weeping over the pillow of the dying Leonardo da Vinci, to understand that we have come into a new age. Culture has suddenly in the course of two short generations come to its own, and kings not only sought for artists all over Europe, but honoured them and paid them handsomely. The first trace that I can recall of this in England is when Henry VII—the last king of the Middle Ages but also the first king of the Renaissance—sent all the way to Italy to find Torrigiano, and to entrust him with the building of the splendid Renaissance tomb in Westminster Abbey, wherein lie his own body and that of his spouse Elizabeth of York. The new architecture made a complete conquest of England, as can be shown in the classical detail of all late Tudor tombs, where the lingering Gothic outlines are modified by profuse classical detail. The same change may be seen in contemporary France and Germany. The King's architect and the King's painter and his music-master became important personages at court—much sought after by obsequious magnates who wished to be in the fashion. In Italy every prince and doge covered his once arrased or frescoed walls with immense pictures in the classical taste, and spared no expense. Alas that the art of Raphael or Titian was destined to degenerate into that of Bassano and Tintoretto, whose once-esteemed productions cover acres of now unappreciated canvas !

Another product of the sixteenth century is the literary layman. I do not mean that there were no literary laymen before the Renaissance, from the forgotten authors of the Chansons de Geste and the Troubadours down to Dante or Chaucer, or Charles of Orleans or the tedious Gower, or dozens of others who escape notice by their obscurity. But the lay memoir writer, the essayist, the scholar, the political controversialist, even the novelist (as opposed to the old composer of tales of chivalry), are as numerous in the sixteenth as they were scarce in the fifteenth century. Clerics are rare for the future in the literary ranks, though I do not forget Rabelais or Erasmus—who was in such minor orders that though technically a clerk he was never a priest. If he had been born twenty years later, I do not think that he would have been in orders at all. But setting aside theological controversy, where they naturally appear as specialists on one side or another, the ecclesiastics are rather out of the game, so far as fine literature is concerned. I leave the theological sphere alone, and shall not speak of Luther or Calvin or Cardinal Bellarmine or Sarpi.

The layman comes to the front in the sixteenth century in every other line of composition, from solid history to epic poetry and political philosophy. To take England alone, we find, instead of the mostly clerical annalists of Lancastrian days, real historians like Sir Thomas More (it is a pity that he wrote no history save his engrossing narrative of the time of Richard III), Hall, Hollingshed and Sir Walter Raleigh. We are rather short of good autobiographies in

England—Lord Herbert of Chirbury, who wrote after 1600, is really our first interesting autobiographer. But French laymen who wrote their personal adventures in an engaging style are very numerous. I need only mention Comines—who bridges the years between the fifteenth and the sixteenth centuries—Montluc (that delightful self-centered Gascon), Tavannes, Vielville, Fleurange (German by birth but French by breeding), and Sully, who takes us on into the seventeenth century, just as Comines at the commencement of the change takes us back into the sixteenth. Each was a man who started in the one century and went on into the other. Next to autobiographies come biographies : I need only mention the ' Loyal Serviteur ' who wrote the delightful life of the Chevalier Bayard, and Brantôme, who drew the characters of scores of his contemporaries, from the ' hommes illustres ' to the ' dames galantes '. Oddly enough, while England had no autobiographist who could be compared to Montluc or Sully, Scotland produced one first-class specimen of the sort, Sir James Melville, who wrote a most interesting account of his own vicissitudes from the last years of James V, all through the troubled times of Mary Queen of Scots, down to the days of the Gowrie plot, and other misadventures of James VI and I. It is a very long tale, starting from misfortune at the battle of St. Quentin in 1557, and going down to 1590. I know nothing like it for giving personal impressions of the unfortunate Queen, the ruffianly Bothwell (who nearly murdered Melville on one occasion), and the various regents who kidnapped or controlled James VI during his prolonged and much-troubled minority. It is a thousand pities that Walter Raleigh did not write about the court of Elizabeth instead of starting on his immense torso of a universal history ! He had the literary power to do it. Or that Philip Sidney had left behind him some personal impressions rather than a tedious pastoral romance.

Meanwhile, Italy swarmed with historians of considerable merit, such as Paolo Giovio, Guicciardini, and, so far as his narrative output goes, Machiavelli, though one thinks of him as a political philosopher, or a military critic rather than a historian, when one has been reading the *Prince*, the commentaries on Livy, or the *Arte di Guerra*.

Political philosophy is naturally closely connected with history, though it may swerve off into social economy, or discussion on morals in general, or divagations on the relations of Church and State, or discussions on the foundations of law. The Middle Ages had their contributors to this sort of literature, some of them scholastically minded, some of them severely practical like the author of the *De Regimine Principum*, some legally-minded like Marsilius. Naturally, the relations between the Papacy and the emperors had produced a certain amount of controversial literature. But the sixteenth century, largely influenced by newly discovered classic lore, which had been unknown to the preceding ages, launched out into much wider and more universal methods of thought, unknown to their predecessors. Scientific discovery had also its influence—the philosopher who starts from the geocentric theory, envisages the world somewhat differently from him who has to grapple with the new heliocentric conception of the universe. But I cannot go off into discussion of a sphere of thought which has to embrace all manner of thinking from More's *Utopia*, Montaigne's *Essays*, Calvin's views on the relation of Church and State, down to Bacon's *Novum Organum*, which I take to be really sixteenth-century thought, though the 'wisest, greatest, meanest, of mankind' lived some way into the following age. But by the end of the sixteenth century we are well launched in methods of thought that are comprehensible to the modern mind, and the days of scholasticism are far away in the past.

As to pure literature, so called, poetry, drama, *belles lettres* in general, the change is just as evident. Compare English poetry, lyric or narrative, of the fifteenth and the sixteenth centuries—the former practically non-existent, the latter at best ballad-mongering, in the earlier age. Not that I wish to deny all merit to the ' Lay of the Lady Bessie ' and certain others of the later ballads. But Skelton was the best rhymer that we could show even in early sixteenth century, and he is unreadable save to professional historians

Man and the Universe 57

of literature. While, starting from Surrey and Wyatt, English lyric poetry takes a sudden uplift, which soars into the highest possible merit in the days of Elizabeth. The fifteenth century was unaccountably dumb—the later sixteenth as unaccountably vocal. Whence exactly came the inspiration? Renaissance *joie de vivre* hardly seems to account for it, nor conscious or unconscious copying of continental models.

This is not the place to discuss literary history in general, but one must make a space for the mention of the drama—the Middle Ages give us no more than miracle-plays (generally very prosaic and trivial) and 'moralities', which are sometimes a shade better. The sixteenth century launches out into the modern drama, whose beginnings may be sought in queer combinations of survivals of the miracle-play with its inevitable 'fool' or 'vice', with inspiration sought from Terence—inexplicably popular in the Renaissance time—and even Plautus. Italy starts with the obviously classical imitation like Machiavelli's *Clizia* and *Casina*: in France Jodelle's *Cleopatra* and *Dido* and such things superseded 'mysteries' and 'sottises' from 1550 onward. In England the development was rapid and extraordinary from miracle-plays, via *Ralf Royster Doyster*—which is rustic Terence adapted to Tudor taste—through blood-and-thunder melodramas with a pseudo-historical foundation, like Gorboduc, up to the highest tragedy and comedy in Shakespeare—that wonderful man who could make good plays out of every sort of timber. He could adapt Plautus' Menaechmi into the *Comedy of Errors*, or rather inferior Italian stories into *Othello*, or the *Merchant of Venice*, and turn the apocryphal prehistoric legends of Geoffrey of Monmouth into *King Lear*, which is very live stuff, or make *Macbeth* out of a few hints from Hollingshed's boil-down of early Scottish history, which is all that he knew of the original story. One must not go into the personal element in his play-making, which has been so much emphasized in recent years, but rather look at the way in which an individual of genius born in 1564 could envisage human nature, and the humours and ironies of life. One cannot imagine a fifteenth-century English writer elaborating the absurdities of Falstaff, Nick Bottom, or Dogberry, any more than one can imagine him drawing and understanding the psychological difficulties and mental agonies of Hamlet. I count Shakespeare as pure sixteenth century, though he lived some sixteen years into the seventeenth, for he was well started in his work before the turn of the centuries, and there was nothing cataclysmic in the accession of James I to make a change of outlook on the world natural to a dramatist—or to any one else, save perhaps a bigoted exponent of the necessity of a perpetual war with Spain.

I think a parallel might be drawn as to the sixteenth-century development of mind between Shakespeare and Cervantes—equally clear exponents of their age. The one dwelt for practically all his working years in London, and retired, as a successful man in the eyes of the everyday world, to live as a small squire in Warwickshire. The other, a soldier who battled all over the Mediterranean lands, was a leading instance in the history of literary men's ill-luck, and died in poverty, a disappointed veteran. Perhaps Shakespeare may have been a disappointed man also—but the world judged him lucky. Had he not (a thing wholly unprecedented and incredible) made a fortune out of the play-house? But he and Cervantes had in common the humorously cynical outlook on mankind and its frailties ('Lord, what fools these mortals be!' says Puck), and an inimitable power of expressing it—the one in tales, the other in dramatic shape. And both combined the humorous outlook with the aspiration for something deeper and nobler, and had their ideals, though they sometimes concealed them. Don Quixote, for all his absurdities is a tragic figure, most tragic, perhaps, because Cervantes, laughing at romances of chivalry and their belated admirer, must have felt that his knight was—after all—a much more sympathetic figure than the contemporaries—dukes or innkeepers alike—among whom his lot was cast. He would not have written of Don Quixote unless he himself, in earliest years, had felt the romantic urge also, and had come to bitter disillusionment. When one has realized *vanitas*

Man and the Universe 59

vanitatum, it requires a very well-tempered mind to express one's experiences in a humorous form. There is a strong temptation to the commentator to look upon Shakespeare, the successful opportunist so far as material matters went, and Cervantes the broken idealist, as national representatives of the struggle between the England of Elizabeth and the Spain of Philip II—they were almost exactly contemporaries (1564–1616 and 1547–1616). This is dangerous work: for I fear that Shakespeare was not a typical Englishman, nor Cervantes a typical Spaniard—though both were typical representations of aspects of the sixteenth century. They had cast medievalism behind them, and could see its absurdities, and realized that they were living in the modern world —which had a new set of puzzles of its own—which might be faced with some sort of a new philosophy of life—cynically humorous or humorously cynical perhaps—but not wholly optimistic, and most certainly not medieval.

The sixteenth century had its literary men who were moral misfits : I am not going to say that such did not exist before 1500—Villon was a fine example. But there is plenty of difference between the Parisian and Christopher Marlowe —a misfit of a much more complicated kind. The one is purely 'picaresque'—a companion of burglars and cutpurses—the other tempestuous and rather satanic, with a queer acquaintance among political spies and shady secret agents—at the hands of one of whom he met his death, not in a mere tavern brawl (as legend said), but in some undiscernible intrigue. Yet he was a master of the 'Ercles vein', and could 'crush, quail, conclude and quell' with the best of his contemporaries, or 'make and mar the foolish fates' with sonorous dignity. And he is not merely 'full of sound and fury—signifying nothing', but has glimpses of the eternal ironies and verities.

But the main difference between the medieval and the modern conception of good and evil in mankind, is that the evil is objective and merely perverse in the Middle Ages : tyrants are tyrants because they are tyrannical—ogres and giants are cannibalistic and treacherous because they are ogres or giants—and therefore to be feared, or disposed of by some simple sword-thrust or ingenious trick. They rank with dragons, as undesirable abnormalities, which need no explanation. The sixteenth century came to see that villains have a psychology like other people. Tyrants are tyrannical because they live in perpetual fear of an assassin, or because they have become megalomaniac by seeing their worst ambitions accomplished. Traitors are not merely traitors for the pleasure of treason, but because they have some old grievance, some well-nursed plan of revenge, or (less frequently) see a short cut to some otherwise unattainable end (power or wealth) by an unscrupulous act. Shakespeare could even arrive at the psychology of the hired assassin, when he set forth the two confessions of the first and second murderers to Macbeth. Generally the psychology of murderers did not trouble earlier generations—they were taken for granted, as toads and adders are. And the sentiment of the man in the street was 'I'll teach you to be a toad' by prompt and drastic suppression. When we set about to analyse our villains we are becoming modernistic, and shall some day come to find Tiberius, Nero, Richard III, Philip II, or Robespierre comprehensible human beings, and not merely monsters of evil, like King Herod in the miracle-play—though monsters of evil they incidentally were. Philip II and Robespierre were undoubtedly unaware of this simple fact about themselves, and conceived that they were faithful ministers of the Church in one case, and of the *Être Suprême* in the other. Glimpses of the obvious are proverbially difficult to get—when we ourselves are concerned. Hamlet—a glorious exception—was quite aware of this. But introspection—except morbid religious introspection by those obsessed by the consciousness of sin—was as rare in the Middle Ages as it was to be common in the seventeenth century.

We are on the way to 'the noblest study of mankind is man'—but have still some distance to traverse before that conception is to become popular. There were many stages of thinking to go through before we reach it, from Calvin's absolute division between the saved and damned, and Hobbes' 'natural man' with his short, brutal, sensual, miserable life, to Rousseau's absurd picture of the virtuous noble savage, untroubled by the arts of priests and princes. Hobbes, I suppose, was nearer the mark as to primitive man, as the spade of the archaeologist bears witness. But it is only a limited number of us who are prepared to accept his deduction as to the necessity for a dictatorial one-man power to build and control the unitarian state—without which we are to relapse into prehistoric barbarism. The theory is much in vogue at present, as witness the positions of Herr Adolf Hitler and others, save that the divine king is replaced by the almost divine Führer. Constitutional monarchy and parliamentary government are no longer the universal panacea that they were supposed to be in the nineteenth century. We realize the change when we read of ' Parliamentarianism ' used as a term of abuse in many a twentieth-century screed. Nevertheless, neither can we raise the slogan ' back to Hobbes ', nor can we acquiesce in the easy-going formula that

> Whate'er is best administered is best.

For it remains as true as ever that

> How small of all that human hearts endure
> The part which laws or kings can cause or cure!

Mankind is heterogeneous, and what is one race's panacea may be another race's poison. The sort of administration that seems best to the one unit, may be execrated by another. Sad as the fact may be, there is no universal remedy for anything, whatever authoritarian theorists may say.

CHAPTER V

TENDENCIES AND INDIVIDUALS. THE POPES
AND THE KINGS OF FRANCE

Two generations have now passed since the blessed word 'Evolution' was invented, and was applied as a universal panacea to all the problems of the universe—historical no less than physical. By this I mean that a whole school of historians have set forth the thesis that history is a continuous logical process, a series of inevitable results following on a well-marshalled table of causes. Of course the logician may tell us that every consequence is the summing up of its antecedents. But that is hollow formal logic. And to my mind it is impossible to turn all history into a continuous and mechanical panorama of logical causes followed by inevitable results. My humble opinion is that things might generally have happened otherwise than they actually did. The history of mankind is often accidental, even occasionally cataclysmic. It is not a logical stream of cause and effect, but a series of happenings, affected in the most inscrutable fashion by incalculable chances, which were not in the least bound to occur, ranging from natural phenomena such as plagues or earthquakes, to the appearance of outstanding human personalities who 'put on the clock' or occasionally 'put the clock back'. The Whig historians who pontificated on the theme that 'history is the history of peoples, as opposed to the personal adventures of kings and statesmen' were far more wrong in their general conception of the world than Thomas Carlyle preaching of the all-importance of the individual in his book on 'Heroes'.

Those who proclaim that they will write the history of a century or a country with 'the people' as the protagonist, are infected with the 'equalitarian' dislike for figures that

The Popes and the Kings of France 63

are too abnormal to fit into a theory of continual logical 'progress'. They try to whittle down the Superman into a mere typical product of his age and race, whose greatness shall not offend the susceptibilities of smaller folk—such as historians—and sin against the precious doctrine of equality. If our researches end by making the Hero into a mere incarnation of his race, or the *Zeitgeist*, it is all the more flattering to the man in the street. I have read arguments to prove that Julius Caesar, Charlemagne, Martin Luther, and Mussolini are no more than typical developments of their age and their surroundings—even that some one else would have taken their places if they had not been born. This I take to be absurd: there have been countless crises in history where the opportunity did not produce the man, as according to this doctrine it should have done, and when things paltered on without the solution which to us seems obvious, if only there had been some strong personality to provide it. And on the other hand, the man has sometimes made the opportunity, rather than found it waiting for him.

The opportunity was obviously waiting for the man or men who could seize it at the end of the fifteenth century, and no single dominating personality appeared—no Julius Caesar, or Charlemagne, or Hildebrand, or Bonaparte. But instead we find a group of figures each exercising wide influences over his contemporaries, but none of them of universal compelling power. Some of them neutralized many of the activities of the others. The interesting thing is to find that the mere political opportunities got mixed up in the second quarter of the century with the religious complications, and remained so tangled up for a century. At the beginning of the period we might think that we were to study a struggle for domination in Europe between the houses of Hapsburg and Valois. By the middle of it we find Christendom torn across by internal scissions in each country on the question of religion, so that at one moment half Germany is attacking the Emperor with the assistance of France, and at another half France is assailing the Valois government with the aid of countless levies from the Protestant half of Germany. There were times when Dutch subjects of the Hapsburgs, French Huguenots, and English Protestants regarded each other as brothers and allies, 'those of the religion', as French and English contemporary writers call themselves. While at the same time French and English Catholics were looking to Spain for aid against the heretic. Nationalism seemed for the moment superseded by international religious alliances between sectarian parties in each country.

How did the established figure-heads, kings and popes, face the problems, merely political at first, but presently completely complicated by religious cross-currents? And outside the list of kings and popes, what other personalities directed the course of events?

The kings of France from Charles VIII to Henry II were flamboyant figures with no touch whatever from the spirit of the oncoming age, save that the last two of them were affected by Renaissance culture. They had all one misplaced ambition, the establishment of a French empire in Italy, to which all other considerations were subordinated. The religious movements outside France in the times of Francis I and Henry II were regarded by those monarchs, who had no religious inspiration whatever themselves, merely as useful happenings, which distracted their enemy the Emperor Charles V. They leagued themselves with Schmalkaldic German princely allies, just as at other times they leagued themselves with the Turk. Some Frenchmen —as La Noue for example—urged that it was a mortal sin to enter into alliances with the infidel: others, pious Catholics, thought that it was equally immoral to help the North-German Protestants—open rebels against the Holy Roman Church. But such considerations of propriety had no influence whatever on Francis I or Henry II, who for their personal convenience were prepared to enlist the help of any enemy of Christendom. Most of their subjects agreed with them; in the words of the old swashbuckler Montluc, 'Princes on the other side made much ado about our master calling in the Turk to his aid. For my own part, I would call up all the devils of Hell to break my enemy's head when he is trying to break mine.'[1]

For sixty years the kings of France ignored the great spiritual problems of the age, merely striving to set up their empire in Italy. Sometimes they fought with, sometimes against, the Pope—who was for them not a religious but a secular Italian power. Sometimes they were excommunicated—occasionally they tried to set up an anti-papal synod of cardinals, who should bless where the Pope banned. For the first thirty years of the struggle for Italy the French kings were not so very wrong in their estimate of their papal contemporaries. Alexander VI, Julius II, and Leo X were essentially statesmen with a local Italian policy—which varied with the individual pontiff for personal or family reasons. No one could mistake them for religious leaders, or for personalities with any inspiring influence, save that which their official position gave them. Alexander VI was universally acknowledged to be a public scandal to Christendom : Julius II was a hasty-tempered, belligerent old man, much set on the prosperity of the house of Della Rovere as well as on the extension of the limits of the papal states. The one general thesis attributed to him was that ' the Barbarians ought to be thrust across the Alps ', but this was not because the Barbarians were barbarous or foreign, but because they interfered with papal politics. He was not an Italian patriot, and hated some of his countrymen and neighbours as much as he hated the French. Leo X was primarily a member of the House of Medici, for whose advancement he was ready to risk much, and secondarily a dilettante and a patron of the fine arts. Cultural rather than spiritual problems interested him, and contemporary malevolence put into his mouth the cynical epigram that ' Christianity was a profitable religion for priests '. It was one of the humours of history that his great plan for the rebuilding of St. Peter's at Rome was the indirect cause of Martin Luther's first outbreak of rebellion against the Papacy. For the indulgence-certificates which Tetzel sold so abundantly in Ger-

[1] Montluc, ii, p. 137.

many, and which provoked the hitherto unknown professor at Wittenburg, were to contribute their proceeds toward the reconstruction in high classical style of the great Basilica. Who could have conceived that a zeal for classical architecture could bring about a religious cataclysm?

The French kings therefore were not to be blamed as enemies of Christendom because they fell out with certain very unspiritual popes in the course of their invasions of Italy. That condemnation may be reserved for their conduct of a few years later, when they leagued themselves with Sultan Soliman, while the Turks were overrunning the Hungarian and Austrian lands on the Danube, and threatening to sweep away all the barriers of eastern Europe. But real blame falls upon them for not understanding that the establishment of a French empire in Italy was a vain dream, for military and geographical reasons, if not for racial or national ones. Seven disastrous expeditions from Charles VIII's first march to Naples in 1494, to the last misguided raid into the southern kingdom under Guise in 1557, were required to prove to the House of Valois that 'Italy was the grave of the French'. Italy could not have been held by any power that had not a permanent command of the sea, and an enormous army for purely garrison purposes. No French king ever enjoyed the first, nor had the resources for the pay of the second. French armies in Italy always melted away, as much from want of financial maintenance as from the chances of war, or the diseases bred by free living in an unfamiliar clime.

The net result of sixty years of misdirected energy on the part of four French kings was to crush out the spirit of the Italians—the land was devastated from end to end, and the old civic enthusiasm dead. The French had worked for the Hapsburgs—and, as it turned out, for the Spanish branch, which retained none of the more genial inspiration of Maximilian I and Charles V, but was purely dull and decadent. With Philip II reigning in Milan and Naples, with bastard houses connected with popes in Tuscany and Parma as vassals of the Spaniard, with Venice and Genoa permanently reduced from first-rate to second-rate powers,

The Popes and the Kings of France 67

Italy was to start on the century and a half of Spanish domination which meant spiritual death and cultural decay. Without professing an illimitable worship for Pre-Rafaelite art, or 'standing mute before Botticelli', we may lament the taste of an age which patronized Ribera and Caravaggio and Bassano, one may add the Carracis and Tintoretto, and erected all the baroque churches of seventeenth-century Italy. That taste was the outward and visible sign of the loss of inspiration and the general decadence which came from that subjection to the Spanish yoke, which was completed when the French retired hurt from the long struggle for domination in the Peninsula, and found occupation in forty years of civil war between the Huguenot and the Catholic factions. Perhaps the most distressing thing in Rome is the fresco by Vasari outside the Sistine Chapel which represents the Massacre of St. Bartholomew, and in particular the murder of Admiral Coligny. It used to bear the inscription *Ugonottorum Strages*, but that has been removed, and the uninformed tourist often asks in wonder what the picture chances to represent. It was painted in the moment of enthusiasm which led Pope Gregory XIII to strike a medal with the same inscription, whereon a winged angel is represented slashing down with his sword a number of cowering figures of unprepossessing aspect. On the other side of the door of the Sistine it is balanced by a fresco, representing the triumph of Don John of Austria (1571) over the Turks at the naval victory of Lepanto—an exploit to which the Massacre of St. Bartholomew was evidently regarded as an appropriate pendant. This seems odd to the modern observer, for the murder of an unarmed old man and his friends by a gang of midnight conspirators hardly seems a fair parallel to the defeat of a dangerous fleet of infidels after a hard battle. And after all the Huguenots were *not* exterminated on the night of St. Bartholomew, but survived to wage twenty years more of war, and to win themselves toleration by the sword.

Italy, however, had certainly been ruined by the great wars of 1493–1558, and ceased for a century and more to be the focus round which all European politics centred.

And the kings of France, whose personal ambitions were all important in the first half of the sixteenth century, count for nothing in the second, till at its very end Henry of Navarre succeeded in establishing himself on the throne of his very distant cousin of the House of Valois. And even he, the ruler of a devastated land where civil war was only just dying down, had not the time to do much more than show the beginnings of a policy before he was assassinated. He was, after all, one of the great opportunists with whom we shall be dealing presently, an important figure, but not the exponent of one of those enthusiasms which shake the world. Toleration by compromise may be an excellent thing, but it leaves both parties to that compromise discontented, when each regards its own faith as not only true but morally bound to be militant and propagandic.

The kings of France then left no personal impression on the spirit of the century, though they bulk so largely in any narrative of its annals. All that we can say is that if some of them had been other men than they were, the course of history might have been very different. If, for example, Francis I had been another Louis XI—ascetic, economical, unchivalrous, given to intrigue more than to war—the struggle between Valois and Hapsburg would not have taken the shape of successive invasions of Italy always ending in disaster. Or if Charles IX had been a vigorous, self-reliant, strong-handed king, like his grandfather Francis I, there might have been no Huguenot wars. The personal element counted for much, but the individual left no permanent influence on his times.

To a large extent this was also the case with the popes —a series of persons who had to deal with a crisis which was so unprecedented that for many years not one of them could comprehend its meaning, much less dominate its development. Some of them were men with a strong will, some of them merely time-servers and opportunists—trying to discover ' a pill for the earthquake '. All of them with the exception of the short-lived Adrian VI were Italians, and nearly all of them allowed Italian politics to occupy their minds as much as the general crisis in Christendom with which they had to cope. Moreover, they were generally old men already when they came to power, and had but a few years in which to exercise their authority. It may not be generally realized that there were no less than *eighteen* popes in the hundred years between 1500 and 1600. Even after deducting five who reigned but for a few months, in some cases but for a few days (Pius IV, Marcellus II, Urban VII, Gregory XIV and Innocent IX), there were thirteen popes to the century. Of these only two, and those both men of no particular mark, Paul III and Gregory XIII, enjoyed more than ten years of possession of the throne of St. Peter. The average was more like five or six years. When it is remembered that each was elected after a stormy, and sometimes a long, conclave, and required some time to assert his authority over his late rivals, it is easy to understand that there was a sharp break of continuity between each reign. The newly chosen Pope was often precisely the man whom his predecessor especially disliked. Most inaugurations meant the bringing in of a new batch of cardinal-nephews, and new secretaries in every department of Church management. The wonder is that there was even so much continuity in the general policy of the Papacy as can be detected.

It is therefore no cause of wonder that no individual pope of the whole thirteen who covered the century can in any way be called the dominating spirit of the period. Several of them are sufficiently prominent personages, as a pope would naturally be in any case. But prominence does not necessarily imply dominance, spiritual or political. It may be said in a rough general fashion that the popes down to 1554 were men of the preceding century—Italian princes primarily, witnesses of a world-convulsion whose full meaning escaped them. The short-lived Adrian VI, the last non-Italian pope, was the only exception. As to the rest Alexander VI, whose disgraceful pontificate opens the century, was a public scandal, even in those days, for nepotism, cruelty, political fraud, and personal immorality. Julius II was a politician of military tastes, whose violent schemes usually came to disaster. Leo X was a patron of all culture (and of his relations of the House of Medici) entirely destitute of any moral or spiritual enthusiams, whose contemporaries doubted even if he were a good Christian, but were certain that he was a good art-critic. His dealings with the rival foreign powers who aimed at the subjection of Italy were shifty and unscrupulous, and his treatment of the first symptoms of the reform movement in Germany show that he wholly misunderstood its character and importance. The Dutchman Adrian VI, an intruder thrust in by the Emperor among the long line of Italian popes, had hardly time to announce his policy of inquiry into abuses, before he was carried off by the Roman climate, so deadly to northerners. Clement VII, another Medici, had to face a situation in the Church which had grown far more dangerous than had been the case in the time of his cousin Leo X. So far was he from realizing this, that his first care was not to attend to religious matters, but to stir up a purely political war with the Emperor Charles, which ended in his seeing Rome stormed and sacked by a horde of famished landsknechts. Having humbled himself before Caesar, and crowned his conqueror at Bologna in 1520, he had three years left him for indulging in shifty negotiations with Henry VIII of England, on the disgraceful marriage-question—negotiations which reflected credit on neither party.

Clement's successor Paul III was essentially a 'family man' more interested in the planting out of his bastard son Pier Luigi Farnese in the duchy of Parma—he would have liked to get him Milan too—than in the summoning of the General Council at Trent, which the Emperor persisted in forcing upon him (1545). He had the old papal notion that General Councils, and emperors also, were dangerous to the supremacy of popes, and actually succeeded in breaking up the first sessions at Trent by recalling the Italian bishops to Bologna on the pretence of a scare of plague. When Charles triumphed over the Protestant princes of Germany at Mühlberg (1547), Paul is said to have shown some disappointment over this complete

The Popes and the Kings of France 71

discomfiture of the heretics. He had hoped that the war might be a protracted one, and would distract the Emperor from Italian affairs for a year or two. He was a pure opportunist, and though he enjoyed the longest reign of the century (1533-48), left nothing decided among all the religious problems of the time. As a sample of his procrastination it may be noted that though he drew up his bull of excommunication (well deserved) against Henry VIII of England in 1535, he did not publish it till 1538. The final blast was caused by the fact that Henry 'so far from profiting by the leniency of the Curia had proceeded to further excesses, having dug up and burned the bones of St. Thomas of Canterbury', the greatest martyr of the medieval Church.

Julius III, the successor of Paul III, had but a short reign of five years. He yielded to the Emperor in the matter of reopening the Council of Trent, having perhaps a better notion of the absolute necessity of some sort of settlement of Church affairs than his suspicious predecessor, who thought only of the danger to his own power from conciliar pressure. But he was far more interested in the idea of endeavouring to oust Paul's bastards from the duchy of Parma, and in his plans for adorning Rome with gardens and new buildings, such as his *Villa Giulia*. For he was an easy-going and luxurious personage, without any very marked political or spiritual ambitions. In a way he may be called the last of the Renaissance popes— who appreciated the good things of this life, and failed to take with sufficient seriousness the crisis of the times in which his lot was cast.

His successor, Paul IV, was a very different character : he left some mark behind him and may justly be called the first of the popes of the Counter-Reformation, for he visualized the religious situation with a clearness to which none of the popes of the last forty years had attained. Oddly enough, however, he was also the last inheritor of the old dislike of the Papacy for the House of Hapsburg, and in his early years chose to make an attack on Philip II, the head of the Catholic party in Europe, on account of old family grudges concerning local Neapolitan politics. For he came from a house of Neapolitan nobles, the Caraffas, which had always taken sides against Philip's ancestors. In 1556 this policy seemed to savour of insanity. Paul, no doubt, was thinking of similar assaults on the Hapsburgs made by his predecessors : had not Clement VII, at the League of Cognac, endeavoured to stir up all Europe against Philip's father ? But in 1526 the scission between Catholic and Protestant was not yet the dominant fact in European politics. By 1557 it was : and an attempt by the Papacy to strike down the strongest Catholic power was wrongheaded ; it was also a sheer impossibility : Philip's general, the Duke of Alva, swept away the Roman army, and its French auxiliaries, with ease, and imposed a dictated peace on the old Caraffa. The terms were not hard, for Philip was a pious man according to his lights. But they sufficed to teach popes for the future that Italy was now a Spanish domain, and that it was hopeless to think of breaking loose. No later pontiff was unwise enough to kick against the pricks.

But the really important part of the doings of Paul IV was that he put himself at the head of the intransigent Catholic party at the restored Council of Trent—though he would have preferred to work the Counter-Reformation by purely papal authority rather than by that of a Council— and to stand firm on the resolve that there must be a reform of morals in the Church, but no trace whatever of any change of doctrine. There must be no further attempt to lure back Protestants to the fold by concessions on disputed points, such as justification by faith, the sacrament in both kinds, the marriage of the clergy, the sole authority of the Scriptures as opposed to pious tradition. The Protestant must for the future be regarded as an enemy to be suppressed by force, not as a lost sheep to be coaxed back into the flock by argument or persuasion.

Hence the two sides of the activity of Paul IV—he raged against the financial corruption, for which the courts of Rome were famous : he made a clean sweep of clerical officials convicted of blackmailing and embezzlement—

The Popes and the Kings of France 73

including some of his own relatives—enforced sumptuary laws, and started on an attack upon simony, pluralities and non-residence, the besetting sins of the higher clergy. He was especially keen on the suppression of unseemly luxury and frivolity among the countless dependents on the papal court, and insisted on gravity of manners and frequent attendance at the Mass and the Confessional. So unpopular were these puritanical measures that the population of Rome is said to have begun to go down during his pontificate.

But the other side of Paul's work was for the repression not of corruption but of unorthodoxy by the use of the stake and the axe. He introduced a more rigid Inquisition into the Papal States, and proceeded to hunt down all persons whom he considered as fair game—not only Lutherans and relapsed Jews, but persons suspected of free thinking of any sort, philosophers, deists, agnostics and professed Catholics who were found to be unsound on cardinal points of the faith. Of these there was no small crop to be harvested, for the revival of learning and classical studies had not been favourable to orthodoxy. But the Protestant victims were comparatively few : Lutheranism and Calvinism had never taken any strong root south of the Alps. The Roman Inquisition, carried on with zeal both by Paul and by his successor Pius IV, produced more recantations than burnings—as had been the case in England, when the Wycliffites were persecuted in the fifteenth century. But the total of victims of the axe, cord and stake (many were hung or beheaded before they were burned) was considerable, and included some notable names such as that of the scholar Antonio Paleario (1570) ; the fate of the more celebrated Giordano Bruno, who mixed pantheism with Protestantism, belongs to the last year of the century (1600).

Along with the Inquisition Paul IV introduced the famous invention of the Index Librorum Prohibitorum, the list of books of evil tendency, the possession of which would get the owner into trouble with the Inquisition. The two sides of Pope Paul's mentality are beautifully represented in the Index. On the one hand it contains all the works of Luther, Calvin, Zwingli and such people, along with the more cryptically heretical translations of the Bible into the vernacular tongue, and certain controversial works in which good Catholics arguing with Protestants had slipped into error of doctrine, through compromise or over statement. On the other hand were books judged immoral, either like Machiavelli's *Prince* on political grounds, or like Boccaccio's *Decameron* and Aretino's satires by reason of their indecency and shamelessness. Scientific works like Copernicus's refutation of the geocentric theory slipped into the list as attacking the first chapter of Genesis, concerning the creation of the world. But, indeed, almost any scientific book could be made to figure in the Index by an ingenious board of censors. The most humorous working of the Index was perhaps the passing of an expurgated edition of Boccaccio's famous stories, the expurgation consisting not in the removal of their lewdness (an impossible task, for it is essential) but in making the perpetration of sexual offences not monks or friars but laymen, and not nuns but burgesses' wives! This absurd censorship was destined to endure for centuries, and the Congregation of the Index still exists to-day, to deal with the heterogeneous mass of twentieth-century political and religious books which are considered unwholesome reading for the unlearned laity.

Pius IV, like his predecessor Paul IV, had but a short reign, but left some impression on the time by his successful and persistent manipulation of the Council of Trent, which he guided to its end of leaving all doctrine unchanged, all influence of national particularism and lay statecraft excluded, a considerable amount of administrative reform accomplished, and the theoretical supremacy of the Papacy fully acknowledged. In Rome he was mainly remembered for the clean sweep which he made of his predecessor's disreputable nephews. The cardinal Carlo Caraffa was strangled, his brother Giovanni Caraffa decapitated, not without good reason, and several other nobles of the family group with him. But while severe on the relatives of his predecessor, Pius was not exempt from this same habitual weakness of popes himself. He gave the cardinal's hat to two of his own nephews, and made another nephew Secretary of State and Archbishop of Milan at the age of twenty-three. It is true that this last relative, Carlo Borromeo, was a man of great ability, made a fine figure at the Council of Trent, and restored decent order in his great archdiocese, in which it is said that no archbishop had been a permanent resident for some eighty years. Being (a rare thing among cardinals) an enthusiast and an ascetic, careless of money, and living a spotless private life, he was honoured with canonization some twenty years after his death, and is still regarded as the chief patron saint of Milan, in whose cathedral his embalmed body rests in state before the high altar.

The same honour of canonization fell to Carlo Borromeo's uncle's successor at the Vatican, Pius V, a Dominican friar and ex inquisitor-general, whose ascetic and rigorous life, combined with his untiring zeal in persecuting heretics—Lutherans, relapsed Jews and agnostics alike—commanded the veneration of his contemporaries. It was something new to have a pope who not only enforced regular behaviour on others, but practised austerities on himself—Pius IV and Paul IV had not been noted for personal abstinence or neglect of the comforts of life, and Pius IV was a very irregular attendant at church ceremonies. Their successor's typical and best-remembered action was a sudden expulsion of all courtesans and panders from Rome—there are said to have been 25,000 of them—which seems a large estimate. Under him the precept *Si non caste tamen caute* had certainly to be practised in the Holy City.

This was the pope who excommunicated Queen Elizabeth (1570) and divorced Mary Queen of Scots from Bothwell, in a vain attempt to turn all English Catholics into traitors. He was a patron of the Ridolfi plot, though there is no evidence that, like Philip II, he encouraged Ridolfi to procure the assassination of the English Queen. No one can blame him for the excommunication: Elizabeth's tricky and hypocritical policy had well earned the papal censures. But its indirect result was to convert the majority of the adherents of the old faith in England into conformists : they refused to regard rebellion against a heretic queen as a necessary religious duty. From the point of view of expediency the famous Bull of 1570 was a mistake.

The successor of the canonized Pius V was by no means such a marked character, nor one who in a reign which extended to twelve years—a very long term for a sixteenth-century pope—left much impression on the Church. Indeed Gregory XIII is best remembered for the useful change which he made in the Calendar. The year was now ten days 'out of reckoning', and the spring and autumn equinoxes had long ceased to correspond to the dates to which they were attributed. The error was, of course, not so tiresome as that of the Mohammedan Calendar, which with its 360-day year shoves the religious obligations into inappropriate seasons—compulsory fasting for example at midwinter—but it was beginning to be serious. Gregory suppressed the days between the 4th and 15th of October 1582, and his calculation was accepted in all the Catholic countries of Europe : sectarian prejudice kept the Protestant states from accepting a Roman innovation, however reasonable. It will be remembered that England kept the old Calendar till the reign of George II—and that its supersession was followed by riots to the popular cry of 'give us back our eleven days'.

Gregory's non-astronomical activities were different from those of his ascetic predecessor. He was rather of the old-fashioned papal type—had a bastard son whom he made governor of the Castle of St. Angelo and commander of his army, and two pushing nephews who received the purple. Of his unseemly rejoicings at the reception of the news of the massacre of St. Bartholomew we have already had occasion to speak. A great foe of Queen Elizabeth, he subsidized Sir Thomas Stukeley's abortive expedition against England in 1578, and Fitzmaurice's equally disastrous one against Ireland in 1579—which ended at Smerwick. But when he sent the first Jesuit missionaries to England in 1582—he was a great patron of their order—he was

The Popes and the Kings of France

aiming a much more effective blow against the heretical sovereign than either of his military expeditions could deliver. Indeed the days of papal armies were over, and it was by the Spanish armed power alone that popes could strike.

Gregory died in the midst of violent riots and disorders in his own dominions, caused by no religious friction but by feudal troubles. Like Edward I of England he instituted a 'quo warranto' inquiry—requiring the barons of the Papal States to show by what legal grants they were holding their lands. So many of them had usurped Church lands during the old days of the Avignon Captivity and the Great Schism, that he expected to win back much valuable property. He reaped the reward of civil war, as the barons made open armed resistance, and subsidized brigand bands. The consequent ruthless taxation to raise troops, in a year of famine, provoked riots in Rome itself, and Gregory died in April 1585 in great distress of mind murmuring, 'Awake, O Lord, and have pity on Zion.' His hard-handed successor, Sixtus V, had some difficulty in suppressing the local troubles, but made himself feared by his successful hunting of brigands and his interminable rows of gallows.

Sixtus, who is said to have secured the Papacy by an adroit simulation of ill health and simple piety, which deceived rival candidates into electing him as a stop-gap, not likely to last long or to do much, turned out a highly political pope and no ascetic. He was no humble friend of Spain, joined with reluctance in the support of the Armada of 1588, and was no favourer of the League in France. Though he had to excommunicate Henry III for his murder of the Duke of Guise and his brother the Cardinal, he did not wish to see France fall into the hands of Philip II, and may indeed be considered as in a timid way the successor of the policy of Paul IV. But the Papacy had by now ceased to be a dominating factor in international politics. The Jesuits had grown into a much more redoubtable power, as will have presently to be shown.

After two ephemeral popes (Gregory XIV and Innocent IX), who between them only occupied the years 1590–91, the century ended with the Pontificate of Clement VIII, a figure of no importance, only remembered for his tardy acquiescence in the reception into orthodoxy of Henry IV of France. Like Sixtus V, he was no friend of Spain, the Jesuits, or the League. For the last time under him the Papacy reappeared as a winner of Italian territory : when the last Duke of Ferrara died in 1598, Clement by armed force expelled his cousin Caesar, who tried to maintain himself as the heir of the Estes, though his illegitimacy was certain. The reunion to the Papal States of this much-coveted duchy had been the dearest ambition of Julius II ninety years back. In those days its fate was an important question : by 1598 Italian local politics had come to be viewed with comparative indifference by the rest of the world.

From this short sketch of the history of the Papacy between 1500 and 1600 it is obvious that the only popes who left behind them any permanent impression on their times were Paul IV, Pius IV, and Pius V, all of whom had their share in the genesis and development of that very definite movement which we call the Catholic Reaction. Their predecessors were mainly engrossed in the continuation of the futile game of local Italian politics—playing off Spain against France, and trying to add duchies to the states of the Church. Incidentally some of these pontiffs of the first half of the sixteenth century did something for the cultural side of the Renaissance—they were patrons of painters, sculptors, architects, even of scholars. But their main interest was in Italian politics, and they thought and lived as Italian princes—good or bad, wise or unwise. They entirely failed to see that they were confronted with a crisis in thought and moral conscience which affected the whole of Christendom, and while the foundations were shaking under their feet imagined themselves to be dealing merely with the old question of the lax administration of the Church, and with a group of German malcontents who had raised the old Augustinian doctrine of Justification by Faith. They imagined that the really important problem at the moment was the holding of the balance between the Hapsburg and Valois intruders into Italy, not the preventing of a schism which was to tear half Europe away from the Roman allegiance.

Things had gone too far before the Papacy woke up to the true condition of affairs, and all chance of the reunion of Christendom had disappeared by the time of the Council of Trent. Forced by Charles V into assenting to the summons of that Assembly, Paul IV and his successors finally saw that all that could be accomplished was the retention of the Roman sway over half Europe, by a league with the intransigent and reactionary party in Christendom, and a drastic reform of the worst of the abuses which had made the old system hateful. Holding fast to all medieval doctrine, while collaborating in the removal of many medieval scandals of administration, Paul IV and Pius IV saved the position of the Papacy—and Pius V by his well-advertised asceticism made Rome respectable. Oddly enough it was the more worldly-minded popes who made most use of that wonderful machine, the Jesuit order, which Ignatius of Loyola and his successor James Lainez placed at the disposition of the Roman see for the defence of the old faith. Paul III, Pius IV, and Gregory XIII showed confidence in it, and utilized it, Paul IV and the ascetic Pius V were less confident in its trustworthiness. Apparently they had some suspicion that the machine might turn to managing its master, and while professing obedience might endeavour to force a policy on him. This was indeed the danger, as after ages were to show : but even before the sixteenth century was out, we sometimes find the Jesuits working against the Pope of the moment—as for example in France in 1593, when they backed the League against the now-converted Henry of Navarre, whom Clement VIII had resolved to take under his special protection. How far the popes would have succeeded in their effort to preserve the old hegemony of the Roman see without the help of the untiring and all-pervading Jesuits is a question worth discussing. On the other hand, could the society of

Jesus have saved the situation for the Papacy if they had been forced to collaborate with a series of old-style pontiffs, set on a purely Italian and secular policy, and destitute of the religious fervour which inspired Paul IV and the sainted Pius V? The collaboration was needed.

CHAPTER VI

TENDENCIES AND INDIVIDUALS. CHARLES V AND PHILIP II

THERE was one personage whose activities cover all the most important years of the century, and whose position was so abnormal and unprecedented that at the first glance it might seem that he ought to have become the dictator of Europe, and to have set his impress on the whole of Christendom. Yet he failed to do so. Napoleon, whose knowledge of history was somewhat sketchy, once expressed his surprise that Charles V did not succeed in mastering the world. Certainly his opportunities appeared to be great, and his personal character was high: though not a genius, he was a most level-headed, intelligent and hardworking monarch, not plagued with vices like his contemporaries Francis I and Henry VIII, and entirely destitute of the megalomania or 'kaiserwahnsin' which ruined many princes of less ability in all ages. On the whole he was a moderate, well-meaning, religious man, with a strong sense of duty and an infinite capacity for hard work.

The election of Charles as Emperor in 1519, in succession to his grandfather Maximilian, gave him a position which no sovereign since Charlemagne had enjoyed, since he was not only the sole owner of the heritages of Hapsburg, Burgundy, Castile and Aragon, and the possessor of the southern half of Italy, but also the titular head of the Holy Roman Empire. The imperial title had come to mean little when it was in the hands of princes with a moderate territorial endowment, like Charles' great-grandfather Frederic III,[1] or the Schwartzburg, Palatine, Nassau,

[1] It must be remembered that Frederic III had only part of the Hapsburg inheritance—the duchies of Austria and Styria; Tyrol and the westward outlying lands were still in the hands of another Hapsburg branch till its last heir abdicated (1490).

and Dutch emperors of earlier centuries. But the immense possessions of Charles outside Germany gave him a chance of making the imperial power a reality, after centuries of impotence. For no emperor before him had ever possessed such resources, territorial, financial, and military. Nothing looked more likely in 1519 than the establishment of a Hapsburg domination over all central and southern Europe. For the new Emperor inherited a share of the diplomatic ability of his Spanish grandfather Ferdinand, and no small portion of the magnanimous and adventurous temperament of his Austrian grandfather Maximilian.

This being so, it may appear extraordinary that Charles did not attain to what appeared to be his obvious destiny, and after many wars and many victories, retired in his old age to a monastery, as a broken old man who had failed to achieve his purpose.

The reasons for the frustration of his career were three—one psychological, and two military. The first was, of course, the outbreak of the Protestant Reformation—a religious movement far more complicated and serious than any preceding phenomena of a more or less similar character, such as the waves of indignation that followed on the great schism of 1378, or the national unrest that resulted in certain regions from the teaching of John Wyclif in England or John Huss in Bohemia. The disruption of Germany that started with the Lutheran protest was undoubtedly one of the main causes of the failure of Charles in his life-work.

But the two military causes must be considered. The first was the irruption of the Ottoman Turks into Central Europe. They had been checked on the Danube for a hundred years, and no one foresaw the sudden collapse of the Hungarian monarchy at the battle of Mohacs (1526), or the further advance when the Turk thundered at the gates of Vienna in 1528. These catastrophes gave the Emperor a suddenly developed eastern war-front, which distracted his attention, and drew away his arms from France and Italy. Nor was it only on the Danube that the new peril became obvious. A few years after the disaster of Mohacs Turkish pirate chiefs, who had conquered Algiers and Tunis in 1516-17, offered their allegiance to Sultan Soliman, and placed their fleets at his disposal. The western Mediterranean ceased to be the 'mare nostrum' of the Italians, where for 500 years no non-Christian flag had been seen. A new and serious naval peril grew up for Sicily, Sardinia and Southern Spain—all in the Emperor's charge—and forced Charles during his short intervals of peace in Europe to direct his efforts against the pirate-scourge. His two great African campaigns against Tunis (1535) and Algiers (1542) were the one a transient success, the other a dreadful disaster, which destroyed an army that would have been invaluable in Italy a year later. It was the misfortune of Charles V that he had to deal with the most capable and ambitious of all the sultans who ever reigned at Constantinople, a monarch as steadfast and as obstinate as himself, and even more physically vigorous, for Soliman died in his tent, still campaigning, at seventy-three, while Charles had retired, worn out, to his monastery at the age of fifty-six.

If he had been engaged with the Turk alone the great Emperor might possibly have restored the boundary of Christendom on the Danube, and swept the Mediterranean free of the Barbary pirates. But the Turk was only his secondary enemy, against whom he marched or sailed at moments of special crisis or opportunity. His real foes were the Kings of France, still set beyond all reason on continuing the vain venture which had been started by Charles VIII, the conquest of Italy, though it had already led to a dozen lost campaigns, and drained the best blood of France in many disastrous battles. This persistent attempt to establish a French domination beyond the Alps was pursued with obstinacy, not only by Francis I, whose military career had started with that brilliant success at Marignano which obsessed his mind for many years, but by his son Henry II, who never had any such intoxicating glimpse of personal glory. It was not only the kings who were besotted, but the whole nation—an appeal to the charms of adventure and easily-got gain never failed in its effect on the French noblesse. Though regularly beaten off, the invasion of Italy was resumed again and again, whenever Charles V was distracted by some urgent problem in Germany or Hungary, or on the High Seas that face Africa.

The most immoral and the most effective policy of the French kings was alliance with the Turk, the common enemy of Christendom, which both Francis I and Henry II took up without shame. There was some protest against it among Frenchmen of the better and more religious type, as has been mentioned before, but no effective opposition, even when a combined Franco-Turkish fleet was ravaging the coasts of Corsica or Nice, and sending thousands of Christian captives to be sold in the slave-market of Constantinople.

As it turned out, the systematic stab in the back which the French kings used to deliver when Charles was deeply engaged with the Turk in Africa or Hungary, or worried by rebellions of Protestant princes in Germany, just sufficed to keep the Emperor from making a success of his reign. He had to have armies everywhere—on the Pyrenees, in Italy, in Flanders, on the Meuse and Rhine, and in his precarious African garrisons. And money to pay them was not always forthcoming—for the treasures of Mexico and Peru, on which his son could depend, were only just beginning to drift across the Atlantic to his treasury. He was often in a semi-bankrupt condition. When his mercenary troops were unpaid, they indulged in mutinies, or fell upon the civil population, or simply deserted. The princes of the empire grudged the money and contingents which they ought to have provided under the rules of the *Matricula*. Some of them, like Charles of Guelders and Robert of Bouillon, openly took sides with the French in the earlier years of the strife. Later on the Protestants of the Schmalkaldic League were far more dangerous in 1547, when a new king, quite as perverse in his ambitions as his father Francis, had just come to the throne, and eagerly linked his fortunes with those of the German heretics.

Victorious for a moment at Mühlberg over the rebel

princes, and vainly in hopes that he had settled the religious troubles of Germany by the *Interim*, Charles was destined after a short pause to face the last and most unhappy of all his wars. He was attacked by Henry II, by Sultan Soliman, and by the German rebellion that flared up again under the leadership of the unscrupulous Maurice of Saxony. After some years of indecisive and sometimes disastrous campaigning the French had taken Metz, and had once more got a foothold in central Italy at Siena—the Turk was threatening Naples. Charles failed to get his son Philip elected as Emperor in his stead—the favourite scheme of his old age—and then feeling himself no better than a gout-ridden invalid, whose life's work had been a failure, abdicated, and retired to spend the short remainder of his life in the very remote Estremaduran Monastery of Juste. The legend that he spent his last months in the vain endeavour to make several clocks keep exactly the same time is probably an allegory, hinting that he had so many problems under his hand at one time that the happy moment when all should be solved simultaneously never arrived.

The life of Charles was not all failure—he had won the domination of Italy for the House of Hapsburg, and he had fought the Turks to a standstill. The French danger had been staved off, and before the old emperor had been long dead, France fell into the interminable wars of Catholic and Huguenot, and ceased for a long generation to be an aggressive power. The Ottoman empire, a few years later, passed from the hands of the great Soliman into those of a sot, who was followed on the divan by a miser. But Charles did not live to see the passing away of the perils which he had spent his life in confronting.

Nevertheless his career was a disappointment in its main lines. He had failed to make the Emperor once more a dictatorial ruler in Germany, and he had failed equally in the attempt to reunite Christendom under a reformed Roman Church. By the end of his life he had come to regard Protestantism as no less a danger than the Turk, but his method of dealing with it by reviving the great

Conciliar Movement for the consideration of all religious questions, was foiled at Trent, by the triumph of the intransigent elements and the diplomacy of the popes and the Jesuits. For the future neither councils nor lay sovereigns could meddle with the Papacy or with doctrine.

There had, of course, been many conjunctures when Charles might, if he had chosen, have put himself at the head of a national German demand for Church reform and revision of doctrine, a move which would have crushed the Papacy—for the popes were still behaving as intriguing Italian princes of no spiritual insight. But his personal character rendered this course impossible. He was a respectable and sincere Conformist, quite uninterested in such questions as Justification by Faith, or Free Will, or the meaning of the Sacrament of the Eucharist. And he had been profoundly shocked by some of the freakish developments of Protestantism, such as the antinomian outbursts of the Anabaptists, and the iconoclasm which devastated churches. The conduct of his own army in the sack of Rome in 1527 had made him feel ashamed— no good Christian should have had any responsibility for the wrecking of St. Peter's, or the ransoming of cardinals, however tiresome and provocative the conduct of Clement VII might have been. He was all for reforming the administration of the Church, but not by violence, or by the breaking up of all time-honoured institutions. And, looking at matters from the point of view of an emperor, he naturally resented the conduct of his vassals—German princes and free cities—who introduced sweeping changes in Church government without consulting him or getting his permission. If he accepted the extraordinary decision of the Diet of Speier in 1526, running to the conclusion ' *cujus regio ejus religio* ' (15 August), it was because the Pope and the King of France had formed the League of Cognac against him on 22 May, and he had no attention to spare for German quarrels at the moment. His real religious policy was embodied in the *Interim* of 1547, published after his victory at Mühlberg, and this imposed a creed on Germany founded on his good pleasure alone. His defeat was marked by the treaty of Passau (1552), which conceded local liberty of conscience, and his failure was formally proclaimed at the Diet of Augsburg (September 1555), where it was enacted 'that no emperor or prince should offer any violence to any state on account of its religion or faith, but leave them quietly alone', while religious differences should be adjusted by 'peaceful Christian methods'. In the same autumn (25 October) Charles announced his approaching retirement, and in January 1556 transferred the administration of his Spanish possessions to his son. In the following autumn he carried out the ceremony of resigning the Imperial Crown to his brother Ferdinand, and retired to Spain.

By assenting to the conclusions of Passau and Augsburg he had acknowledged that his whole policy had failed, so far as religious matters went. He handed over to his son not only the charge of the last act of the French war, which was soon brought to a successful close at Cateau Cambrésis, but a recommendation that peace with France should be accompanied by a joint action of both powers against heresy. A firm adherent of the old religion, he had permitted the persecution of heretics in his own hereditary states, though he had been forced to watch their multiplication in Germany ever since the Diet of Speier in 1526. But he was neither fanatical nor personally cruel, and his efforts to suppress Protestantism by the stake and sword were not very vigorous. It was reserved for his dull and ruthless son to make the Netherlands smoke from end to end with *autos-da-fé*, and to root out heresy completely from his Spanish and Italian dominions.

Putting aside the matter of religious persecution, a custom to which all princes in that age were equally addicted—there is little to criticize in the character of this laborious and not ungenerous emperor. He was courteous and even genial to his subjects—an extraordinary contrast to his awkward and arrogant heir. He was not revengeful or wilfully cruel—most victors would have beheaded the prisoners of the campaign of Mühlberg instead of merely imprisoning them. He was liberal when he had the wherewithal for liberality, which was not at all times. He was an enlightened patron of art—and was well repaid by Titian's magnificent picture of him in his old age. Though he won battles by the sword of his great captains, not by his personal guidance, he took the field in several years, and showed himself deficient neither in courage nor in endurance, though he was accused of lacking initiative and showing over-caution in his last campaign on the northern frontiers of France. The indictment that he played false to Henry of England both in the campaign of 1523 and that of 1544, when his armies on each occasion failed to join hands with the English expeditionary force, may be parried by the allegation that Henry on his side failed to carry out his part of the co-operation—Suffolk's army on the one occasion, the King's own army on the other, never struck deep into France according to the original plan of campaign. Nevertheless a certain shadow of broken pledges hangs over the peace of Crépy, which left the English army stranded alone around Boulogne and Montreuil : though Charles perhaps knew that his ally also was intriguing for a separate peace with France.

Charles was a competent man, on the whole a man of laudable aspirations, he bestrode all Europe for nearly forty years, yet he left no permanent impression behind him. This was due partly to his own limitations, but much more to the extraordinary complication of hindrances which fell to his lot—the simultaneous attacks by the Kings of France and the Sultan coming precisely at the moment when the outbreak of the Reformation in Germany produced an unforeseen religious cataclysm with which no ordinary sovereign, however capable, could cope.

Oddly enough the great Emperor's detestable son left more of a trace on the history of the century than his brilliant father. The one had been a prince of the Renaissance, the other was a most perfect example of a prince of the Counter-Reformation. Considering the opportunities for evil that lay before 'el rey prudente', we can only express a feeling of relief that his procrastination and indecision, his distrust of his best friends and his nearest kin, his leaden hand and his faithless pen, his secret treacheries and his open persecutions, saved Europe from falling under the black tyranny of a hypochondriac.

His armies fought many a good fight, his generals were the best in their generation. Fortunately the inspiration at the centre was missing. Philip himself was neither a general nor an organizer, and the strength which he wielded was due to his father's work, and to the line of great leaders bred in the old Italian wars. He himself, shut up in the Escurial, an ascetic Tiberius in a very bleak Capreae, contributed nothing to his wars but orders difficult and sometimes impossible to execute, always received with dismay by the reluctant commanders of his formidable hosts.

When we say that Philip left a permanent impression on his age we mean that he accomplished the remarkable feat of ruining the great empire which his father had left him, of leaving Spain drained of vitality and condemned to spiritual lethargy. A series of unsuccessful wars, combined with the deadening influence of systematic persecution and espionage worked by the Inquisition, broke the spirit of the Spanish race. Not all the gold of Peru and Mexico would compensate for the loss of initiative and energy caused by Philip's minute and detailed tyranny. For the misfortune of Spain his reign extended over more than forty years—destined to be almost exactly parallel with those of his shifty and unscrupulous rival Elizabeth of England— he started three years before her (1555 as against 1558); she outlived him by five years (they died in 1598 and 1603 respectively). By the time of his death he had crushed the spirits of a whole generation of his subjects, and left ruin behind him.

Philip, therefore, may be reckoned as one of the dominating figures of his age, though his domination was entirely of the negative sort—he saw to it that the inspiration alike of the Renaissance and the Reformation was killed in southern Europe—having the effective but not always willingly given co-operation of the Counter-Reformation popes and the Order of the Jesuits. They would not have accomplished all they did without the help of his sword, nor he have carried out his policy without the aid of their propaganda. But being a single figure with forty years of activity before him, he stands out more prominently as an individual than Paul IV or Pius IV or Pius V, all of whom were short-lived rulers, working for the same general end, no doubt, but in ways determined by their personal idiosyncrasies. Between them, Philip, the popes and the Jesuits kept half Europe in the Roman obedience, though the other half slipped free after a final struggle.

It should be noted that Philip was, in the early years of his reign, after the Peace of Cateau Cambrésis (1559), in a much more favourable position for exercising general influence in Europe than his father had ever been. The two great hindrances which had stood in the way of Charles V had been removed. France, after the death of Henry II (1560), had plunged into a long series of civil wars, and was 'out of the picture'. Turkey, after the death of Soliman the Magnificent, had fallen into the hands of incompetent and eccentric sultans. The German problem had been taken out of Philip's hands by the fact that his uncle Ferdinand and his cousin Maximilian successively wore the imperial crown, and had to deal with the situation created by the Augsburg compromise, with which they worked on an opportunist policy, anxious to keep the peace at all costs. They were not of much use to the fanatical Philip, and could not prevent their Protestant vassals from sending intermittent help to his revolted subjects. But on the other hand they took off from his shoulders the weight of the German burden, which had broken down his father's strength. If they gave him little help, they at least guarded his rear, and saved him from any serious interference on a large scale on the part of the German Protestant princes. It may be added that they took over the land-front of Christendom for defence against the Turk, though the Turk was growing very much less formidable than he had been in the days of Charles V.

Absolutely dominant in Italy by virtue of his possession of Milan, Naples, and Sicily, and his predominance over the minor states—the Dukes of Savoy and Parma served as generals of his armies, while the popes had reluctantly dropped their ambitions as secular princes—Philip had no danger to fear in the lands which his ancestors had won by so much hard fighting. Spain was already tamed by his father—the days of the *Communeros* and the rebellious feudal nobility were long past. In the middle of his reign Portugal fell into his hands by inheritance—unwillingly, but with hardly a blow struck to preserve its independence, and with Portugal went all its empire in the eastern seas, 'the wealth of Ormuz and of Ind', which Pope Alexander VI, with such splendid disregard of other people's rights, had granted to Manuel the Fortunate eighty years back. But the Portuguese colonial empire, great as it was, was far less important than the American empire which the *Conquistadors* had won for Charles V, while he was engrossed in his Italian wars. The gold and silver of America had begun to pour into the Spanish treasury in the later years of Philip's father, but not in such regularity as was to be the case when exploitation had replaced military conquest. The Emperor had profited from the hoarded wealth of Montezuma or Atahualpa, captured once in bulk and irreplaceable: his son got the regular produce of mines worked systematically by slave labour, a vast annual income. He could depend upon it as a normal item of his revenue, till in the second half of his reign the buccaneering English began to interfere in the Atlantic with the precious ever-welcome *flota*. The American gold, long the monopoly of Spain, upset all the scale of prices in Europe, when it began to be dispersed around, mainly in war expenses. Already in the time of Charles V it had caused financial troubles in many lands, the gold-owning sovereign having an immense advantage over his political rivals. But Philip was a much greater gold-monopolist than his father: he found ways to get rid of his primary advantage by means of unsuccessful wars and lavish subsidies to allies, till all that was left to him was the fact that prices were higher in Spain than in any other country of Europe, and that national industries flagged, because they could not compete with those of countries where the costs of production were not so abnormally high.

With such resources it might have been supposed that Philip might have controlled all Europe, or at least all southern and western Europe. That he failed to do so was entirely his own fault. He was governed by a curious mixture of obstinacy and procrastination; when he had made up his mind he was hard to move from his resolve, even when circumstances continued to prove that his decision had been unwise. But it took a very long time for him to arrive at any decision, because he profoundly distrusted all advice given him by his ministers or generals. He was always suspecting interested personal motives in any course suggested to him by his subordinates: and their reports, preserved in the Spanish archives, show countless marginal notes arguing criticism and distrust in his own hand. For he read everything, important or unimportant, that came into his chancery, and wasted endless hours in commenting on things trivial as well as on things of real moment.

If Philip had been merely an honest fanatic, ready to wade through any amount of blood, and to kindle any amount of fires for heretics, he would have been much less hateful than was actually the case. But he was also a systematic liar and hypocrite, who thought no means too base to secure his two great ideals—autocratic power for himself, triumph for the Roman Church. He made no scruple of violating the most solemn written engagements—other princes did that in his time—but his habit of subsidizing hired assassins even contemporary opinion thought unworthy of a man of ostentatious piety. He lured suspected persons into his clutches, and put them secretly to death without a trial:[1] suspicion was as fatal as proved treason. But the word treason might be made to cover almost any action that savoured of criticism or disobedience. His chosen tool, the Duke of Alva, once wrote a letter to him which expresses the whole mental attitude of master and man: 'Lawyers are only accustomed to pass sentence on a

[1] See the case of Montigny, the envoy from the Netherlands in 1567.

crime being *proved* : that will never do here.' One of his most odious habits was to utilize the Inquisition for his own political interests, where religion was not in the least in question. Indeed, it may perhaps be said that he was a tyrant first, and a fanatic only in the second place. It will be remembered that he dealt most drastically with Paul IV when the old Neapolitan pope ventured to assail him by force of arms and with French aid. But it was seldom that the interest of the autocrat clashed with that of the orthodox Catholic. And his faith was as sincere as his belief in his own essential infallibility—the two inspirations generally worked together with perfect ease when some particularly treacherous scheme was afoot.

A certain additional distaste has—perhaps a little unfairly —attached itself to the unamiable figure of the despot from his unsocial and secretive habit of life—a curious contrast to that of his blatant and boisterous father-in-law Henry VIII of England. Henry loved to show himself off, to advertise his wit, his learning, his taste in costly apparel and in tournaments and pageants, to appear surrounded by a splendid court, and to show ostentatious liberality. Philip disliked all public ceremonials save *autos-da-fé*, at which he was a regular attendant : it was hard to interest him even in the obligatory official shows which attended his third and fourth marriages. He was awkward in company—as had been very much remarked in his father's day, when he was in Germany and Flanders. He had no gracious small-talk such as some kings successfully cultivate, and disguised his unreadiness of speech by a rebarbative affectation of haughty silence. In his mature years he shut himself up for months in the Escurial, where the gloomy bed-chamber in which he died looks out on the high altar of the chapel. The habit of mind which induced him to rear this great palace-monastery in a rocky corner of the most uninviting mountain-range in central Spain is obvious. He disliked human society, and preferred to seclude himself with a few secretaries in apartments that are more like cells than ordinary rooms. Here he carried out his interminable desk-work in bleak surroundings. Louis XI of France, a spider of the same sort, had at least the lovely country-side of Touraine around him at Plessis-les-Tours. Philip looked out on nothing but barren rocks—sun-blasted in summer, wrapped in rain-fogs in winter. Here he could in his more hypochondriacal moments practise self-maceration with the celebrated scourge, which he bequeathed on his death-bed to his insignificant son Philip III.

Philip's character explains his failure to be a world power, even in days when France was become a battle-field of civil wars, and Elizabeth of England was practising all her shifty diplomacy to put off her inevitable fight with Spain for as long as possible. If Philip had been wise he would have declared war on her in her earlier years, while she was still hardly safe upon her throne, and had not accumulated the navy which was to foil the great effort of Spain in 1588. He imagined himself a diplomatist of great finesse—but the English Queen was almost as unscrupulous and quite as cunning as himself. A study of their insincerities is amusing, but leads to the conclusion that her procrastination was politic, and his temperamental and misplaced. He would have been wise to declare war on her in 1568 over the matter of his seized treasure ships, just before the 'Rising in the North'; she had given him quite sufficient provocation.

Despite the distractions of his Algerine wars (1559-65) and Morisco rebellion, Philip's main interest was in the furthering of autocracy and the suppression of heresy in the Netherlands. Here both his ambitions were concerned: he was determined to govern the curious amalgam of old Low-Country duchies and counties, not by their ancient customs as his father had done, but by his arbitrary will. And he was also determined to root out the growing Protestantism which had survived the old Emperor's comparatively mild persecutions. He first imposed on the Netherlands as regent his bastard sister Margaret, the wife of Ottavio Farnese Duke of Parma, with Cardinal Granvelle, a stranger from the Franche Comté, as her minister (1560-64). It was wrongly supposed that the change in the spirit of government, and the terrible increase of executions for heresy, were due to Margaret and Granvelle. This was entirely an error : everything done by the regent was under strict orders from Madrid. Protests proved futile, and only led Philip to send to the Netherlands his ruthless general Alva, with 10,000 veteran troops from Italy (1567). Alva practically relieved Margaret of all power, and set to work to govern by the sword, the axe, and the stake. His decisive act, which made revolt inevitable, was the seizure under circumstances of gross treachery of the nobles who had headed the protest to the King against misgovernment in 1565—the Counts of Egmont and Horn. The former was the victor of the battle of Gravelines, the last defeat of the French in the great war ; the latter High Admiral. They were both Catholics of unimpeachable orthodoxy, perfectly loyal to the Crown, and idolized by all the nobility of the Netherlands. For the idiotic cruelty of their execution, under a ridiculous charge of treason, Alva was responsible ; but he took the precaution of getting the King's leave. Philip signified his complete approval—the counts were kept for several months in prison till the royal mandate arrived (May 1568). Alva's ' Council of Blood ' put to death many hundred Netherland nobles and citizens, by no means confining its attention to Protestants : all constitutional protests had become treason. Hence in its earlier stages the Revolt of the Netherlands was not in fact an entirely Protestant movement—some Catholics joined in the rising as directed for the repression of tyranny, not for the protection of heresy. Philip's two foibles co-operated to make the discontent general : many of the old faith disliked tyranny, though they had no love for Lutherans.

It is surprising that Alva's reckless governance by the sword and stake, accompanied by crushing financial exactions, went on for several years before any general explosion. Partial risings backed by German help he succeeded in crushing : the real war only began with the seizure of Brill by the ' Sea Beggars ' on 1 April 1572, after which it never ceased for the rest of King Philip's life, despite an abortive pacification on terms of compromise made by Don John of Austria, the most moderate of Alva's successors, in 1577. The terms would never have suited Philip; he disavowed the acts of his able and ambitious bastard brother, who was aiming at building up a kingdom of his own in the Low Countries. The war that went on against the unaided Netherlands from 1572 to 1585, and against the Netherlands backed by the parsimonious aid of Queen Elizabeth from 1585 down to the end of the century, was the 'running sore' that sapped all Philip's resources, drained his treasury, and finally broke his heart. The only small measure of success that came from all his efforts and intrigues was that the seven southern provinces of the Netherlands were reconquered, and remained in his hands—half ruined by the expulsion of all their Protestant inhabitants. Pressed in between France and the new Dutch republic, they were more of a charge than a profit to Spain. Aware of this, in his last moments, Philip separated them from the Hapsburg monarchy, and bequeathed them at his death to his daughter Isabella. If she had left heirs a kingdom of Belgium would have come into existence two centuries before its time!

Though hampered for the last thirty years of his life with the interminable Dutch War, Philip found energy enough to interfere with the internal affairs of France on the side of the Catholic Leaguers—some of whom promised him the French crown—and to plan a number of attacks on the dominions of Elizabeth of England. His great Armada of 1588 was only the largest and the most unlucky of several naval ventures. At sea he was always unfortunate, and the most humiliating episode of his old age was to see Cadiz, his most important harbour-city, taken and sacked by an English expedition (1596). His pose during his last years was that of the blameless man afflicted by inscrutable decrees of Providence—like Job of old. But he never realized that his own character was the cause of all his misfortunes.

If we designate Philip II as one of the figures dominating the sixteenth century, it is firstly because he might, if his character had been different, have turned the fate of

Charles V and Philip II

Europe into ways very different from those which his father had tried ; but secondly (and this is most important), because he accomplished a definite feat—he left Spain ruined in reputation, finance, and spirit, though when he took over her rule she was by far the most powerful state in Christendom, and had not only Europe but 'the Two Worlds' at her feet. I have failed to find in him any redeeming traits save his quite genuine affection for his daughters, and his dislike for the paintings of El Greco.

CHAPTER VII

TENDENCIES AND INDIVIDUALS. HENRY VIII
OF ENGLAND

THE individual figures which we have hitherto been contemplating—the succession of popes and of Valois and Hapsburg sovereigns—had to deal with the main central problems of Christendom. They settled the course of events in Italy, France, Spain, and Germany. But the same spiritual and political questions which they had to face were also to be found in the more outlying parts of Europe, and these came under the control of some personages of outstanding interest to the historian, though their doings had not the world-wide importance of the activities of popes and emperors.

It may be a little humiliating to English students to have to recognize that the history of the reign of Henry VIII is only a side-show in the general history of Europe—interesting certainly, depressing, still more certainly, but having no decisive influence on the great struggles, temporal and spiritual, of the central years of the century. It cannot even be said of Henry, as of certain later statesmen, that

> He made the name of England great, and sunk her deep in debt.

The debt was certainly produced by his reckless finance, but the great name did not appear. The egotistic flamboyant policy of the King of England made his title prominent in every league and many wars, but its general result was unimportant in the main stream of affairs. It may be said that he was usually the dupe of his allies and the butt of his enemies. Whichever power was ally or enemy at a given moment—and the designation often had to be altered—he always came badly out of his bargain or his war. The net result of a reign of thirty-eight years was the gain of the single town of Boulogne, desperate bankruptcy, the contempt of the neighbouring sovereigns, and the well-earned hatred of every orthodox Catholic and every conscientious Protestant. This 'majestic lord' had broken the chains of Rome indeed, but only to leave his subjects enchained with the absurd fetters of 'the King's Religion'. He had gutted the shrines, smashed the monasteries, humbled the bishops, but left medieval dogma untouched. The whole of his elaborate system had to crumble at his death, because it rested on nothing but his own overweening will. As a crowning political example of 'how not to do it' his career is almost unrivalled. As the opposite example of how a king with much less opportunities fought through equally great difficulties, and left a new monarchy founded on the love of his people, I propose to tell the story of Gustavus Vasa of Sweden—a character much neglected by English historians.

Henry would have been a striking figure in the roll of sovereigns wherever his lot might have been cast. Tall and strong, with a handsome face, and a pleasing address, he had all the physical advantages of his grandfather Edward IV, as well as the keen intellect of his father Henry VII. He was a child of the Renaissance, better educated than any king before him—he had been intended for the Church while his elder brother lived, and had been taught by the best scholars. He had picked up while quite young a taste for theological controversy which never left him. He was no mean musician—could write pleasing accompaniments to his songs—he had an eager interest in architecture, and was always building in the new style, where classical detail was working into the main 'perpendicular' structure, in what we now call the Tudor fashion. He appreciated the development of painting—Holbein made many a portrait of him and his court—and of all the decorative arts. In short, he had all the makings of a typical Renaissance king of the cultured sort.

Unfortunately his dominating motive was self-conceit and a boundless desire to shine in every sphere of life. He would not only be a mighty hunter, a musician, an architect, a scholar, but also a brilliant general in the field and a superfine diplomatist in the cabinet. His ambition was to display himself as a sort of universal genius, and he was entirely lacking in tact and modesty, whether he was displaying himself before his own subjects or before the rest of Europe. He was serenely autolatrous, and so thoroughly convinced of his own essential righteousness that the failure of others to recognize it drove him into ill-restrained rage. In his early years he saw himself as the destined arbiter of Europe, and had the strange presumption to put up his candidature for the position of Holy Roman Emperor when the aged Maximilian died in 1519. He spent much money on the Electors, none of whom had the slightest real intention of favouring his suit. This was a beautiful example of the way in which he overvalued himself on every possible occasion. He was in truth the ruler of a state of second-rate importance, but aspired to play a leading rôle in Europe, in virtue of his very considerable personal ability, and the immense riches which his thrifty father had left behind him. The money, though it lasted over many years, was spent at last, and contemporary sovereigns had taken his measure, and discovered that he could be cajoled and deceived by wellmanaged appeals to his superabundant vanity, and his illjudged conviction that he could impose on others as he imposed upon himself.

It was only as the years rolled on that his many detestable characteristics became gradually evident. He was not only self-indulgent but ruthlessly selfish, and absolutely destitute of any sense of gratitude or of obligation to those who had served him. Deliberate cruelty gradually emerged as one of his foibles : there had been a hint of it in his first year of reign, when he sent his father's unpopular ministers, Empson and Dudley, to the scaffold in order to please the public, and also slew, a little later, his unlucky cousin the long-imprisoned Duke of Suffolk, whose crime was nearness to the Crown. But after this there was a term of years when the axe had a respite : its reappearance for the disposal of Edward of Buckingham in 1521 was the first sign of the growing blood-lust that marked the second half of Henry's reign. Buckingham's only guilt was his Plantagenet blood—the hasty and foolish words for which he was adjudged to have incurred the penalties of treason were mere excuses. This was a deliberate judicial murder, intended to warn all other nobles with a royal descent that they must show complete subservience to the King and never mention their ancestry. After this isolated piece of cruelty there was another pause, till the great divorce question and the breach with Rome had driven Henry into complete ruthlessness, and killed in him all sense of decency and all regard for justice. It would be profitless to detail the list of his atrocities, which ranged from the execution of conscientious objectors like More and Fisher to the extermination of the Pole and Courtenay families, on suspicion of having remembered that they were near of kin to their master on the Yorkist side. Almost more discreditable to Henry's record than these crimes was his dealing with Thomas Cromwell. The man was an unscrupulous ' climber ', but he had served his master faithfully for many years, and taken the responsibility for his most unpopular acts ; when he had ceased to be successful in all the business entrusted to him, and had provoked sufficient enemies, Henry callously struck him down. He intended thereby to discharge some part of the disrepute which he had earned himself on to the ' Vicar-General ', who had been his docile instrument. The charges brought against him were preposterous, the only cause of his fall was that he had earned sufficient hatred in many quarters to make his execution a popular move. Henry had no sense of gratitude whatever, even for the most useful and faithful service. The end of Cromwell somewhat recalls those of Empson and Dudley thirty years back : the King was merely making an indecent bid for popularity by sacrificing faithful if unscrupulous servants of the Crown.

Henry's matrimonial infelicities are often cited as the whole cause for his breach with Rome ; and certainly if Clement VII had shown for him the same easy complaisance in the way of granting a divorce which many popes had shown to many kings, matters might have gone differently in detail, for there was no doctrinal difference between 'the King's Religion' and that of the Pope. To the end of his reign Henry was executing Protestants for heretical views on the Eucharist, or eating flesh on a Friday. The 'Six Articles' commanded the approval of all orthodox Catholics. But a doubt arises whether this autolatrous monarch would not have involved himself in the struggle with Rome on two other points of attack. He wanted to secure the wealth of the monasteries—and, incidentally, a good deal more of valuable ecclesiastical revenues, which were not in monastic hands—annates and other moneys which had been going to Rome. But he also wished to make himself the spiritual as well as the lay head of the English nation, and this involved a breach with the Roman system: no mere 'Gallicanism' or *concordats*, such as Francis I secured, would have satisfied him. He was fully aware that the papal supremacy was breaking up all over Europe, and the conception of a national Church with a national king, not merely 'Defender of the Faith', but 'Supreme Head over all causes both spiritual and temporal', was very fascinating to one who was a theologian as well as a tyrant, and loved to control men's souls as well as their bodies.

Nothing is more absurd than Gray's satirical line about Henry's seeing

> The gospel-light first dawn in Boleyn's eyes.

He never saw the Reformation light at all, being colour-blind in such matters. But the involuntary reluctance of Clement VII to grant him a divorce from the Emperor's much-enduring aunt, enraged him with the Papacy at a moment when the Papacy seemed to be breaking down. And there was an old-established English grudge against all the Roman abuses, provisors, and annates, and pluralities held by Italians, and Peter's Pence, and endless costly lawsuits before the Roman courts. Parliaments and kings had shown themselves restive before on the point of the practical inconveniences of the appeal to Rome. And here certainly

Henry VIII of England

was an opportunity such as had never before occurred for cutting the connexion. The King imagined himself quite competent to continue looking after dogma, but he was equally certain that he could manage all religious jurisdiction and administration. After 1532 and the submission of the 'last Free Convocation' he had the Church well in hand.

Hence came fifteen years of a nightmare reign. It is astounding that it lasted so long—down to the last the atrocities continued : only twelve days before his death Henry, his body already a mass of festering corruption and his fingers unable to grasp a pen, sent to the scaffold the heir to the greatest name in the realm, a brilliant soldier, the first of the new English lyric poets, all on a flimsy charge of having dared to quarter the royal arms in the escutcheon of Howard. How his people continued to endure his freakish cruelty is one of the puzzles of history. Yet the 'Pilgrimage of Grace' was the only rebellion that ever menaced his throne ; and this dangerous rising of the old Catholic party he contrived to put down not by arms but by faithless diplomacy and broken promises (1536). He then slew its leaders, whom he had cajoled into dispersing their formidable host by gracious words, and by undertaking to summon a free parliament and to stop the persecution of those of the old faith. It is strange that a strong will, a fluent capacity for plausible explanations, and an absolute lack of conscience or scruple should have carried him through all his self-created troubles. He had an astonishing personal ascendancy over all men that he met, and an undeserved reputation for magnanimity and geniality, acquired in his early years when he was still the spectacular sovereign of a loyal people. In those days all unpopularity would be shifted on to Cardinal Wolsey—just as in later years it could be laid on the shoulders of Wolsey's old pupil Thomas Cromwell. Both Wolsey and Cromwell have been made to bulk too large in the history of Henry's reign : both were really the King's tools, though each had his personal idiosyncrasies. Wolsey was no doubt proud and ostentatious, with absurd ambitions for the Papacy—as misplaced as his master's ambitions for the title of Emperor. Cromwell, more cynical, and capable of any turpitude, had a private distaste for his employer's adherence to old dogma, being a man of the Renaissance, and a contemner of the traditionary theology which Henry cherished. But he allowed Lutherans or Anabaptists to burn for the royal pleasure, while he saw to the hanging of abbots and friars of the non-juror type with, as we gather, more personal satisfaction. And no doubt he enjoyed the mutilation of miraculous images, and the destruction of relics of dubious authority, as any 'intellectual' of his age would have done. Possibly he and his precious band of commissioners may have gone a little farther than the King desired in the way of the destruction of art-work. But Henry got the gold and silver of the shrines, and the valuable lead of convent roofs—wherefore he pardoned over-zeal.

The really important thing to note in the careers of these two great ministers of the 'Defender of the Faith' is that they could be disposed of without the slightest difficulty, and among general rejoicings, the moment that their master got tired of them. A fortunate fever probably saved the broken-hearted Wolsey from an execution on Tower Hill. Cromwell's end was more spectacular—created Earl of Essex and apparently high in royal favour on 17 April 1570, he was arrested for treason on 10 June and beheaded on 19 July! One of the queerest freaks of King Henry's mentality is that he allowed Cromwell's insignificant son Gregory to sit in the House of Lords for the rest of his reign, just as Thomas Boleyn, the father of the unfortunate Queen Anne, retained his earldom of Wiltshire till his death, six years after his son and daughter had gone to the scaffold. This, I suppose, was from ostentatious magnanimity : Gregory Cromwell or the old Thomas Boleyn might have been got rid of without any trouble if the King had so desired.

When we look down the whole record of King Henry's foreign policy and wars it is astonishing to see how little he accomplished at the cost of so much energy and wealth expended. In military affairs he was obviously behind the spirit of the age : he raised large miscellaneous levies of untrained men, and packed them off under untried commanders to Biscay or Picardy. When their pay came late, or the season turned unpropitious, they mutinied wholesale, or died of camp fever, or quietly deserted. Twice Henry took the field himself, bringing with him an ostentatious accumulation of costly lumber and unnecessary hangers-on. It will hardly be credited that on his Tournay campaign of 1513 he took with him the whole establishment of his Chapel Royal, 115 priests and choristers, as also a 'house of timber', requiring fourteen wagons for its transport, an immense tent of cloth of gold, and an innumerable list of minor pavilions : his wardrobe-tent alone was 45 feet long by 15 feet broad ! No wonder that with such impedimenta his marching record was about equivalent to that of a snail. The only benefit secured by the presence of the King in his campaigns of 1513 and 1544 was that the terror of his presence was good for discipline. He hanged sleepy sentinels, or unlicensed marauders, or deserters, so freely that the whole army trembled, and waited for his departure till it fell back into its normal habits. In 1544 Norfolk reported that after the King had returned to London his whole army was going to pieces—some had sick leave, some no leave, but they all got back to Dover somehow, so that he had but a fraction left of his original contingent.

All this was in an age when the continental sovereigns were raising standing armies and keeping them embodied, instead of trusting to hastily raised accumulations of untrained men, disbanded at the end of each campaign. Moreover, it was the age when the smaller firearms began to be all important in battle—as was shown at Bicocca (1522) and Pavia (1525). Henry, a great archer himself, retained his preference for the bow—the old victorious weapon of Crecy and Agincourt. At the end of his reign he was forced to hire companies of Italian and Spanish arquebusiers, because his subjects were still unaccustomed to the new weapons, which were becoming recognized everywhere as an indispensable necessity for a competent army. When raising troops for the suppression of the

'Pilgrimage of Grace', the Duke of Norfolk complained that he had not 100 arquebusiers among 6,000 or 8,000 of his Midland levies. In the campaign of 1544 round Montreuil and Boulogne, though the King had bought a considerable number of small firearms from Germany, he seems to have had not 2,000 arquebusiers in an army of some 34,000 men, and many of these were foreigners. In the vanguard division there were only 181 men with firearms to 2,300 'bows and bills'. The only military sphere in which Henry seems to have kept up with the times was artillery. He started foundries at Greenwich and elsewhere, cast many brass cannon, and even introduced the use of shells for mortars—'hollow shot of cast iron stuffed with fireworks, fitted with screws of iron to receive a match to carry fire : the fireworks, being kindled by the match, did break the iron shot into small pieces, whereof any smallest piece hitting any man did kill or spoil him'.

As a warrior Henry did not shine : the one successful episode in his whole military career was the 'Battle of the Spurs', at which a French cavalry force, which had left its infantry far behind, turned to sudden rout when attacked by an English division of all arms, and was hunted for many miles. The King did not get the opportunity of breaking a lance, for his staff kept him back till the French gave way, but he had the delightful experience of chasing a defeated enemy as long as his horse would go, and of capturing dukes and counts and the Chevalier Bayard himself. He never forgot this exhilarating afternoon—but had no chance of ever repeating its joys in all his life.

It is to be feared that Henry had more appreciation for the decorative side of war than for marches in the mud and rain. Hall and his other chroniclers have much to tell of his musters and reviews, the magnificence of his apparel and his retinue, and the elaborate ceremonial with which he took over the surrender of Therouanne, Tournay, and Boulogne. This was quite in keeping with his character : all through his reign he loved occasions—tournaments, pageants, like the 'Field of the Cloth of Gold', Church ceremonies, or openings of parliament—in which he could figure as the central figure of a splendid show. His subjects, it cannot be denied, enjoyed them too, and only reflected afterwards on the amount of money which they had cost.

Reckless financial extravagance, indeed, was one of his most prominent foibles. He wasted his father's treasure, all the tremendous spoils of the Church, and the taxes which his people regarded as intolerable, on schemes of all sorts which came to ignominious ends, because he was regularly outwitted by his enemies and betrayed by his allies. The idea of balanced accounts never appealed to him—the great expedient of his last years was a debasement of the coinage, which ruined the poor, and made all foreign exchanges impossible without loss of the most heart-breaking kind to unfortunate treasurers.

As I have already observed, all Henry's pompous interference in foreign affairs had no very great effect on the general trend of European history. He was a dominating figure to his own unfortunate subjects, but not to contemporary sovereigns or statesmen, of whom two successive generations deliberately cajoled him. In the great international crisis of the Reformation he lost the opportunities which might have come to him from a resolute adherence to one cause or the other. He defied the Pope, and persecuted the Protestants. If he had chosen to throw himself in with the cause of Reform, he could have established a national Church of a much more attractive kind for many of his subjects than the Church of 'the King's Religion' which he actually invented—an institution hateful to all honest men of any faith. If he had refused to quarrel with the Papacy, and had made up his mind to stifle his desire for Anne Boleyn, or had insisted on possessing her in a less formal capacity than that of a crowned queen, he could undoubtedly have held England in the Roman obedience—at least for as long as he lived. His inordinate sense of his own self-sufficiency undoubtedly kept him from either course. As an orthodox theologian he would have nothing to do with new-fangled Lutheranism : as the head of a powerful state, he would not be bullied by popes. An English divorce from the unfortunate Queen Catharine would suffice if he could not get a Roman one.

There is no doubt that to obtain a male heir for the House of Tudor was to Henry a strong incentive for getting rid of the staid princess with whom he had lived for some eighteen years of wedlock. The strange thing is that he should have persisted with such obstinacy in choosing for her successor a lady of many charms, but of quite unequal condition from his own : she sprang from a pushing but very new family, and her elder sister had already fallen a victim to his volatile affection. The idea of marrying her was obviously preposterous from the point of view of policy. There were plenty of princesses in Europe, and Henry had not yet acquired the reputation of a Bluebeard. On the whole, it would seem that he was inspired by obstinacy and self-assertion, as much as by an overwhelming passion for the lady. He would marry just as he pleased, though the Pope might protest, and the more scrupulous English clergy might conceal their private dismay with difficulty. The King was determined that his will should override all difficulties, and dashed down his faithful servant Wolsey not for opposing the marriage—which the Cardinal did not —but for failing to make the Pope consent to it. This was as ungrateful as it was illogical—but gratitude (as has been said before) had no part in Henry's composition. It would have been unpopular to make the breach with Rome solely a matter of the marriage question—for Anne was regarded as an adventuress and Catharine as a martyr—so the King engineered the rupture by causing his subservient parliament to pass the 'supplication of the Commons' against the practical grievance of papal administration, followed up by the 'Annates Act' (1532) and the Act against Appeals to Rome (1533), which cut off the supply of moneys from England to Rome, and the third Act (1554) which forbade all oaths of spiritual obedience to the Pope, and named the Archbishop of Canterbury as the person who should grant all licences and hear all appeals for the future. This was called 'a bill for the abrogation of the usurped authority of the Roman Pontiff'.

Henry VIII of England

The breach was now complete, and after Cranmer had declared Catharine's marriage null and void (23 April) he crowned Anne as Queen on 1 June 1534. In just under two years from the day on which she attained her ambition, the wretched woman was indicted and executed on a complicated charge of adultery with no less than six gentlemen of the royal court (19 May 1536). The incredible details of her trial only cause the reader to wonder whether her abominable husband was more moved by wrath with her for bringing him no male heir, or attracted by newer and younger faces, or determined to get rid for political reasons of a spouse who had brought him much unpopularity. Probably all three reasons told with him : his conduct shows cold-blooded calculation rather than sudden irritation. It was a curious nemesis for his treatment of Queen Anne that five years later he made himself the laughing-stock of all Europe by marrying in a hurry another wife, whose reputation was far worse than that of her predecessor, and detecting her lurid past (and present) only after he had taken her round all England on exhibition. Catherine Howard was a failure : but what sort of wives could such a king expect?

To sum up. What had King Henry accomplished by his last twenty-five years of intriguing with France and the Emperor, his hanging of scores of pious Catholics, and his burning of scores of pious Protestants? He had failed to make any permanent impression on the balance of power in Europe, and he had established in England a brand of religion of his own, which nobody loved. He had outraged his Catholic subjects, and kept down by force the strong and growing Protestant party that he hated. Practically he had 'stopped the clock' for a quarter of a century so far as England was concerned. The moment that he was gone, its hands began to move again—in a way which would have caused him wild anger. Seymour and Cranmer and their friends could reveal their real tendencies and views, which they had been forced to keep hidden for so many years, under pain of death. The overpowering will of Henry which sufficed to terrorize all his subjects while he lived, ceased to have any effect the moment that the breath had gone out of his bloated body. His worst legacy to his country was the group of unscrupulous politicians whom he left in power : the kind of men who had been content to bear with this tyranny, and to become the instruments of his administration, were (with the possible exception of his brother-in-law Seymour) a disreputable gang. But being opportunists, they set to work to keep the machine of the State working, in the manner that would be least dangerous and most profitable to themselves.

So much for the King who kept England out of the Reformation for so many years, and made his own good pleasure the only guiding principle of his policy. I have to compare with him another king, a few years his junior, who also had to face the problem of the Reformation movement, in a country which lay even more outside the central focus of European politics than did England. He also carried out a policy of his own, under great difficulties, and lived to see it succeed, as Henry's did not.

CHAPTER VIII

TENDENCIES AND INDIVIDUALS. GUSTAVUS VASA AND SCANDINAVIAN PROTESTANTISM

SWEDEN had been for the last 130 years nominally linked to Denmark and Norway by the Union of Calmar (1397). But national spirit was opposed to the Union, and though several Danish kings had been duly crowned, it was only intermittently that they had been in real possession of Sweden. For the last fifty years a line of capable statesmen—'administrators' as they were called—of the great noble house of Sture had reigned with quasi-royal power. John, the last Danish king who had been crowned and striven to assert his authority, had been beaten in battle and expelled in 1501 : his father Christian had suffered exactly the same fate in 1464.

In 1513 there came to the throne in Denmark the most extraordinary prince who had been seen in the north for many a generation. He bore a strong resemblance to his contemporary, Henry VIII, being strong-willed, cultured, ready to interfere in matters religious with the same confidence as did the King of England, absolutely unscrupulous in keeping his word, and relentlessly cruel. We may add that he was tall and handsome, and had, like Henry, amatory tastes of the most pronounced. He was under the impression that he was a great diplomatist, and that everything could be done by well-managed deception. He had married the most wealthy and distinguished bride that had ever been seen in the Baltic lands, Isabella, the sister of the Emperor Charles, and at the start of his career hoped to get much help for his ambitious schemes from his brother-in-law.

Christian's main desire was to restore the Union of Calmar, by the conquest of Sweden, from which his father and grandfather had been ignominiously expelled by the Stures. He could count on some help from factions which were opposed to the great administrators, notably from the clergy—the primate Gustavus Trolle, Archbishop of Upsala, was a personal enemy of Steno Sture the Younger, who had burnt his castle and put him in prison. When liberated, he proffered his help to Christian, and induced Pope Leo X to put Sweden under interdict, and to excommunicate the administrator.

It was therefore in the disguise of a crusader for the rights of the Church, and as an enemy of heretics, that Christian invaded Sweden in 1520, with an army strengthened by 2,000 French mercenaries, and a corps of landsknechts raised in north Germany by the leave of the newly elected Emperor, his brother-in-law. The Swedish army— a levy of the medieval sort of nobles and peasant bands— was completely defeated by the King's troops at the battle of Bogesund (19 January 1520), fought at midwinter on the ice of a frozen lake. The administrator was mortally wounded, and for want of a leader the Swedes made their submission—only the widow of the administrator maintained a resistance for a few months in Stockholm, at the head of the relics of her husband's party.

Having the capital in his hands, and garrisons in the most important towns, Christian proceeded to carry out a plan which would have commanded the admiration of Caesar Borgia, but which was destined to be fatal when tried in a stubborn northern country. Having been crowned in state on 4 November 1520, he summoned all the notables of Sweden to a series of banquets and festivities which were to follow the ceremony. As he had proclaimed a full amnesty for those who had fought for the late administrator, the whole of the nobles and magistrates of the realm came into Stockholm. On the 6th of November, while Christian was presiding over the diet, the vindictive Archbishop Trolle, acting as had been arranged between him and the King, stepped forward and raised the point that although the late rebels had received the royal pardon, they had not been released from the excommunication issued by the Pope, and were all under the ban of the Church —the execution of which had been delegated to the King. Professing to be suddenly convinced by this plea, Christian arrested ninety-six magnates, including practically the whole of the nobles of the nationalist party, two bishops, and the burgomasters of Stockholm and other towns. They were all executed next day after the semblance of a trial : this atrocity is generally known as the ' Blood Bath of Stockholm ', and Christian obtained the well-merited title of ' Christian the Cruel '.

After handing the administration of Sweden over to the venomous Archbishop, Christian returned to Denmark, leaving garrisons in the more important castles and towns. He imagined that he had won a complete victory, by the extermination of the whole of the leaders of the Particularist or national party, and returned to Copenhagen in triumph. But Christian appeared in a completely new character in Denmark ; instead of being the champion of the Church he began to pose as the reformer of clerical abuses and the friend of the peasants. With the assistance of a Westphalian clerical adventurer, Dietrich Slaghoek, whom he had made Archbishop of Lund and primate of Denmark, he proposed to confiscate the monastic lands, to restrict the power of the bishops, some of whom he imprisoned, and to set up a national church court to which all appeals should go, instead of to Rome. He also invited Protestant preachers from Germany, and gave them preferment in his kingdom. At the same time—with the most utter folly—he provoked the lay nobility, by proclaiming the abolition of serfdom, and of the exemption from taxation which (like all barons of the Middle Ages) they had hitherto enjoyed in consideration of their military service. He promulgated other laws, favourable to the peasantry and the burgesses of towns but offensive to the aristocracy, on his own authority.

Apparently Christian's head had been completely turned by his success in Sweden, and he had come to regard himself as omnipotent—he lacked the calculating brain of Henry VIII. All his troubles presently burst on him at once—Pope Adrian VI excommunicated him, ostensibly for the judicial murder of the two bishops executed at Stockholm, and at the same time declared Archbishop Trolle suspended from the discharge of his functions for complicity in the same atrocity. More effective was the action of the Danish nobility, who threatened the King, terrorized him into allowing the execution of his tool Archbishop Slaghoek, and finally held a diet, at which they declared him deposed, and raised his uncle, Frederic, Duke of Holstein, to the throne. Christian fled with his wife and children to the court of his brother-in-law, Charles V. For eight years he lived as a pretender, raising trouble when he could; he kept up a pirate fleet based on Gothland, which interfered with Danish commerce, he set going several peasant-insurrections against the government of his uncle, whose power lay in the support of the noblesse, and finally, taking advantage of particularist troubles in Norway, which was (like Sweden) never reconciled to the union with Denmark, he landed near Oslo in 1531, and was proclaimed king by a Norwegian diet—though without much enthusiasm, his character being by this time pretty well understood all round Europe. Even Henry VIII, though feeling some sympathy with his activities, had refused any practical help when they met at London in 1523. Christian's end is the only thing which provokes some sympathy with this detestable person: he was kidnapped at an interview on shipboard (to which he had most unwisely come) by Gyllienstierna, the admiral (incidentally a bishop!) of his uncle Frederic, and sent to Denmark, where he was shut up for twelve years (1531–43) in a one-windowed dungeon in the castle of Sonderborg, with no companion save a Norwegian dwarf, who had been his fool in better days. This confinement failed to kill him, and when his crimes and his career had been partly forgotten, he was moved to another castle, where he could see the light of day and occasionally stir out of doors. He lingered on till 1559, when he died at the age of seventy-nine, having outlived all the sovereigns contemporary with his youth, including his brother-in-law Charles V—a much younger man— whom he survived for a few months Twenty-seven years of solitary confinement was not too great a penalty for the shameless atrocities of his early years. His character and activities show so many parallels with those of Henry VIII that it is interesting to note the difference that was made by the fact that the English King had, and the Danish King had not, a streak of common sense mixed with his autolatry and ruthlessness.

During the two years (1521–23) when Christian was working up the Danish nobility and clergy to revolt, trouble began to appear in the conquered Sweden. Gustavus Ericson Vasa was a member of a family of some note : he was personally as well as politically connected with the great Sture ' administrators ' by the fact that his paternal grandmother had been a sister of the elder Steno Sture. Luckily for him, he was not at home at the time of the Stockholm ' Blood Bath ', or he would have been one of its victims. His father Eric of Vasa, his brother-in-law and several more distant relations perished on the scaffold that day. But he himself happened to have been taken prisoner by King Christian in 1518, and to have escaped to Germany before the Swedish national cause went down at Bogesund. Reaching Sweden shortly after, he was one of the few who tried to keep up the resistance against the Danish conquest. But he was still a young and comparatively unknown man of twenty-five, and at first got little support. For months he wandered about in the mountains of Dalecarlia, going secretly from farm to farm, hiding in haystacks or barn-lofts, and sometimes working as a miner or a farm-labourer to conceal his identity. He led a life much like that which tradition ascribes to Robert Bruce ; indeed, there is much similarity between the stories of the two adventurers—save that Bruce had a decent claim to the Scottish throne, and Gustavus Vasa none whatever to that of Sweden. He was merely (like William Wallace, to take another parallel) a determined rebel, the exponent of nationalism, with a price on his head. The Swedish government had made its surrender to Christian in March 1520 : it was not till November that the King showed his hand, and slew off all the notables of the Sture party at the ' Blood Bath '. Gustavus had now the blood of a father to avenge, and found himself the sole heir to the patriotic tradition, for the whole generation of his elders and contemporaries had been swept away by the axe. The news of the 'Blood Bath' fired many hearts, and on 20 December 1520 Gustavus was able to collect a band of peasants, at whose head he fell upon the bailiff of Dalecarlia, and slew him in his own house. In February 1521 a meeting of miners and yeomen elected him 'administrator'—the title borne by the Stures—but only a remote mountain region was in arms : the greater part of the land still lay crushed under the catastrophe of the past November. However, discontent was bound to spread—the treacherous Archbishop Trolle's rule was execrated, and it was found that the garrisons of King Christian's mercenaries were not collected together in any place, but billeted about the country in trifling detachments. Gustavus had at first to depend on the peasantry alone, and his armies were like those of Charles Edward in Scotland in 1745—they were continually going home to till their fields or reap their harvests. If they won a battle, they would disperse to stow away their plunder, and disappear for weeks. Gustavus's army sometimes rose to 15,000 spears, sometimes sank to 1,500. He continued, however, to hold his party together, and when he was in force took the offensive. In April 1521 he defeated the Archbishop's mercenaries at Westerås, and got possession of Upsala, the old capital of the realm, in July. Stockholm he could not capture : Trolle and all his supporters had taken refuge in it, and he could but put the water-girt city under blockade. The Archbishop sailed to Copenhagen to ask help from his master, but found Christian too busy with new Danish troubles to recommence a regular reconquest of Sweden. He deposed the Archbishop from his regency,[1] and sent a fleet to relieve

---

[1] Trolle's turbulent career, however, was by no means at an end. He took part in all Christian's attempts to recover his throne, went with him on his Norwegian expedition of 1531, and after his master's captivity joined in the revolt of the Danish Catholics, after the death of Frederic I, and was killed in battle in 1535 on the isle of Fünen, fighting against the partisans of Frederic's Protestant successor.

Gustavus Vasa and Scandinavian Protestantism 117

Stockholm, but could do no more. In April 1523, as has been already said, the Danish nobles deposed their tyrant, and made his uncle Frederic king. The Stockholm garrison thereupon made overtures for surrender, and Gustavus took the opportunity of getting himself elected king, instead of administrator, at Strengnäss (7 June 1523), and entered Stockholm in triumph on 20 June.

King Frederic wrote to Gustavus that he had been elected king and that according to the tradition of the Calmar Union, he was prepared to give all guarantees of good government under national administration to Sweden. He was told that he was too late in his offer, that Sweden had now a king of her own, and that the Union of Calmar was gone for ever. It remained to be seen whether Denmark would fight; but Frederic, seated on a shaky throne, and with partisans of Christian still in arms in many places, gave Gustavus a quasi-recognition, by meeting him at the Conference of Malmo, and entering into a truce between the two realms. The Danish kings, however, would not formally resign the claim to the Swedish throne, and continued to place the shield ' azure three crowns or ' in their blazon for centuries, much as the English kings kept using the title of France, and showing the lilies in their quarterings, right down to the Peace of Amiens.

Gustavus's election as king was, in a way, only the beginning of his troubles. The land was desolate, there was no money in the treasury, and the new generation of nobles, the sons of those who had perished in the ' Blood Bath ', regarded him as an upstart, and no better than any of themselves. He was taunted with being ' the Peasants' king ', which was true enough, for it was with a peasant army that he had won his crown; the peasants looked upon him as their own man, whom they had made, and could possibly unmake if they grew discontented. Immense tact was required to keep them from being unduly casual, disobedient, and slow to pay taxes. Many of Gustavus's early troubles came from his original partisans, and their presumption in dealing with him. He got some advantage from having been reared as a private person, and knew his contemporaries of all ranks through and through, in a way impossible to those born in the purple. This, of course, had the corresponding disadvantage, that he had none of the prestige that comes from hereditary royal descent. He was only the surviving party leader of the old Sture faction.

Gustavus was a large, handsome man, with a portly presence, genial and good-tempered in his usual mood, but when provoked or in presence of a crisis he could flare up into very drastic action. Occasionally he used the gallows or the axe—but it may be said that he was never unjust, and that any one whom he struck down had always deserved his fate. He never slew from suspicion or from deliberate politic cruelty like Henry VIII, nor did he ever sacrifice an old servant as a scapegoat—as Henry sacrificed Thomas Cromwell. Unlike his Tudor contemporary, he was a happy father and husband, with many children—three of his sons were destined to wear the crown. His private life was pure: 'though he enjoyed converse with fair ladies, he never brought scandal on any, nor was it ever said that a child was born to him out of wedlock, for he kept to his true nuptial vows'. Most important of all, he was a sincerely religious man, and no one ever ascribed his dealings with the Reformation to mere sordid political ends.

He had suffered bitterly from the treason of Archbishop Trolle and his adherents to the Swedish national cause. That their conduct had been disastrous to the whole realm was advantageous to him, because it had to a great degree sapped the strength and reputation of the Church. But it is clear that he was a God-fearing man set on reforming the old abuses when he came to the throne, and not an enemy of religion. The medieval Church in Sweden, as elsewhere, had been too strong as a secular power: its archbishops had often been men of great houses, heads of baronial factions; its wealth was inordinate, though Gustavus may have been exaggerating somewhat when he said that a third of the realm was held as Church-land and half its castles. The lives of the higher clergy were no better than those of their contemporaries in other lands—political bishops, baronial abbots, non-resident canons and

Gustavus Vasa and Scandinavian Protestantism 119

idle monks were as common in Sweden as elsewhere. Moreover, the churchmen had, as a whole, been hostile to the Sture party during the fifty years' rule of the great ' administrators ', and were looked on askance by the nationalists. The particular form which the attack on them took was undoubtedly influenced by the fact that Protestantism was by now gaining ground in North Germany. There was no Lutheran party in Sweden, though preachers of the new learning had begun to drift into Sweden. The important thing, however, was that protests against the subjection of national life to the policy of the Roman See were things that could not but appeal to the nation, after the Stockholm Blood Bath had been carried out under the ostensible direction of a bull of Leo X. And no one could forget that the primate of the national Church had adhered to Christian II, and joined in the responsibility for the King's atrocities.

Still at first Gustavus made no attempt to break away from the Roman Church, or to encourage Protestant propaganda. He filled up the places of the patriotic bishops who had been murdered at Stockholm, as well as those of Trolle and the other unpatriotic bishops who had fled to Denmark, with orthodox Catholics of his own political party. But he permitted no persecution, and allowed Lutheran ministers to come freely into his realm, and to lecture and dispute with the orthodox clergy in his capital. The first trouble came from these lectures : the bishops clamoured for the arrest of heretics, who preached Justification by Faith, the complete authority of the Bible against tradition, and the uselessness of the monastic life. He would hear nothing of persecution, and made one man of notoriously Lutheran tendencies his chancellor, and another a professor in the University of Upsala.

Misjudging the strength of the King's position, and trusting to the efficacy of a cry against heresy in a nation where heretics were barely known, the newly appointed Archbishop of Upsala and the Bishop of Westerås raised open rebellion in 1525, on a complicated programme of grievances —over-taxation, the favouring of Protestants, and the plea that Gustavus ought never to have been elected king while any of the old House of Sture remained alive. There was, in fact, a boy of twelve, son of the last administrator Steno II, who had fallen at Bogesund in 1520. To propose the election of a child meant, of course, anarchy, and reaction under clerical administration.

The rising failed, Archbishop Cnut was captured and executed in 1526, but the rebellion lingered on for a year longer, under curious conditions. A lad was produced to represent the Sture boy—though he was a year or two too old for the personation. This is a curious parallel to the story of Lambert Simnel in England, for the real Niels Sture was visible at Stockholm, just as the real Earl of Warwick had been visible in London. But some rebels wanted to be deceived, and were deceived : they held out in fastnesses on the Norwegian frontier for some time, till they were hunted down. The pretender escaped to Germany, and was hung for highway robbery at Rostock a few years after—a less happy end than that of Lambert Simnel, who grew old in the kitchen and the falcon-mews of Henry VII.

The suppression of this clerical rebellion encouraged the King to show his private tendencies in religion. He refused to displace priests who had married, allowed of the printing of a Swedish translation of the Bible, and began to talk of the absurdity of church-services in Latin, and the uselessness of most of the monasteries in the land.

He showed his hand finally at the famous diet of Westerås held on Midsummer Day 1527, which may be considered as the starting-point of the Swedish Reformation. The King's intentions were known, and he had warned all his trusted supporters to come to the diet with large retinues. This so scared John Magnus, Archbishop of Upsala, the recently appointed successor of the fallen Cnut as primate of Sweden, that he fled to Dantzig, having drawn up, in company with a majority of his suffragans, a protest against any legislation that might be passed at the diet, as done without their consent.

The diet, as John Magnus had expected, proceeded to

Gustavus Vasa and Scandinavian Protestantism 121

pass a large measure of disendowment of monastic property and other Church-lands. The Chancellor explained that the King's expenses, for the recent year of rebellion, worked out at about two and a half times his revenue. The country was in a state of bankruptcy, unless some new source of revenue could be discovered, and the one which was obvious was a large resumption of Church-lands. Bishops like Gustavus Trolle, who had let in the Dane, were the curse of the realm because of their great lay fiefs and many castles. 'The King's present revenue was about one-third of that of the bishops and monasteries put together.' The only way out of bankruptcy was a large measure of disendowment; let the clergy be given a liberal and reasonable maintenance—but their present possession of great lay-fiefs was an intolerable abuse. As to accusations of heresy, the King had permitted certain preachers of the Gospel to set forth their views : he saw nothing contrary to the Gospel in them ; but much that was consonant with the teaching of the Bible and the primitive Church. He was not going to persecute them because certain prelates wanted to keep up all ancient traditions, were they right or wrong. But the main thing that was to be borne in mind was the bankruptcy of the monarchy. If nothing could be done to save it, it was his intention to abdicate and wash his hands of all responsibility!

The King then asked for an answer from the diet. One of the two surviving bishops from before the War of Independence answered with a bold *non possumus*. He was the King's subject, but also bound to render to the Pope obedience in things spiritual. He could neither consent to vote away Church-lands, nor to tolerate the preaching of heresy. An old baron, one of the few survivors of the Sture faction, said that he considered that Bishop Brask spoke fairly enough. Thereupon the King said that if the majority of the diet held this view, he could no longer accept the responsibilities of the throne, and walked out of the hall.

Immense confusion and interminable debate followed in his absence. The spokesmen of the burghers and the peasantry said that the State could not endure without the King, and that chaos must not be allowed to come again. Finally a large majority—though it included only one bishop—sent to petition the King that he should abandon his idea of abdication, and state his proposals for the better ordinance of the realm.

It was only after he had been three times petitioned to return that Gustavus reappeared to state his 'propositions'. They amounted to a large but not complete measure of disendowment. The bishops were to surrender all their castles and lay-fiefs to the Crown, and were to receive instead an endowment either in land or from rents and dues. The same was to hold for canons and prebendaries. Monasteries 'in which there has been woeful misgovernance' were to be regulated by the Crown, which should have power to inquire into their lands, and, where it was thought necessary, to dissolve or unite houses found to be unprofitable or scandalous. For the future all elections to bishoprics should be by the chapter, but dependent on the King's approval of the nominee. Finally, all clerical persons were to be tried in the lay courts for civil offences, the spiritual courts only retaining jurisdiction over morals and doctrine. To protect the growing Protestant minority from attacks in the spiritual courts for heresy, a special clause set forth that preachers had liberty to set forth the Word of God as proclaimed in the scriptures, and that the Bible was to be read publicly in churches and schools in the native tongue.

The diet accepted all these propositions, which were called, when ratified, the 'Recess of Westerås'. Most of the bishops and clergy tried to 'make the best of a bad job', and accepted the re-endowment. Gustavus therefore had not to make a clean sweep of the hierarchy, but contented himself with filling up the sees vacant by flight of their holders. The new primate, Laurence Petersen, was an avowed Lutheran, and was the first Archbishop of Upsala who did not get his pallium from the Pope.

The policy which the King carried out from 1527 onward was one requiring much patience, and a very cool head.

It could not have been worked by a man of a passionate temper, or by an impetuous enthusiast, who might have tried to hurry things because his conscience was goading him. He had the extraordinary good fortune to survive for over thirty years, so that there was not the break of continuity which follows from a change of personal administration. On the whole his work much resembled that which Elizabeth carried out in England a generation later. This policy was the slow re-manning of the Church-establishment by clergy conforming to the new faith, without any eviction *en masse* of those who clung to the old doctrines and ceremonies. The University of Upsala, which he had put under Lutheran control, provided the bulk of the Swedish clergy, and trained generation after generation of Protestant ministers, who gradually replaced the elder men as they died out. None but Lutherans got promotion to any high office, so that by the end of thirty years every important place in the Church was filled with conformists. Meanwhile the old incumbents were not evicted or molested, so long as they gave no trouble, and offered no public opposition to the changes which were going on around them. The widest variety of ritual prevailed in neighbouring parishes : those who chose among the elder men continued to use the Latin Mass, which was not prohibited, though the King declared his own personal aversion for services not generally understood by the congregation.

A growing proportion of the clergy accepted the new Swedish ' Manual ', which was permissive and not compulsory. In its original form it was a close translation of the old Catholic Mass-Book. The translator, Olaf Petersen, brother of the first Lutheran Archbishop of Upsala, explained that ' he had allowed most of the ceremonies to stand which had been used heretofore, and were not clearly contrary to God's Word '. The character of the new ' Manual ' made transition easy ; people and priest alike could feel that practically they were using the old service in a new tongue. This was as the King desired : letters exist in which he warns zealous Protestant ministers not to go too fast. ' Zeal may be unreasonable, and improvement must be slow till the mass of the people are better instructed.' But the future, of course, was in the hands of the young, and as the older clergy died out, the body of the Church grew more and more Protestant, and the survival of the old ritual became exceptional.

As to the monasteries, the King's policy was slow and gradual suppression, quite differing from the two clean sweeps which Henry VIII made with the English religious houses. He began with closing small, poor, or scandalous establishments, transferring their surviving members to larger and better-ordered foundations. Inducements were offered to monks of suppressed houses to take up parish work, and many did so, some marrying and becoming conforming pastors. But the main scheme that worked was the cutting off at the bottom of the supply of novices to keep up the existence of the monasteries and nunneries that were spared. The greater part of their lands having been taken over by the State, there was not sufficient maintenance for large bodies, and the survivors, in self-defence, let their numbers drop, rarely accepting a novice. In twenty years they were nearly all elderly men : for the younger generation, who would in the Middle Ages have turned to the monastic life, or been thrust into it by their families, had for the most part other ideals and aspirations by 1540 or 1550. Hence a slow dwindling in the numbers in most religious houses, and when they reached a minimum the King declared the foundation 'decayed', and drafted the survivors into another house of the same order. The disappearance became progressively more rapid as the older generation died off. In 1545 it was said that there were only four nunneries surviving instead of forty which had existed in 1500, and the proportion with the monasteries was not very different.

On this principle the Reformation Settlement naturally took a very long time to work out—fortunately for Gustavus his life and reign were to be protracted : he survived till 1560, and had brought his scheme to a practical conclusion before he died, leaving behind him a well-organized national Church without any cataclysm in religion having taken place, and, what is more surprising, without any religious persecution having been practised. The Diet of Westeras, however, did not quite mark the end of Gustavus's troubles, either religious or political. He had yet to deal with several rebellions of different types. The first and most important was in 1529 : this was a composite affair, semi-baronial, semi-ecclesiastical. The nobility, as has been already pointed out, had been hard hit by the ' Blood Bath ' of 1520 ; and many of them had been conciliated by a clause of the Recess of Westerås which permitted the resumption of lands given to the monasteries since 1450 by the descendants of the original donors and founders. The King wrote sarcastically on one occasion, ' to resume old manor lands from the Church, or to get chattels from a dissolved monastery my nobles are most willing ; in that way every one is ready to be " Christian " and " Evangelical " '. But there were some who looked deeper into things, and were not to be bought in this fashion, seeing that the King was building up a strong monarchy on the confiscated church-endowments, a thing hateful to feudalism. But still more did they dislike his reliance on the support of the free yeomanry—was he not the ' peasants' king ' ? To the discontented barons were joined some of the elder clergy, wroth at the King's quiet and consistent promotion of Lutheranism. The rising was headed by the High Steward of Sweden, Thuré Jensson, and by Magnus, Bishop of Skara. The appeal was to good Catholics to overthrow a heretic king, and it was promised that Clement VII should absolve Swedes from all oaths of allegiance to him.

This rebellion was much like the ' Rising in the North ' in Elizabeth's day in England, and flickered out in a similar way. The peasantry refused to stir, because they distrusted baronial leaders. The high-steward and bishop escaped to Germany ; only two West-Gothland nobles were beheaded —the rest merely fined. This was the only feudal rising in Gustavus's long reign.

But he was more troubled in his latter years by insurrection of a different sort—sporadic effervescence of lawlessness among the peasantry, and (oddly enough) mostly in Dalecarlia, where he had been proclaimed 'administrator' at his first appearance in 1521. They were seldom serious enough to cause any very great trouble, but were very tiresome. The King himself used to ascribe them to mob-psychology—the innate suspiciousness of uneducated people. 'Whenever I want to make some sort of a change for the better in administration, they straightway take to their pole-axes, and send round the Fiery Cross : and most of all the Dalecarlians, who boast that they made me king, and are therefore entitled to immunities which no subjects should dream of claiming : they think that they ought to have the management of the State.' The yeomanry, indeed, looked upon themselves as the victorious party at the end of a long period of civil war, and found it irksome to settle down, even under a king of their own. Regular taxation was especially hateful, as also Gustavus's creation of a small standing army.

On the whole the King showed himself very patient, and used persuasion and diplomacy in dealing with rioters. But occasionally he flared up into a burst of wrath, punctuated by executions. He could not afford to be a tyrant, nor did he wish to be one—a king without ancestors had to be careful of his popularity, when there were both disgruntled barons, unruly peasants, and survivors of the old Catholic party among the clergy to be taken into consideration. The worst troubles were in 1541–42, when there was a rising in West Gothland of peasants out to restore ' true Christianity and the Good Old Times '. They attacked indifferently royal officials, unpopular barons and Lutheran clergy. It was something like a Wat Tyler's rising, but much more like the Devonshire riots of 1549. So great was the stir that Catholic princes on the Continent began to take some notice of it. But it was tiresome and sporadic rather than dangerous, and its most important practical result was that at its end the King kept on foot a much-increased standing army. In the last year of his reign it is said to have numbered 15,000 men—whose annual pay required much careful finance. Gustavus kept them going

Gustavus Vasa and Scandinavian Protestantism 127

not merely by taxation but still more by developing the resources of the realm in the way of mines, forestry, and the setting up of new colonies of peasantry in the hitherto waste lands of the north.

It was after the rebellion of 1541–42 had been quelled that Gustavus got his diet to pass supplementary legislation prohibiting pilgrimages and saint-worship, and cutting down the inordinate number of religious holidays in the Church calendar. The number of malcontent Catholics was not now so great as to provoke more risings at these attacks on the surviving incidents of the old faith.

Gustavus died in 1560, having—as has been shown—achieved all the changes made by Henry VIII without any of the atrocities which had disfigured the English break with Rome, and left Sweden with much the same organization that Elizabeth carried out a few years after his death —by means not dissimilar from his.

CHAPTER IX

THE OPPORTUNISTS. QUEEN ELIZABETH
AND CATHERINE DE MEDICI

MANKIND may be divided into two general types of mentality—some people—the minority—work on a definite scheme of life directed to a realized end. It may be, like that of Plato's old man in the *Republic*, merely to live an honourable life on the lines of a respectable ancestry, distracted neither by over-great ambition, nor by idleness and pleasure, and leaving a straight record for the next generation. Or it may be to serve a cause or an ideal. Or the end may be that of the ' climber '—self-assertion, and the urge to win distinction in some sphere of activity—ranging from that of a small king who would like to be an emperor, down to that of an apprentice who would like to be a foreman, or of a girl who would like to ' marry well '. The desire to climb will be affected in different degrees in each individual by the moral factor—some think honesty is the best policy, and they are often justified ; others think that all methods are good ' *quocumque modo rem* ', and discover that there are limits to the efficacy of unscrupulousness, when one has acquired a well-established celebrity for it. Such was the fate of Napoleon after the affair of the kidnapping of Ferdinand of Spain—a nicely managed job which was, as he afterwards confessed, ' *trop louche* ', and damned his moral reputation for ever. His previous efforts in self-assertion had not quite accomplished the feat—Charles James Fox believed in him, even after Brumaire, as a possible neighbour !

But of course there are many individuals whose desire for self-assertion is wholly altruistic—or so appears to them —who work for a cause without any primary idea of personal profit—from saints to fanatics of every shade.

Such were in our period Ignatius of Loyola and Calvin—whose predecessors and successors are to be found in every century, but equally some less-remembered prophets of one inspiration or another whose enthusiasm perished with them. On the whole it is these people who count in the history of an epoch.

But the large majority of mankind are not guided from first to last by some logical scheme of life, moral or immoral, but are more or less of opportunists. I mean that external circumstances rather than the internal will-power settle the course of their careers. In a time of moral chaos like the sixteenth century they face the situation more or less with Hamlet's despairing ejaculation :

> The time is out of joint ; O cursed spite,
> That ever I was born to set it right !

This necessity for dealing with the strange and unprecedented leads, save with the small minority of those who have a definite purpose before them, almost certainly to opportunism in conduct. But it is inevitable, of course, that when an old system of thought, administration, and daily custom, disintegrates, the effects should be very diverse, in proportion to the different personal mentalities of the individuals on whom the crisis has fallen.

A man may become a ruthless conservative, or rather reactionary, set on keeping the old system going by every possible means, even by the use of brute-force—the gallows or the stake—because he considers that things may be bad enough as they are, but any change must be for the worse. We must try to stop the clock, or even to put its hands back.

More common is the conservative opportunist, trying to retain as much as he can of the old, but timidly conceding much in the way of change, though he dislikes it, if it seems absolutely necessary. This frame of mind was normal in the sixteenth century.

Equally normal was the progressively minded opportunist, who was anxious to make changes, but shrank, from prudential reasons, from introducing them as rapidly, or in such complete measure, as he would have liked. Often he only succeeded in carrying out a small portion of the programme that he had conceived in his mind.

But the egotistic opportunist is also to be considered—who thinks of his own safety alone, without any sentiment or prepossession for either the old or the new, prepared to put aside either, or both, provided that his personal ambition, convenience or survival is secured. He has no objection to complete changes of policy or attitude, if he thinks that his own interests may best be served by the swerve. To this category belong many monarchs who were ambitious for themselves rather than for any cause, and still more servants of such monarchs, who in pursuit of place, power, or wealth were ready to follow out the most contradictory orders of such masters.

Opposite to all these classes of opportunist we place the comparatively few men who have so much self-confidence that they can construct a new moral or material world of their own, contemning all ancient experience and custom, because they consider that in many respects they have been found misguided. This type—call them doctrinaires, theorists, or (with Napoleon) *idealogues*—may be influenced by philosophic, religious, or social conceptions, or by any two of such impulses working together. They believe themselves to be affected by no personal considerations, but only by right reason. They are generally intolerant, and often destructive. Such folks, call them saints, heroes, fanatics, or what you will, are the dominant influence in forming the character of their age.

It may, perhaps, be necessary to give instances, that the different classes of sixteenth-century mentality may be understood. But the same types range through all ages of recorded history, from the kings of Judah and Israel down to the twentieth century. As examples of the ruthless conservative or reactionary we may instance such people as Philip II and his worthy lieutenant the Duke of Alva, who were blind enough in their fanaticism to put aside all ordinary restrictions of honour, charity, common sense, or expediency.

Elizabeth and Catherine de Medici 131

The fundamentally conservative man, who yields unwillingly to the times, keeps as much as he dares of the old, but bows to the necessity of letting in the new, may be exampled from the Emperor Ferdinand I and his son and successor Maximilian II. Both of them yielded for expediency many points that they would since gladly have contested. Ferdinand had to be tolerant. His son found toleration quite congenial to his temperament in face of national prejudices, now grown too strong to be contradicted.

The fundamentally progressive person, who is forced to hang back and to ' leave undone the things that he ought to have done ' in his own estimation, may be instanced by Frederic I of Denmark, a Protestant by conviction, but bound to subserve the wills of the barons and bishops who had given him his nephew's crown. He pleased nobody. Gustavus Vasa, a little bolder, was more fortunate.

The egotistic opportunist, quite unscrupulous as long as he gets his own way, and indifferent to causes so long as he can assert his personal will, is not at all uncommon. Christian the Cruel of Denmark, with his reckless atrocities and his frequent changes from rampant assertion of Papal claims to fostering Protestantism, is a fine example. Henry VIII only fails to be placed in line with the Scandinavian tyrant because he had a fixed policy, hard though it sometimes is to realize the fact, and if he sometimes seemed to waver in practice, was really adhering to a definite programme. If we go below the rank of sovereigns, we need seek no better examples than those of Thomas Cromwell, and John Dudley—Protector Northumberland—who were capable of any intrigue or atrocity or subservience that was profitable to their ambition. The former pandered to every humour of his master, and carried out his most arbitrary and inhuman orders without the least conviction that they were reasonable or necessary—because he loved the power that lay with him as ' Vicar-General ', and aspired to the short-lived earldom that came to him only a few weeks before his disgrace and execution. If he had any preferences they were those of a man of the ' new learning', but these could always be thrust aside when the King had dirty work to be done. Oddly enough Thomas Cromwell had an exact prototype in the unscrupulous minister of Christian the Cruel, Dietrich Slaghoek, an adventurer who had been a surgeon, a quack or charlatan, a canon lawyer, and a man-at-arms, and who was made chancellor and archbishop merely that he might sign away the rights of the Church to his master. Christian sacrificed him when he had failed, just as Henry VIII sacrificed Cromwell, to get some responsibility for unpopular doings off his own shoulders.

Protector Northumberland I take to have been quite as disgusting an example of the egotistic opportunist as Cromwell or Slaghoek. He had not in his later career the excuse that would cover his earlier years, that he was serving a ruthless master whose will could not be gainsaid. His ambition was inordinate: he aspired to be sole ruler of England by controlling puppet kings or queens, and to serve this ambition he posed as head of a party in Church and State for which he had no real sympathy. After ruling for three years in the character of a Protestant zealot, he confessed on the scaffold that he had been a Catholic at heart all through, and had been misled by simple love of power. Northumberland was so consistently false-hearted that even his dying speech may have been insincere, though then it is difficult to see what object he could have in blackening his own reputation when *in extremis*.[1] If his confession was true, this persecutor of Catholics was consciously and deliberately committing something very like 'the sin against the Holy Ghost'. If it was not, we stand convinced that he was simply an egotist with no religion at all, which is the more probable hypothesis. The astonishing weakness in his intellectual make-up is that he conceived that English public opinion would tolerate his preposterous plan for the

---

[1] One hypothesis of explanation is that he had received promises that, if he grovelled sufficiently, his sons Ambrose and Robert should not follow him to the scaffold. He was so selfish that I doubt this eleventh-hour impulse of paternal affection.

Elizabeth and Catherine de Medici 133

transference of the crown to his own family. There were limits to the politically possible even in Tudor days. Though she has gone down in the record of history with many more pages of abuse tacked to her name than Thomas Cromwell or John Dudley, I am bound to state that I consider Catherine de Medici a decidedly less objectionable character than either of them. She was an opportunist and unscrupulous : she has the dreadful stain of responsibility for the massacre of St. Bartholomew to her discredit. But she was fighting and intriguing not, like Northumberland, to usurp power to which she had no title, but to assert her responsibility for keeping together the French monarchy, which had fallen to her by the death of her husband and the minority of her sons. Undoubtedly she was contending for the survival of the House of Valois, and incidentally for the preservation of peace in France. Of course, as she was an Italian, the peace of France cannot have had any sentimental patriotic meaning to her. But the preservation of the House of Valois could only be secured by keeping France quiet, and peace (if not an end in itself) was a necessary means to the end. If she commands little sympathy from the historical commentator in her various shifts and intrigues, her opponents command less. The grasping Guises as champions of orthodoxy, and the vain and inconsequent Louis of Condé as champion of Protestantism, are equally unconvincing in their assumed rôles. The complete triumph of either would mean the downfall of the Valois monarchy, possibly the disruption of the French kingdom which had taken so many centuries to build up. One cannot suppose that Catherine de Medici found any attraction in the idea of religious toleration, but practically she arrived at it, and this should go down to her credit. She tried to keep the realm of France together, if she was very unscrupulous in her methods—and little was the help that she got from the succession of degenerate sons whom her deceased husband had left to her. An acute historian of our own generation [1] has pointed out that there was a considerable similarity

[1] Pollard, *History of England under the later Tudors*, pp. 179-80.

between the position and policy of Catherine de Medici and that of her contemporary Elizabeth Tudor in England. They were both shifty politicians with little regard for oaths or even for consistency in oath-making, but the one died in deep despair, muttering that her last surviving son had ruined the royal cause, while the other survived to a famous if lonely old age, with the record of having brought her kingdom through a long series of crises, and having left it a first-class not a second-class power in Europe. As she was decidedly to be ranked among the few individuals who left behind them a permanent impression on her age, I have dealt with Elizabeth at some length elsewhere. Catherine de Medici, with statecraft of much the same sort, registered a complete failure in her policy, and if she had lived only one year longer, would have seen the transfer of the French crown, for which she had contended so long, from the last of her worthless sons to his distant cousin the detested King of Navarre. Her name was written on water—very dirty water—and she left no trace behind her, save a rather exaggerated reputation for wickedness in the works of romancers.

There are, I suppose, limits, moral as well as practical, to the successful practice of opportunism in every sphere of life. One need not 'serve the times' to the loss of one's own soul, or even of one's self-respect. Tactless assertion of one's own convictions, when their revelation may lead not only to personal danger but to public trouble, is perhaps to be deprecated. But interested silence may run very close to hypocrisy or to cowardice. One can have no respect for the conduct of William Cecil (Lord Burleigh) and so many others of Elizabeth's councillors of later days, who quietly conformed to Catholicism throughout the reign of Mary, though it is eminently comprehensible. Indeed it is curious to observe that the list of the Marian martyrs contains hardly the name of a single gentleman—the few Protestants of superior rank who could not bring themselves to conform, quietly absconded overseas, like the Duchess of Suffolk. There was a corresponding body of Catholic time-servers in the early days of Elizabeth, who saved their fines for recusancy by attending the English Church service once a year, but retained a quiet adherence to the old faith. 'Bowing in the House of Rimmon' was excused by most of their contemporary co-religionists on both sides. The quiet survival of Crypto-Protestants in some Catholic states, and of Crypto-Catholics in some Protestant states, was a known fact. It was only in southern regions that the prying Inquisition set itself to hunt out concealed and unobtrusive heretics—relapsed Jews, or Marani, or Calvinists or Agnostics. In the Protestant countries a heretic had to be noisy or propagandic to attract attention, such as the Anabaptists received in several Protestant countries, and the unfortunate Brownists from Queen Elizabeth, and Servetus from Calvin.

As has been very frequently remarked by English controversialists, the numbers of Roman Catholics who suffered death under Elizabeth—nearly all Jesuits or else political rebels and conspirators—were ostentatiously treated not as heretics but as traitors—hung that is, not burned like the few unfortunate Anabaptists who went to the stake. Putting aside actual conspirators like Norfolk or Babington or Dr. Lopez, the remainder were propagandists, according to the views of the Queen and her ministers, who were pervading England to preach the efficacy of the bull of Pius IV, issued on 25 February 1570, which declared Elizabeth deposed and excommunicated. Roman Catholic laymen who paid no attention to the bull, and did not harbour Jesuits, had nothing to fear, so long as they paid their recusancy fines. The distinction between hanging and burning may not appeal to the modern mind, and one can quite understand the beatification by recent popes of the unfortunate Jesuits who suffered in England. They did, no doubt, regard the bull of 1570 as effective, and teach that Elizabeth was no lawful queen, but their religious activity in keeping alive the faith of the dwindling Catholic remnant in England is the thing remembered by their co-religionists to-day. To Elizabeth and her councillors the matter that was evident was that Jesuits were mixed up with the schemes of the

Pope and the King of Spain for a Roman Catholic restoration, and the deposition of an excommunicated sovereign—they were 'adhering to the Queen's enemies'. And these enemies were perpetually hatching plots, and presently launching Armadas against England. That the missionaries were devoted men who were ministering necessary spiritual sustenance to brothers deprived of their ordinary facilities for worship and the sacraments, was a point that would not appeal to the Elizabethan lawyer or juryman—though it may to the student of to-day.

Toleration is a plant of late growth in the human breast. If the votaries of any creed, pagan or Christian, have a perfect confidence in their own scheme of the relation between man and the Divinity, then all deliberate opponents of that scheme are obviously misguided persons. Hence the orthodox are entitled to bring them to a better state of mind by persuasion, or if needful by more drastic methods. Indeed it is their bounden duty so to do. When two families, races, kingdoms, or empires happen to have developed different theories of the universe, clashes are bound to come. For as every one knows, 'orthodoxy is my doxy', and this being the fact I am in conscience required to impose my correct views on all and sundry, as Herr Adolf Hitler very clearly understands to-day. The legendary Nimrod, or the real Khuenaten, Jezebel and Jehu, the early Moslem with his alternative of 'the Koran or the Sword', Charlemagne in Saxony, the famous abbot of Cîteaux at Béziers, or Alva at Brussels, were all logical according to their lights. The only toleration known to the ancient world was that curious form of it which rested on the view that one's own gods were local and not universal, and that other nations also might have gods—of an obviously inferior sort. One might allow contemptible neighbours to go to their own devils in their own miserable way, as some rulers—Romans especially—whether cynical or 'broad-minded' were content to do. With a monotheistic religion this is of course impossible, for other people's gods must be either myths or evil spirits. The early Christians often identified Apollo or Venus with

Elizabeth and Catherine de Medici 137

myrmidons of Satan, if not with Satan himself—as witness the weird story of St. Gregory Nazianzen and the oracle of Apollo at Daphne, or the strange medieval legend of Tannhäuser and the Venusberg.

The misfortune has often been that heretics of our own religion, who have the same fundamental beliefs as our orthodox selves, and therefore ought to know better, have in all ages provoked more wrath in their quasi-co-religionists than the misinformed votaries of inferior creeds. One might merely pity and contemn a sun-worshipper or a snake-worshipper, perhaps try to convert him. But a learned and argumentative person who is perfectly well acquainted with the main tenets of one's own creed, but is perversely wrong on some one important dogma, is much more hateful, because much less likely to see the error of his ways. Hence the awful proverb of the Suni Moslem that 'it is more profitable to kill one Shiah than ten infidels'. Hence also the perverse attempt of the Papacy in the fifteenth century to exterminate the Utraquist Hussites of Bohemia, just when the Turk was thundering at the gates of Christendom. I can never forget the English archbishop who said to the Lollard Oldcastle, 'Hah, Sir John, in this schedule of yours there is much good stuff and Catholic doctrine, but you must answer me whether or not you believe that the material bread remains in the sacrament of the altar, after consecration duly performed'. Every one knows what happened to Oldcastle in the end.

But there have been few witnesses who, standing before their inquisitor, have dared to speak out so boldly as Sir John did in reply to Archbishop Arundel. Lollards in the fifteenth century, Protestants in the sixteenth, often quibbled or equivocated, and ended by going as penitents to carry a faggot at Paul's Cross—humiliating enough, but not so trying as being burned above a number of faggots at Smithfield. Henry VIII was rather fond of cross-questioning Lutherans who were likely to break down ; one whole day in June, from nine in the morning to seven at night, he spent in the examination of a heretic. When the unfortunate man recanted, the King was gracious, and the audience expressed their wonder at his divine learning. It is marvellous that there were so many who took the hard road to the stake, rather than that there were many others who took the easy road of submission. Wherefore let us not be too severe in our judgement on William Cecil and his fellows of the council, who went to Mass in the reign of Mary. Or on Cranmer for his shifts and hesitations before he took the final plunge, and recanted his penultimate recantation. Despite of many conformists in hard times, both from those of the old faith and those of the new, I am under the impression that the moral fibre of the nation had vastly improved since the fifteenth century. The proportion of Lollards who recanted under the Lancastrian persecutions is immensely greater than that of either Catholics or Protestants who, when brought to the last trial, failed to keep their troth. This was specially true of the clergy : friars and Jesuits went to the gallows, Protestant preachers to the stake, with a good grace and a splendid confidence, when their party was out of power. I imagine that this was due to the new spirit of the sixteenth century. The lethargy of the Middle Ages was over, and many men braced themselves up to face the hard duty imposed by conscience and a sense of moral obligation. The opportunists were, no doubt, still in the majority, but it is not the opportunists who set the spirit of the time, though they may have to fall in with its waves of change.

So Martin Luther's 'Here stand I : I can do no otherwise : God help me !' at Worms, or Thomas More's 'I pray God preserve me in my just opinion even to death', are the things that counted in history.

I would not ascribe too much importance in the formation of the age to the great movement which has been vaguely called the Renaissance. It was coming, nay had already come, in 1500. But I must venture to differ from the opinion of many famous writers. I do not think that there was any salvation for man's soul in the Renaissance. It was in many ways a thing of beauty, an intellectual awakening, a cultural revelation, but it was not a moral movement. As every one knows, though few are prone to stress the point, the votaries of the Renaissance included many of the most immoral spirits of the age—high and low, clerical and lay. Popes like Leo X and princes like Ludovico Sforza were its patrons. Some of its literary exponents were foul-minded people like Aretino. Among its typical products were the cynical Machiavelli, and the scoundrel-artist Benvenuto Cellini. The cult of old classical beauty was accompanied with the revival of the old classical vices and immoralities—deliberately discovered and revived. Looked at from the moral point of view it was an attack on medieval ideas, not because they were often noxious and evil, but because they were absurd or ugly. It was a freethinking movement of a dissolvent kind, and it had no positive and profitable reconstruction of the world to offer. One can admire or practise art and literature without being a better man for the study or the practice. To employ a skilled chisel, a facile pen, or a paint-brush that attracted the judicious purchaser's eye, did not make the artist or the littérateur the prophet of a better age to come. The ages of the best art have, all down history, often been the ages of the worst morals. The way out of the disillusionment and spiritual apathy of the late fifteenth century was not by the cult of beauty, nor the study of the models of antiquity.

I do not say that the Renaissance had not an immense influence on the spirit of the time. But neither the destruction of old delusions, nor the introduction of new standards of art, are necessarily effective agents of spiritual regeneration. I do not think that the abominable condition of Europe in 1500 could have been cured by good scholarship any more than it could be cured by good art. The intellectual revolt against scholastic ignorance was felt by many whose personal lives were no more seemly than those of the worst patrons of the old system. And it cannot be denied that intellectual revolt often led to the development of wild outbursts of antinomianism—not merely curious revivals of pantheistic or dualistic doctrines, but notorious evil living—defended with blatant insolence, or wit.

Conceivably if this movement had not happened to synchronize with the spiritual revolt against the corruptions of the Church—of which revolt I deny that it was the parent —the net result of the Renaissance might have been only morally destructive. Something of the same sort was seen in early imperial Rome, when the old religion of the Republic had been laughed out of court, when ' no one but children and fools believed in the old gods ', and a highly cultured aristocracy, ruled despotically by Neros and Domitians, lost all touch on decency, civic responsibility, and any serious conception of life. Things were tending that way in the Italy of the early sixteenth century, and there would not have been even that very imperfect reform of abuses which was carried out by the Council of Trent and the popes of the Catholic Reaction, if there had not been the moral revolt of the Protestant Reformation to set the defenders of the faith on their mettle.

Italy with a succession of popes of the old type, and princes of the great tyrant-houses, Sforzas, Gonzagas, Medici, &c., would have shown even worse corruption than did the Italy of the second half of the sixteenth century. Even as it was, the social annals of the time sufficed to supply English dramatists with sufficiently horrid tales, on which Elizabethan admirers gloated, like the *Duchess of Malfi*, or Vittoria Corrombona '*the White Devil of Italy*'. If there had not been popes like Pius IV to indulge in general bloodletting among titled miscreants, things might have grown to such a general anarchy of evil as is hard to conceive. I do not say that households like the Cenci, who so inexplicably attracted the attention of Shelley, or nunneries like Sta. Margherita at Monza, or nests of *bravi* and spies such as Cosimo de Medici kept, were necessary results of the Renaissance. But I do hold that cultural splendour free from all moral restraint may be co-existent with all the vices and the crimes that the human heart can conceive. The counter-Reformation, with all its hypocrisies and inquisitions, did represent some sort of a check on notorious evil living. It is interesting to note that the greatest miracle of St. Carlo Borromeo, the typical saint of the counter-Reformation, was that he was preserved from certain death while saying Mass at the high altar of his cathedral, by the providential deflection of a pistol ball fired straight into his back not by a Lutheran or an Atheist, but by a friar of a corrupt order, the Umiliati, into whose moral turpitudes he was conducting an inquiry. The incident may be considered typical of the times, and entirely creditable to the sainted cardinal and his activities. It is commemorated in many pictures, though somehow gunpowder does not fit in well with one's conception of the representation of a miracle. I must confess to have felt the same incongruity when, in a group of votive pictures in a small Italian church, I noted a saint leaning down from the clouds to snatch a small child from under the malignant wheels of a large red motor-car. But I hate to say that 'the age of miracles is past'—even from the artistic point of view.

CHAPTER X

THE TURKISH DANGER, 1520-1571

EVER since recorded history began, a never-ending strife between the East and the West has endured, and the tide of conquest and invasion has been mounting eastward or westward, only to reach its high-water mark, stand still for a moment, and then commence slowly or quickly to ebb backwards. The writers of the old classical world of antiquity saw this clearly enough; Herodotus, the father of all European historians, began his famous book with a tale of raids and counter-raids between Europe and Asia, mixed with curious legends of abducted ladies, tracing down in legitimate succession from them the Great War of Greek and Persian which had been the all-engrossing interest of his own youth.

Different nations have led the attack in successive ages: the Greek, the Roman, the Frankish Crusader, last of all the Russian and the British powers on the one side; the Persian, the Saracen, the Tartar, and the Turk (Seljouk or Ottoman) upon the other. Three or four times Europe has appeared to submerge Western Asia, and to graft her civilization so firmly therein that the lands of the debatable zone seemed incorporated for ever with the Western world. Alexander the Great, and after him the Romans, made so thorough a conquest of Asia Minor, Syria and Egypt, and planted there so widely the culture and organization of the West, that it seemed incredible for long centuries that these regions would slip back again into complete Orientalism. On the other hand, the Persians in the old days before Alexander, the Saracens of Mahomet in the Dark Ages, the Tartars under the House of Genghiz Khan in the late Middle Ages, the Ottoman Turks in modern times, not only occupied all the debatable lands, but cut great cantles out of Europe, and added them for a time to the East. For six hundred years southern Spain was an Oriental land, looking to Mecca and Bagdad for its religion and its culture—not (as of old) to Rome and the nearer West. For four and a half centuries Constantinople and the Balkan peninsula was in similar case : even now the Ottoman Turk still sits by the Golden Horn, in defiance of all probabilities, and occupies what was once the central focus of Eastern Christendom.

In the sixteenth century there came the last great assault of the East upon the West, the third since the break up of the Roman Empire. I shall not have to speak of the first—the Saracen conquest of Roman Syria, Egypt, Africa, and Spain, nor with the back-swing of the pendulum when in the eleventh century the Crusaders threw themselves upon the Levant, and established a precarious hold upon all its waters and much of its lands, while the Mohammedan powers were weak and divided. The second dangerous assault of East upon West was the awful but transient inroad of the Mongols, under the descendants of Genghiz Khan, in the middle of the thirteenth century. The year of terror for Western Europe was 1241–42, when the immense horde of Batu Khan, after sweeping all over southern Russia and destroying Kief its ancient capital, overflowed into Poland, beat its dukes and their German neighbours at the battle of Liegnitz, and then threw themselves upon Hungary. The Magyar kingdom seemed absolutely annihilated at the battle of the Sajo ' ubi fere extinguitur militia totius regni Hungariæ ', and the Mongols came across the borders of the Bohemian kingdom, and actually pressed down into Dalmatia, and saw the waters of the Adriatic. There seemed no end to their advance, and after a winter of acute panic, which reached as far as Paris, Italy, and England, all Christendom was praying, not with too great confidence, that divine power might send back these Tartars ' ad suas Tartareas sedes '—to the inferno from which they had emerged. But after a year of terror Christendom breathed again. For reasons which seemed inscrutable to the contemporary Western observer, the Tartars swept back eastward again. Hungary and Poland emerged from the deluge, battered but preserved, and it was only in unlucky Russia—with which Latin Europe had little concern—that the effects of the Mongol inroad lasted for centuries—spiritually down to our own day, for Russian barbarism is in one aspect a spiritual survival of the wicked work of the Eastern savages in the thirteenth century—when the old Slavonic freedom and culture was destroyed, and after two centuries and more of slavery the Muscovite czardom emerged with a semi-Oriental mentality, taught by the long subjection to the knout of the great Khan of the Golden Horde.

There was not for almost two centuries any year of panic in Europe from the fear of a sudden and irresistible onslaught from the East, such as that of the Mongols had been in 1241–42. But there grew up from small beginnings a new danger, barely perceived in the second half of the fourteenth century, obvious but not necessarily all-engrossing in the fifteenth, but suddenly coming to a head in the early sixteenth century, just at the time that the French kings were raiding Italy, and Luther was nailing his theses to the church door at Wittenburg.

The Turkish danger had come into existence through two political crimes on the part of Christian powers. In 1204 the cosmopolitan adventurers of the fourth Crusade had, at the instigation of Venice, knocked to pieces the old Byzantine empire, the ancient warden of the gates of Europe against eastern invasion, and had set up nothing in its place. After that date there was no Christian military power left on guard toward the frontiers of Islam. The Frankish principalities of the nearer East—Cyprus, Athens, Achaia, &c., were miserably weak. The restored Byzantine empire of the wretched Palaeologi was no stronger. There was nothing left to resist the Turks of Asia Minor, when they began to unite under the very capable house that descended from the Emir Othman and bore his name. The only first-rate Christian power which was vitally concerned in the danger was Venice, who had sucked up all the trade of the Levant, so that for her profit alone the Crusades seemed to have been fought out to their uninspiring end. And Venice preferred to keep open the trade routes, by commercial treaties with the sultans of Egypt and other Moslem princes, rather than to exert herself for the general defence of Christendom. She did not really awake to the oncoming danger till far into the fifteenth century, when the Ottoman Turks, whose growing power and persistent hostility to Christendom the Italians—Venice and Genoa alike—ignored in their blind commercialism, finally built a navy, and captured the feebly defended Constantinople in 1453—a blow that changed the face of the whole commercial world.

But there was a second Christian power that was responsible for the development of the Turkish danger in a degree only less serious than that of the Italian republics. Behind the moribund Byzantine empire, the vassal of Venice, there lay in the mid-fourteenth century a group of new Slavonic states which had established themselves in the inland after the devastating effect of the Crusade of 1204. The Serbs were divided into several principalities, of which that ruled by the House of Nemanja was the most important: to the east of them the Bulgarians had a solid kingdom between the Danube and the Balkans. Supposing that another push from the East should come—and come it did—these Slavonic kingdoms, and not the depleted and bankrupt empire of Constantinople, would have to bear the brunt of the defence. About 1350 it looked as if the keeper of the gates of Christendom would be a strong power, for King Stephen Dushan (1333–55), the last but one of the Serbian House of Nemanja, subdued the other minor states, made Bulgaria his vassal, drove the Byzantines down to the shore, till they possessed little more than Constantinople and Salonica, and having practically the whole Balkan Peninsula in his hands, proclaimed himself emperor of the Serbs, Greeks and Bulgarians at Uscup in Macedonia in 1340. He was a formidable personage, and commanded such a power as had never been seen in those regions since the fall of the Byzantine empire.

Stephen Dushan died on 28 December 1355, by one

of the most unlucky chances in the history of Europe, leaving his vast realm to a son, who was a minor, and a group of ambitious relatives. A few months before, the Ottoman Turks had been called into Europe, as auxiliaries by the Byzantine pretender (or usurper) John Cantacuzenus, and had been put by him in possession of the fortress of Tzympe on the Dardanelles. When Cantacuzenus gave up the struggle and abdicated, they refused to depart, and seized Gallipoli, in defiance of the protests of the legitimate emperor John Palaeologus (1357). Undoubtedly Dushan could and would have expelled them, had he but survived: but on his death not only did the Bulgarians and other vassals disown their allegiance, but the young Czar's uncle Simon declared himself king in Thessaly, and other local despots ceased to care for orders from Belgrade.

At this precise moment, when the Turks were but just established on the Dardanelles, the brilliant and unscrupulous King of Hungary, Louis the Great, thought it an appropriate opportunity to fall upon his Slavonic neighbours, and add their dominions to his realm. He conquered northern Bosnia in 1359. He took Belgrade and a great slice of northern Servia in 1365, and twice invaded Bulgaria under the pretence of a crusade (1365–69). He had obtained the Pope's approval for the subjection of the schismatic Serbs and Bulgars to the Roman obedience, and his conquests were accompanied by forced submission to the Western Church. This led to revolt, and desperate war between Christian and Christian, at the very moment when every nerve should have been strained to expel the Turks. A partial and scattered resistance only was offered to the advance of the young sultan Murad, who, after two victories over incomplete musters of the Serbs and Bulgarians in 1363 and 1371, conquered the Thracian and Macedonian lands up to the Balkans. Meanwhile, Louis of Hungary, who had destroyed the strength of his Slavonic neighbours, turned off to wars with the Venetians and to a successful snatch at the crown of Poland, and let affairs in the south slide. The chance that the Turkish encroachment might be stopped by the Serbs and Bulgars had been completely

The Turkish Danger, 1520-71   147

annihilated by him—while he himself, with too many 'irons in the fire', went off, after having thrown everything into confusion. He was a purely destructive power, and the damage which he did to Eastern Christendom was to continue for six hundred years. For without his intervention in the Balkans it is more than doubtful whether Murad I, great soldier as he was, would ever have mastered the Balkan Peninsula. The descendants of King Louis and his nobles paid for this crime against Christendom a century and a half later, for he destroyed—or at least mutilated—the buffer-states which ought to have held back the eastern invasion. It was because they were gone that the Turks were finally able to cross the Danube in 1525, to annihilate the last levy of Hungary on the bloody field of Mohacs, to sack Buda-Pest, and to turn the best part of the Magyar kingdom into a Moslem pashalik for nearly two hundred years. The fate of Bulgaria and Serbia was hard—the former was annexed in two slices in 1381 and 1386. The Serbs made a final rally under their last king Lazarus, but were cut to pieces on St. Vitus's Day 1389 at the fatal field of Kossovo, remembered to this day in Serbian ballad poetry. The King, his nobles and his army were exterminated, and the surviving remnant of the race was forced to do homage to the Sultan. Murad I had himself fallen in (or after) the battle, but his successor Bajazet was as great a warrior as his father, and continued for another generation the gradual conquest of all the outlying lands of the Balkan Peninsula.

It may seem extraordinary that the House of Othman, starting from very small beginnings in the mountains of Asia Minor, only one family among several Turkish princely houses, accomplished the task of crossing the sundering waters and taking Orientalism into Europe, when so many greater invaders had failed—the Persians in the seventh century, the early Caliphs in the eighth, the Seljouks in the eleventh. A word therefore must be said as to the Turkish state, at the moment when it became a factor in European affairs. We may commence by pointing out the obvious fact that the descendants of the obscure emir

Othman were for ten generations an exceptionally gifted race—there was only one weakling in the line from 1300 to 1566—a thing quite unparalleled in Oriental dynasties. Some of the nine other sultans were very bad men—according to all human standards—some of them comparatively decent autocrats. But all, with the one above-named exception (Bajazet II, 1481–1512), were great fighting men, able leaders of a miscellaneous horde of adventurers gathered from all the East : for the original Bithynian clan that had Othman for its head formed only a fraction of the host that followed his successors.

It was Orchan, the son of Othman, who formed and shaped the Turkish state into a great military machine, which his son Murad I perfected, and set working for the conquest of the Balkan lands. The two pieces of organization which created the Ottoman power were the raising of the Janissaries—the first disciplined infantry seen in the East—and the introduction of the non-hereditary feudal system which had as its base the 'timar' or fief of the mounted man-at-arms, whom Westerns would have called a knight. This is not the place to describe at length either of these institutions. Every one knows of the Janissaries—the Christian tribute-children levied at an early age in conquered lands, brought up in barracks under a strict military training, and regarded as the Sultan's private property. They were slaves, but privileged slaves, and always promoted to high honour outside their corps if they served him well. So thorough was the physical and mental discipline to which these captives were subjected, that it was rare for them to turn back and fly to their own people. Scanderbeg, the great Albanian hero, is almost the sole example of a Janissary who, after ten years' training, flew to his native mountains and headed a long and successful revolt against his former master. As long as sultans were formidable and masterful, the Janissaries were useful tools : only when, in the late sixteenth century, the line of great sultans ends, did their former slaves become their masters, and, like the Praetorian guard of imperial Rome and the Mamelukes of Egypt, take to making and unmaking rulers for the profit of themselves. In early days the Janissaries were but a small body—Murad I had only a thousand of them in 1360, but by the sixteenth century they numbered over 100,000. A trustworthy infantry—all skilled bowmen—was a thing unknown to the other Eastern powers with whom the Ottoman sultans had to contend, as also to the Christian states with which they had to deal in the fifteenth century. Hungary and Poland were feudal kingdoms, with no army save a turbulent knighthood.

The Timar-system was much more important even than the Janissaries in the development of the Turkish state. When land was conquered from the Christians—first from the Byzantines, afterwards from Bulgar and Slav—it was cut up into fiefs, each fit to support a fully armed horseman, who held his land by the tenure of taking the field whenever the Sultan raised his banner. There was none of the Western folly of stipulating for a forty-days' field service only, or of making the fief hereditary. It fell back to the Sultan at the Timariot's death, and if he left sons of military age they were given land elsewhere on principle, to prevent the growing up of local attachment and regional particularism. The Turks, like other Moslem conquering races, were singularly indifferent to racial homogeneity in their armies: any adventurer with a good horse and a strong lance might get a 'timar' served out to him. The whole Mohammedan East was a recruiting ground for the only state of that religion which was at this moment a rapidly growing power. But many recruits were found among Christian renegades—outlaws of all sorts, or Slavs and Greeks, who in despair threw up their faith in order to keep their personal freedom and find themselves on the winning side. The son of the last king of Bulgaria fell in battle as a Turkish pasha: a considerable percentage of the Bosnian nobility became perverts—whose descendants still survive in Jugo-Slavia as a Mohammedan minority among the mass of their Serbian kinsmen. The Timar system is the thing which accounts for the rapid settling up of the Balkan Peninsula after its first conquest—the effect was very similar to that of William the Conqueror when he cut up all England into fiefs for his military adventurers—by no means all Normans—who joined in his enterprise. But we are concerned with the Ottoman Turks not so much for the interesting history of the development of their power, but for the tremendous onslaught by which they broke into Central Europe in the sixteenth century. Passing lightly over details of their doings between their seizure of the Gallipoli Peninsula in 1357, and their terrifying appearance before the gates of Vienna in 1528, it is necessary to note that though they first appeared on the Lower Danube in the last year of the fourteenth century, they did not pass it in overwhelming force till the third decade of the sixteenth. During all this period the kingdom of Hungary was the buffer-state for Christendom, since Serbia and Bulgaria had been beaten down. Twice in periods of special stress crusades were preached and succours were sent to the aid of the Magyars—both counter-offensives ended miserably: the first at Nicopolis in 1396, when an enemy largely composed of French contingents, though led by Sigismund as King of Hungary (he was not yet emperor), perished miserably through indiscipline and bad leadership. The second, led by Ladislas, King of Poland and Hungary, backed by Cardinal Julian Cesarini and some Western succours, was crushed even more disastrously at Varna in 1444. The Turks were now so firmly settled into the Balkan Peninsula that not even the temporary dislocation of their power by an assault from the great Tartar Khan Tamerlane, who took them in the rear in Asia Minor, could shake their grasp on Thrace and Macedonia. There was a considerable opportunity for Christendom immediately after Tamerlane had beaten and captured Sultan Bajazet I at Angora, in 1404, but no advantage was taken of it. And Bajazet's grandson and great-grandson Murad II and Mahomet II reconquered all that had been lost for a moment both in Asia and in Europe, and resumed a vigorous pressure upon the borders of Christendom. Both failed against Hungary, after long fighting, of which the hero on the side of the defensive was John Huniades, the saviour of Belgrade on two occasions. But though this

The Turkish Danger, 1520–71 151

central advance was beaten back repeatedly, Murad II and Mahomet II cleaned out all the outlying Christian principalities in the corners of the Balkans—Bosnia, Albania, and the Frankish principalities in the Greek Peninsula. They also subdued all the minor Moslem states in the eastern end of Asia Minor—the lands of the families which had once been equals and rivals of the race of Othman.

But of course the central event of this period was the capture of Constantinople in 1453. It might have been had earlier, but the emperors had done obsequious homage to the Sultan, and, if not content to be his parasites, did no more than intrigue behind his back with the Papacy—to induce the popes to launch yet more crusades eastward. The bribe which they could offer was the recognition of the supremacy of the Western Church over the Eastern, the humiliating bargain made at Florence by the penultimate emperor John VI Palaeologus and his Patriarch in 1439. But the tardy and imperfect intervention of the West ended in the disaster at Varna in 1444—after which Murad II might well have closed in on Constantinople, but refrained from doing so, lest he should bring the Venetians into the matter—their naval powers were the one thing which might still have saved Constantinople. The Palaeologi were granted nine years more of precarious existence on the Golden Horn, till in 1453 the young Mahomet II, the son of Murad, picked a wolf-and-lamb quarrel with Constantine XIII Palaeologus, closed in on the almost defenceless city, and took it, after a short siege, by force of artillery. The Venetians, notwithstanding the importance to them of Constantinople as the half-way-house and entrepôt of much of their trade, deliberately refused to send any adequate help to save the Emperor. Their fleet actually ran up to the Bosphorus, just before the siege, and took on board the greater part of their colony, and then departed for good. Yet, if Venice had chosen, she might have sent 100 galleys and 20,000 men to save Constantinople; she preferred to spend her strength in wars with the dukes of Milan for the possession of Eastern Lombardy. In 1454, the year after the end of the Byzantine empire, the peace of Lodi gave her Brescia, Bergamo and other towns. To obtain them she had betrayed the cause of Christendom, and (though she knew it not at the moment) sacrificed her long naval predominance in the Eastern Mediterranean, and the oldest branch of her trading activities.

The nemesis for this political crime worked out slowly, but began from the moment that Mahomet II got possession of the deserted quays and arsenals on the Golden Horn. The Sultan set to work to make the Ottoman state a naval power—which it had never been before—and to cut all the threads of Western commerce. Before he was dead he had effectually blocked the way to the Black Sea, and had practically mastered the Aegean—Christian vessels could get no farther than Crete or Rhodes. Venice at last was forced to fight, after she had allowed the main advantage of position to go to the enemy. But her Golden Age had begun to die away : after 1453 begins that struggle between Turk and Venetian for the control of the Levant which was to last for the rest of the fifteenth century, and for three-quarters of the sixteenth, down to the day of the battle of Lepanto in 1571, which marks the end of the attempt of the sultans to become the dominant naval power in the Mediterranean.

The fall of Constantinople and the establishment of a Turkish war-navy made the Ottoman state doubly a danger to Christendom. It was now no longer only the land frontier, all the length of the Danube and Save, right and left of Belgrade, that had to be defended, but also a new sea-front in the Levant and the Adriatic. From 1460 to 1479 Venice was forced to take up the war which she had long shirked, and attacked Mahomet as head of a curious miscellaneous alliance—not only the kingdom of Hungary, and the insurgents of Albania—still holding out under the indomitable ex-janissary John Castriot, or Scanderbeg as he is more usually termed in his Turkish name—the crusading or semi-piratical little power of the Knights of Rhodes, even Venice's old enemy Genoa for a space, and (what is surprising) the great Tartar Lord of

Armenia and Northern Persia Uzun Hassan, who had been frightened by Ottoman expansion eastward. The alliance was a powerful but an ill-compacted one. To the general surprise of Europe Sultan Mahomet faced it and beat it. The only part where he failed was the Hungarian line along the Danube, where John Huniades once more preserved Belgrade, and all subsequent advances were beaten off. Indeed, there might have been danger to the Turks in this direction, if the new King of Hungary, Mathias Corvinus, the son of Huniades, had not turned off, distracted by unjustifiable and unnecessary ambitions in Central Europe. In 1467 he invaded Bohemia, and got involved in a seven-years' struggle with the Czechs : later he fell upon the Austrian Emperor Frederic III, and drove him out of Vienna, and the greater part of his hereditary domains. Meanwhile, he left the Sultan alone, to deal with his other foes, for most of his reign (1458–90).

On all the other fronts Mahomet triumphed. The Tartar lord of Persia was slain in battle in 1473, the Albanians submitted after the death of Scanderbeg in 1467—some of these clans turned Moslems *en masse* to keep their lands, so did some of the Bosnians in 1464 after their last king had been captured and executed. These instances of widespread apostasy were as disheartening to Christendom as the complete failure of Pius II to get together a Western league for one last crusade—a disappointment which killed the old Pope. The Venetians lost most of their Aegean possessions—in 1470 the Turkish navy achieved its first success by driving off a Venetian fleet and co-operating in the siege of Chalcis in Euboea, the greatest of the harbour-ports of the republic. It fell and its garrison was massacred. At last in 1479 the Venetians sued for peace, and as its main condition surrendered Scutari, their last possession on the Albanian coast. They complained that they had been betrayed by the King of Hungary, who had failed to distract the Turks, as he might easily have done : but he preferred to conquer Austria.

With the withdrawal of Venice from the war, Mahomet, now the owner of a large and active navy, became a danger to all the states of the central Mediterranean. His fleet conquered all the Ionian islands save Corfu in 1479, and (an awful phenomenon for Italy) threw ashore a landing force in 1480 into Apulia, which surprised and took Otranto, the easternmost harbour in the dominion of Ferrante King of Naples. The attack was wholly unexpected—no one had ever dreamed of a Mahometan invasion east of the Adriatic—the whole population was massacred after the usual Turkish fashion. This was a dreadful portent, not so much from the actual loss but for what it promised for the future—nothing like it had been seen since the ninth century, when once before a Moslem invasion had been seen in Southern Italy.

It would seem that Mahomet was set on following up this first success at Otranto; he collected a great fleet and army in his Adriatic ports, and it is said that, reviewing the Janissaries before the beginning of the campaigning season, he told them that their next muster should be under the walls of Rome—an extravagant promise, for a terrified Europe would have rallied to save the Holy City. But whatever were his intentions they were never destined to be carried out. On 2 May, as he was preparing to start for the West, he died suddenly of a fit of apoplexy, aged only fifty-two, and with many ambitions before him.

On what would have been the result of an assault on Italy by the greatest but one, and quite the most cruel and unscrupulous of the Ottoman sultans, we have not to speculate. Certainly it would have upset the whole political system of Christendom, for the danger was appalling. But what followed in 1481 few could have foreseen—all the previous sultans had been great fighting men—several of them endowed with the highest capacity as well as with the instincts of the conqueror and the administrator. But Mahomet II was succeeded by the first weakling in the Ottoman House—his heir Bajazet II was a dilettante, a poet and philosopher; he hated the camp and preferred the palace—was only very occasionally forced into the field by the murmur of his soldiery. He was no beginner of wars, though he was sometimes thrust into them, either by

The Turkish Danger, 1520-71 155

the unruliness of his own subjects, or because his enemies attacked him. His reign commenced with civil war—the rebellion of an ambitious brother—and ended with abdication at the behest of an unscrupulous son. His long reign of thirty-two years (1481-1512) was a complete setback in the history of the expansion of the Turkish empire, which had hitherto grown with such appalling if irregular rapidity. It will be noted that his personality made an enormous difference to the general history of Europe, as his reign coincided with the period of the great French invasions of Italy. Charles and Louis of France, Maximilian of Hapsburg, and Ferdinand of Aragon, fought out their quarrels without the least interference from the East. The recapture of Otranto by the Neapolitan King Ferrante was the first event of Bajazet's reign—the Turkish standard was never again to be seen in Italy.

Almost always unsuccessful in wars into which he was thrust unwillingly, he was beaten by the Hungarian and the Mameluke Sultans of Syria and Egypt, and had little profit from a feeble war with Venice in 1498-1503, mainly notable for the destruction of the Turkish fleet at the naval battle of Prevesa in the Adriatic, which ended for many years the danger to Christendom that might have come from Ottoman interference on the sea during the great Italian wars (1502). He concluded peace with Venice in 1503, and made no effort to stab her in the rear during the awful crisis of the League of Cambray (1508), when he might have had all her eastern possessions for the asking, while she was being set upon by the Emperor, the Pope, and the King of France, and barely maintained her independence behind the lagoons when her last stand was being made.

In 1512 Bajazet was deposed, at the end of long civil wars between his unruly sons, by Selim, the most unscrupulous of them, who had bought the support of the Janissaries. He died twenty-three days after his abdication —perhaps by poison administered by his undutiful heir.

When the thirty-year reign of this unfortunate and ineffective prince came to an end, a new chapter opened in Turkish history. Once more there was an ambitious and capable Sultan on the throne—and the great wars of Italy were still in full progress. The danger to Christendom reappeared, which had been lost sight of since the death of Mahomet II in 1481. But there did not follow at once the assault on Hungary and Italy that might have been expected. Selim was what we should have called in 1918 not a 'western front' man but an 'eastern front' man. He was obsessed with the opportunities that stood before him on his Asiatic frontier, where there lay the decadent and turbulent Mameluke Sultanate on one side, and a new and precarious Persian dynasty on the other, where the adventurer Shah-Ismail had just driven out the old Turkoman rulers of the country. The one was rotten with decay, the other was hardly taking shape as a national power after a period of chaos. After making a systematic slaughter of his relations young and old—hitherto fratricide had been frequent but not absolutely systematic—Selim had even nephews in the cradle bowstrung—the new Sultan plunged into a series of Asiatic wars, by which (astounding as it may seem) he doubled the size of his empire in the four years 1515–19. Such a rapid conquest of ancient historical lands had never been seen. It came from a military fact—that the Turkish state was on a more modern organization for war than any other Eastern power. It had a disciplined infantry of formidable efficiency in the Janissaries, and it had also developed the use of field artillery. Since the bombards of Mahomet II had smashed the walls of Constantinople, the sultans had recognized the future of the cannon, and had organized not only siege-trains but movable battle-guns. The states of the Nearer East were still in complete medieval somnolence so far as the art of war went, depending wholly on hordes of mailed horse, spearmen and horse-archers without a gun or a foot-soldier to back them. The last sultan but one of Egypt had been pressed by his Venetian friends to buy cannon, but refused because they were both cumbersome and cowardly weapons!

Hence the three great battles by which Selim won his eastern empire in such short space were all victories of

The Turkish Danger, 1520-71

foot and cannon, used to support the usual cavalry arm, over enemies who put nothing but horsemen into the field against him. At the fight of Tchaldiran in Armenia (1514) the day wore on with charges of successive bodies of Persian horse, upon the more concentrated Turkish line, where the Janissaries, with the guns in front of them, formed the centre. Partial successes of the Persians against one of the Sultan's cavalry wings had no importance, compared with the fact that the Ottoman artillery blew to pieces every squadron that vainly charged it, and finally broke the Shah's army in two. Selim was able to pursue a demoralized enemy, and took and sacked Tabriz, which was at that time the Persian capital. He annexed Armenia in consequence, and turned next spring (1515) upon Mesopotamia, where he was equally successful, beating another Persian army in the field, and capturing Mosul and other cities by force of artillery.

The Persian war was not over, though the Shah had been beaten from the field, when Selim plunged into his still more important war with the aged Sultan of Syria and Egypt. He was well aware of the political weakness of the Mameluke state, where a dominant alien aristocracy, never more than 20,000 strong, was imposed on millions of discontented or apathetic *fellahin*, who had no interest whatever in the fortunes of their masters. He was also aware that the Mamelukes were an old-fashioned army, without artillery or foot, trusting entirely to their ancient reputation for desperate cavalry charges. When Selim invaded northern Syria in 1516, and brought the Mamelukes to action at Dabek, near Aleppo, the incidents of the day reproduced those of Tchaldiran. The enemy charged gallantly, and even penetrated as far as the Janissary square, in which the Sultan had to take refuge. But the Ottoman artillery broke the Mameluke centre to pieces, the old Sultan fell in the rout, and the survivors of his army rode off the field in despair. This single battle gave Selim all Syria and Palestine—the cities all opened their gates save Gaza, where there was a general massacre after a Mameluke relieving force had been beaten. Everywhere else the Turks met with apathetic surrender of the local population—it had taken the Crusaders of old thirty years to conquer much less than Selim won in three months. But in 1100 Syria had been full of independent principalities—in 1516 it had been stripped of all wish to defend itself by two centuries of rule by the alien Mameluke power.

The surviving Mameluke beys and emirs had retired to Cairo, there to elect a new sultan. A hardy soldier, Touman Bey, nephew of the last monarch, was placed upon the throne. He had a few months, while Selim was receiving the submissions of the Syrians, to prepare for the last rally of the state, but the aristocracy had been much thinned at Dabek, and some faint hearts or jealous chiefs even deserted to the Sultan. Touman had resolved not to trust to cavalry onsets alone, and had fortified lines at Ridanieh, covering the road to Cairo, and even bought some guns from the Venetians to place in them. His precautions were useless—Selim marched round the flank of the entrenched camp and forced the Mamelukes to fight in the open. In one more battle of the former type the Turkish field artillery again settled the day. Sultan Touman in vain tried to keep up a guerilla warfare against the victor for a few weeks, but finally surrendered, and was hung by the unmerciful conqueror on a gallows in front of the main gate of Cairo.

Thus ended the Mameluke dynasty, and with it a most interesting epoch in the commercial history of Europe. Since the Ottomans had taken Constantinople and blocked the way to the Black Sea, the only free access that remained for European commerce with Persia, India, and the Far East was that which passed through the Mameluke ports, from Scanderoon by Tripoli and Beyrout and Jaffa to Alexandria. But the Syrian harbours were of secondary importance; it was Alexandria which was the great depôt for all the trade of the further lands, which crept up the Red Sea, was transhipped at Suez, and came by a short caravan route to the ancient city on the Mediterranean. The Mamelukes had long ceased to be a conquering power, and were on the best terms with the Venetians. Valuable

The Turkish Danger, 1520-71

as this alliance was to the Italians at all times, it became perfectly indispensable after the Ottoman had blocked the alternative trade routes by the Dardanelles and the Black Sea.

The conquest of Syria and Egypt by the same intolerant and non-commercial power which had already stopped all transit by the northern routes to the East, would have produced a complete block of all trade between Christendom and the Far East, if it had not been for recent events which had been occurring in the Atlantic. But just before Sultan Selim slew the Mamelukes a wholly new route from Europe to Asia, completely out of the control of the Turk, had been discovered. The Portuguese explorers, originally set going by Prince Henry the Navigator, the grandson of John of Gaunt, had been for two generations pushing farther and farther south along the west coast of Africa, past Guinea and Angola—this was as far as they got in Prince Henry's own day. But Bartholomew Diaz in 1486 rounded the Cape of Good Hope and saw the Indian Ocean, and only ten years later Vasco da Gama—a better-remembered man—appeared with his three ships in the port of Calicut, on the Malabar coast of India, and found trade promising and prosperous, in 1496.

This was (as it turned out) a providential thing for Europe, but it was at once recognized as an ominous event for the monopolists of the Alexandria route. The wiser heads in Venice saw the meaning of da Gama's feat at once. The diarist Priuli entered in his note-book:

> The whole of our city is distressed and astounded, and the wisest heads take it to be the worst piece of news that we have ever had. For all know that Venice has reached her height of riches and reputation through our Eastern trade, which brings foreigners to the city in such great numbers. But now by this new route the spice-cargoes will be taken straight to Lisbon, where French, Flemings, and Germans will flock to buy them, and they may get them cheaper in Lisbon than they can be here, for before the freights can reach us by the old route, they have to pay heavy toll for transit through the lands of the Soldan of Egypt.

But what Priuli could not have guessed was that not

only was Venice to find a new competitive route opened against her by the Portuguese, but that the much heavier calamity was at hand of the Alexandria route being suddenly blocked by a permanently hostile power. In 1496 all that could be seen was that it would be needful to improve and cheapen the old line of transit, and this was done by elaborate negotiations with the Mameluke Sultan. Not for some years did the Portuguese competition become absolutely ruinous. And ere this conjuncture came, the Alexandria route was suddenly closed for good. The Turk did not want to facilitate Venetian commerce, but rather to smash it.

It is impossible to speculate what might have happened if the weak and futile reign of Bajazet II (1481-1512) had not precisely bridged over the time between the death of Mahomet II and the accession of Selim I. When Mahomet died the first Portuguese voyage to India was sixteen years in the future. But when Selim came to the throne the Cape route had already been fourteen years in existence, and was beginning to be well exploited. Hence his closing of Alexandria and the Syrian ports did not cut off Christendom from the East, but merely precipitated the ruin of the Venetian monopoly, and threw a new monopoly into the hands of the Portuguese.

Selim tarried two years in Egypt after his final victory over the Mamelukes, occupied in organizing the vast regions which he had added to the Ottoman empire in so short a space. He then took his way back to Constantinople in 1519, free at last to take a survey of Western politics, and to renew (if he pleased) the onward march toward Central Europe, which his grandfather Mahomet had begun, and his father Bajazet had proved unable to continue. What exactly his policy would have been we can only guess, the one recorded fact about his last months being that he threw great energy into reorganizing the Ottoman fleet, and spoke of the expulsion of the Knights of St. John from Rhodes as his first object. But he died suddenly in 1520 before he had taken any definite steps, still not far on in middle age—he was under fifty.

The Turkish Danger, 1520-71

We must note at once the importance from the view of Christendom of Selim's complete distraction from Western politics during his eight-year reign from 1512 to 1520. He had turned eastward, and left Europe alone just long enough for the Hapsburg power to grow up, while he was engaged in the conquest of Egypt and Syria. In 1512, when he went off to the East, that power did not exist—Maximilian and Ferdinand of Aragon were both alive, and intriguing against each other. Charles V was a boy of twelve. When Selim came back, all the accumulated dominions of both the Spanish and the Austrian houses had fallen into the hands of a single heir, and that heir was now a grown man, and had been elected emperor in the preceding year, 1519. To meet the Turkish attack that was about to be renewed by Selim's very capable son, there was now prepared the greatest accumulation of territory and resources that any Christian sovereign had ever possessed. There was a new world-power ready, such as Europe had never seen since the days of Charlemagne—and this power (as we have already seen) was just sufficient to turn back the strongest thrust that Islam ever made against Christendom. Yet it was not a whit too strong, considering the energy of the attack that was coming, and making allowance for the stabs in the back that the kings of France always delivered when the attention of Charles V was distracted eastward or southward against the Ottomans. If the Turkish attack failed, it was no fault of the French kings, who did their best to ruin Christendom, looking only to the danger to themselves from a Hapsburg predominance in Central Europe. Of this we have spoken already.

Between the Ottoman boundary on the Danube and the borders of the Holy Roman Empire there still lay in 1520 the 'buffer-state', that kingdom of Hungary which, under John Huniades and Mathias Corvinus, had proved competent to turn back all the invasions of Murad II and Mahomet II. No one in Europe contemplated the idea that this well-tried guardian of the gate of Christendom might be liable to sudden collapse. As long as Belgrade stood firm Central Europe remained untroubled in mind.

Unfortunately things in Hungary had changed since 1490. After the death of Mathias Corvinus the Magyar state had been disintegrating. It was no longer guided by native leaders : a new exotic Polish dynasty had been introduced, not without much discontent among many sections of the nobles. The evil which overhung Hungary during the reigns of the two Polish kings, Ladislas (1490–1516) and Lewis (1516–26) was the same which ruined Poland two centuries later—the turbulence of a powerful nobility, who had at their mercy an alien elective king of no personal ability. Lewis had the further misfortune of having come to the throne at the age of ten, so that the greater part of his reign was spent under a troublesome regency, and he had hardly attained man's estate when the Turkish storm beat upon his borders.

Soliman, not without some reason called the ' Magnificent ', was the ablest of all Turkish sovereigns, and far above the level of his family in moral as well as in administrative capacity. He was not given to oath-breaking or promiscuous cruelty, as had been his father Selim, and many of his ancestors, and was a man of culture and refinement, as well as a good general.

When he had settled down into the seat of empire, he gave signs of his future intentions by taking the minor fortresses round Belgrade—Shabatz and Semlin—as preliminaries for the central advance that was to come (1521) and then the great frontier stronghold itself—which fell, after a resistance by no means equal to that which had been shown on earlier occasions, on 29 August 1521. Having cleared this front, and planted his standard north of the Danube at Semlin, Soliman withdrew for the winter to Constantinople. He had one more preliminary precaution to take—the eviction of the last Christian naval outpost in the Aegean. In 1522 his reorganized fleet beset Rhodes, and dislodged the Knights of St. John : they made a gallant defence for seven months, and finally departed under easy terms of surrender, which the Sultan honourably kept. The Knights retired to Crete, which was still in Venetian hands, but being not at all welcome there—for Venice wished to

The Turkish Danger, 1520-71

keep out of a Turkish war—presently accepted the offer made to them by the Emperor of the desolate and almost uninhabited isle of Malta, which they were to make famous for the first time in its history by their tenacious defence of a very perilous outpost of Christendom, in waters that were soon to be made as unsafe as the Aegean itself by Turkish encroachment.

Rhodes fell in December 1522, and Soliman would probably have turned his attention again to the Danube, but for a tiresome rebellion which broke out in Egypt, and spread to Syria. The Sultan was called off to the south, and was for more than two years occupied in crushing out rebellion, and rearranging all the administration of these new and outlying gains of his father. It was not till the spring of 1526 that he delivered his great attack on Hungary, preparation for which had occupied all the preceding year. This time he advanced, it is well to remember, as the ally of Francis I of France, who in his desperate straits after the battle of Pavia and the repudiated treaty that followed, had sought to distract the Emperor by turning the general enemy of Christendom against his rear. But Soliman needed no such encouragement—being set on playing his own game.

He left Constantinople in April 1526, with an army reckoned at 100,000 men and a great train of artillery, took Essek and Peterwardein in July, and on 29 August brought the young King of Hungary to a general action at Mohacs near the Marshes of the Danube. Hungary was as little fitted to face the storm in 1526 as in 1521—the King was now twenty years of age, but was in truth little more than the leader of a faction—quite half the baronage were missing from his banner on the battle day. He had gathered 20,000 men, nearly all light or heavy cavalry with few infantry or guns—it was not half what the kingdom ought to have provided at a moment of desperate crisis.

The battle could hardly fail to go in favour of the Sultan —despite some brilliant charges of the Hungarian horse, who beat back one of the Turkish wings, and were only checked by the Janissaries. Artillery won the day—as in the time of Soliman's father against the Persians of Shah Ismail and the Mamelukes of Dabek and Ridanieh. King Lewis was drowned in a marsh while flying from the lost field—like Roderic the last king of the Goths of Spain. The victorious Turkish army passed along the Danube, and took Buda, the old Hungarian capital, on 10 September. There was wholesale massacre and devastation wherever the Ottoman passed—over 100,000 captives were sold in the slave markets of Constantinople, and all the treasures which Mathias Corvinus had gathered—including his famous classical library and works of art—went to be stored in the Seraglio.

Hungary, as the buffer-state of Christendom, was annihilated. In a few towns on the Austrian border, where the Turks had not yet penetrated, the dead King's sister Mary and her husband Archduke Ferdinand, the brother of Charles V, were proclaimed king and queen. But this was but a fraction of the old realm : the pestilent feudal party which had failed to help Lewis II at Mohacs made a pact with the Sultan, by which their leader John Zapolya was acknowledged as vassal prince in the mountains of Transylvania. Buda, the old Hungarian capital, that formidable high-lying fortress, was to be for the future the advanced post of the Ottoman Empire against Christendom, just as Belgrade had been till 1521 the advanced post of Christendom against the Ottoman.

It might have been expected that Soliman would have followed up this tremendous victory by a further advance across the few remaining miles of unsubdued Hungarian territory in the next year. And he promised to come back in the spring of 1527, but was prevented from doing so by a revolt on his eastern frontier—a curious business due to the appearance of a local Mahdi, who preached communism and the overthrow of all secular princes, but was put down and duly beheaded. There was a pause in operations on the Danube—Charles V was fully occupied in the renewed struggle with France that followed the League of Cognac (1526) and had no attention to spare for the East. There-

The Turkish Danger, 1520–71 165

fore his brother the Archduke Ferdinand, now titular king of what remained of Hungary, but really king of Bohemia as well as ruler of the Austrian hereditary states, invaded the lost lands with an Austro-Bohemian army, recaptured Buda, and drove John Zapolya, the Sultan's despicable vassal, into the mountains of Transylvania (1528).

This counter-attack, of course, recalled the Sultan to vigorous action. In the spring of 1529 he came up with a vast army—200,000 men as was reported—recovered Buda in May, and then resolved not to waste time in besieging the still unsubdued fortresses along the Hungarian border, but to march straight at the heart of Austria.

Hence came the great siege of Vienna in September–October 1529, the most dangerous thrust against Christendom from the East that was ever delivered. The Emperor Charles was not on guard—his French war still occupied him—as it repeatedly did when the eastern peril was pressing. He was just about to break it off, rather unexpectedly, at the peace of Cambray (August) at the moment when Soliman entered Hungary, in order to have his hands free for the greater danger. But the peace of Cambray came too late to allow him to be present in person on the Danube. The responsibility fell on his brother Ferdinand, as in the previous year: the Archduke did not throw himself into Vienna, but retired into Bohemia, there to raise an army of succour with the aid of all Germany. The friction between the Catholic and Protestant parties was very fierce at the moment, but the bitter religious strife could not blind any reasonable German prince to the peril from the infidel. A great army was raised, but it was not this general levy of central Christendom which turned the enemy back, but the extraordinary courage shown by the garrison and burghers of Vienna, who saved themselves before the Archduke came to their aid.

Several desperate assaults by the Janissaries had failed, for though the Turkish artillery had shown its usual efficiency, the garrison repelled twenty storming parties in the breached walls. An early and exceptionally severe winter set in, and the Sultan, seeing his Asiatic troops perishing of cold and dysentery, and hopelessly discouraged in spirit, abandoned the siege, and retired first to Buda and then to Constantinople.

This was really the culminating point of the Ottoman attack on Christendom, though its significance was not fully apparent at the time. The Turks were never again to see Vienna till 1683, and the second siege, which John Sobieski foiled in that year, was a mere desperate raid, in which the invader had never a real chance of success, since the Ottoman Empire was already failing, and Christendom was far stronger than in 1529. But in the days of Soliman the Crescent was still advancing, and Europe was wholly distracted by the strife between Hapsburg and Valois—not to speak of the impending religious wars about to break out in Germany.

After Francis of France had retired for a moment from the struggle, at the peace of Cambray—which (as we have seen) synchronized with the Turkish siege of Vienna—Charles V enjoyed the unwonted chance of being able to deal with the Ottoman attack in person for six years. Now when the Emperor had a free hand, the chance of the Sultan's breaking into Central Europe was reduced to a much more feeble probability. It was not till 1532 that he took the field again, and this time he did not strike at Vienna, but at the land south of it, the unsubdued strip of Hungary and the Styrian archduchy beyond it. Soliman got as far as Gratz, but was repelled from its walls, and various corps of his army were beaten in detail. His campaign proved a complete failure, though it led to much misery and devastation. Meantime the Emperor's great Genoese admiral Andrea Doria beset the shores of Greece with a Spanish and Italian fleet, cleared the Turkish squadrons out of the Adriatic, and threatened to invade the Aegean.

The Emperor now took the offensive, not on the Danube, but in a new quarter of the Mediterranean. The north coast of Africa had recently fallen into the hands of the famous Barbary pirate Khaireddin, better known to Christendom as Barbarossa, from his big red beard, who had murdered the last Moorish Emir of Algiers, and driven out the Emir of Tunis. This great adventurer, feeling himself too insecure in his conquests—for the Moors of the interior had risen against him, and the Spaniards had been making small conquests along the Barbary coast in the days of the defunct Hafsid dynasty—sent to Constantinople to offer himself as a vassal to Soliman, who accepted his homage, and named him ' Capitan Pacha ' and governor of Algiers (1533). Suddenly, therefore, the Ottoman Empire found itself extended all along the south side of the Mediterranean, as far as the borders of Morocco. The Emperor, seeing that this irruption into the Western waters threatened the Spanish predominance in a region where his power had hitherto been undisputed, left his brother Ferdinand on guard upon the Danube, and delivered his two great attacks upon Africa. The first, the invasion of Tunisia in 1535, was more or less successful—the Barbary galleys were swept out of the way, and an exiled Moorish prince replaced at Tunis as a vassal of the Emperor, where he held his own for some years. The second, the Algiers expedition of 1541, was a sad disaster—storms wrecked the imperial fleet, the siege of Algiers was unsuccessful, and Charles brought back only a remnant of a great army to Italy, to find that Francis of France was once more attacking him in the rear —his fourth French war lasted from 1541 to 1544.

While Charles was conquering Tunis, Sultan Soliman had been distracted by a war with Persia. Shah Tamasp saw in the Hungarian wars of the Ottoman, the same useful opportunity that the Ottoman found in the French wars of the Emperor. This struggle in 1534-36 was on the whole favourable to the Turks—though Soliman took, but could not keep, Tabriz, the northern capital of the Shahs, he made a permanent conquest of Bagdad in 1536 —and incorporated all Irak and the lower valleys of the Tigris and Euphrates in his empire. They were no longer the centre of Mussulman art and culture—for the land had been woefully sacked by Tartar and Mongol invaders again and again, and Bagdad showed but a shadow of its ancient glory—but the conquest was a notable one, and brought the Ottoman borders down to Basrah and the Indian

Ocean—though it never led to any extension of trade or naval power in that remote southern sea.

Meanwhile, when the Persian war was successfully ended, Soliman was able to turn his attention once more to the Danube—encouraged by the fact that the French King had broken the treaty of Cambray and attacked the Emperor once more in the rear. This time the Turkish and French fleets acted in unison, and there was a great project of a joint invasion of Sicily—which failed because Venice, who had held out so long from war—it was twenty years since her fleet had taken the sea—threw herself into the struggle. She was now only a second-rate power, but had been goaded into intervention by the fear of a Turco-French domination in the Mediterranean, which might make an end of her small surviving empire in the Ionian Islands, Crete, and Cyprus.

The general war by land and sea that prevailed from 1536 to 1547 was the final test of the relative strength of the Emperor and the Sultan. For eleven years the two empires stood in constant conflict, while France twice delivered tiresome but ineffective stabs at Charles's back, in the two short wars of 1536–38 and 1541–44, from each of which Francis withdrew when his affairs went badly, to the great disgust of his Moslem ally. Soliman persisted in constant attacks, till in 1547 he was forced in sheer exhaustion to sue for a five-years' peace—the sign that the vigour of the attack on Christendom had expended itself. There were still wars to come, but none of them were so dangerous to Christendom as those which fell in the earlier years of Charles's and Soliman's long reigns. Much blood was spilt by land and by sea—without any decisive result. Charles lost Tunis, and after the Algiers disaster gave up his African ambitions. But Soliman made no further gains on the side of Hungary.

For the next century there was a curious block upon this frontier—the old Magyar kingdom was divided into three sections—Turkish Hungary included the whole central plain of the Danube, with a pasha established as governor-general in the old capital Buda—Hapsburg Hungary, a

The Turkish Danger, 1520-71 169

long contracted slip along the Austrian frontier, with Pressburg (Posony, Braetislava) as its capital: its strength was a long row of fortresses, Gran, Comorn, Raab, Stühlweissenburg, Szigeth, &c., and it extended down into Croatia. Thirdly there was the principality of Transylvania, under the traitor John Zapolya and his successors, somewhat larger than the mountain-block to which that name is properly attached. It was for many years a Turkish vassal state, but one whose rulers often tried to slip out of their bonds, and occasionally did so, when a capable prince like Stephen Bathory or Bethlen Gabor was on the throne, and a weak sultan was to be found at Constantinople.

The last of Soliman's great assaults upon the eastern frontier of Christendom started in 1552 : it was again made with the co-operation of France. King Francis I was dead, but his son Henry II continued his policy, taking advantage of the Emperor's troubles in Germany, where the Protestant princes were in open revolt. Soliman worked in concert with the French, till King Henry withdrew from the struggle at the Peace of Cateau Cambrésis in 1559 but did not relax his efforts even when his untrustworthy ally had given up the game. Once more the war ended as a sort of drawn game. The Hapsburg House, even when Charles V had abdicated in 1556, and his empire had been divided between his son Philip II and his brother Ferdinand, was still strong enough to defend itself, though not to win a decisive victory. The Sultan's attention was distracted by a second Persian War (1553-54) which went badly for him, as all his attempts to push eastward from Bagdad failed. There were also internal troubles caused by quarrels in his family, a thing normal in Eastern dynasties, when a sovereign grows old, and has ambitious sons. But though Soliman's last years were not happy, he never lost his energy ; the last year of his life saw two dangerous blows levelled at his Christian enemies. His great naval expedition against Malta in 1565 was an attempt to evict the Knights of St. John from their strategical position at the narrows of the Mediterranean. It failed after a six-months' siege, ending in a complete victory for the Grand

Master Lavalette, who drove off the Turks even before the Spanish fleet came to his aid from Sicily. In the next spring the indomitable Sultan made his last invasion of Hungary in person. He died in his tent before the walls of Szigeth, just three days before that well-defended fortress was stormed, aged seventy-two and in the forty-seventh year of his long reign.

There were to be three more sultans at Constantinople before the year 1600, but the genius of the line was extinct. Selim II (1566–74) was a sot, Murad III (1574–96) a miser, and Mahomet III (1596–1603) a nonentity. The personal characters of these unworthy descendants of Soliman counted for something, but it was also clear, even before his own death, that the strength of the Ottoman Empire had come to the limit of its possible extension. Looking at things external, it had now run up—to right and to left—against enemies of such strength as it had never faced in the fourteenth and fifteenth centuries—not powers like Serbia, Venice, Hungary, or the Mameluke sultans of Egypt, but the solid block of the Hapsburg dominions on the West, and the new vigorous Persian state on the East. The Hapsburgs were both a naval and a military power—and they disposed of large fleets and well-disciplined standing armies, not to speak of a line of fortresses laid out in accordance with the new military art of fortification. The Hapsburgs justified their existence in the history of Europe by their constant service as Wardens of the Eastern March—which ended triumphantly in 1571 with Don John of Austria's great naval victory of Lepanto, after which no Turkish fleet was ever a danger to Europe, though the Barbary Corsairs continued to be a petty nuisance to Sicily, Sardinia, and Andalusia. But the disciplined standing armies of the West had also proved themselves a solid hindrance to Turkish expansion, such as the tribal levies of the Slavs, the Hungarian knighthood, or the Mameluke aristocracy had never been. The Landsknechts and the Spanish tercios of pikemen and musketeers were an even better-trained force than the Janissaries whose bows had settled so many an earlier field.

The Turkish Danger, 1520-71

This famous corps itself was beginning to decline in Soliman's day—he had granted them the often-urged, but hitherto denied, permission to marry and yet to remain in their ranks. Later he permitted the sons of Janissaries to be enrolled, along with the ordinary slave-recruits. This had two results—the Janissaries grew into an hereditary caste, and were no longer a body of disciplined fanatics knowing neither home nor family. They came to have relations with civil life, and interests other than those of their master. This, it was observed, made them much less tough and reckless than their predecessors. Another breach in their organization was that, while originally the Janissaries were simply the Sultan's bodyguard, and never took the field save in his suite, Soliman in his later years, when he was no longer always on campaign himself, took to planting bodies of them out to do garrison duty in remote centres of military importance, such as Buda or Cairo. After a few years of outlying garrison duty, these detachments became localized and particularist, one corps very jealous of another, and all grudging at the select companies which lay at Constantinople. These last, when sultans grew weak, took upon themselves the habits of a pretorian guard, deposing weak or unpopular sultans, and claiming immense donations from the prince whom they had placed on the throne. Their military efficiency went steadily down, when compared with that of the standing armies of the West.

A similar decline of quality was about the same time beginning to be detected among the feudal horse, who formed the bulk of the Ottoman armies. Not only were sons allowed to slip into their fathers' fiefs, contrary to the old rule, and so to become tainted with local and provincial jealousies and particularisms, but 'timars' began to be given as rewards for other than true military service. Court officials, secretaries, and clerks, even the eunuchs of the royal harem, were entrusted with them—always, of course, with the liability to produce a fighting man for each timar. But the sort of deputies, cheap adventurers, who served as the representatives of civilian masters, were far less efficient soldiers than the old type of feudal horseman, who had earned his fief by the lance, and fought to keep it. A Turkish state-document of the early seventeenth century complains that the Timariots were going down in numbers no less than in quality, because court favourites, who had received many fiefs, cheated the State by producing far less horsemen than their acreage of granted land should have furnished. And such as appeared were often poor stuff, not trained soldiers, but landless men driven into the warrior's trade by mere poverty. All this developed under the miserable Sultans who followed Soliman on the throne—as long as he lived the enemies of Turkey detected no degeneracy in the formidable Timariot horse ; but the moment that he was gone, and the eye of the master ceased to survey every detail of the machine, degeneracy set in, and was widespread before the end of the sixteenth century.

The Ottoman Empire had lived for two centuries by annexing and exploiting new and wealthy conquests : when it ceased after Soliman's day to be an expanding power, and had to live on its own resources and not on the plunder of new regions, it began to feel the gradual impoverishment that comes from internal maladministration. Tax-farming, the curse of all Oriental monarchies, played a part in the ruin. Constantinople became the centre of a corrupt bureaucracy of pashas intriguing for place and power, who were always ousting each other in the favour of weak sovereigns. Occasionally a Janissary mutiny swept away both sultan and pashas, and let a new set of leeches loose upon the central administration and the Treasury.

Hence it came, fortunately enough for Europe, that the period of the Great Wars of Religion in Europe coincided with a period of anarchy and decadence in the Ottoman Empire. The Thirty Years War, 1618–48, was fought out without any interference from the East. The last rally of the Turks, and their final advance against Austria, came fifty years too late. It would have been a peril in 1630 —by 1683 it was only a transient scare.

CHAPTER XI

THE WARS OF THE SIXTEENTH CENTURY: (a) THE ITALIAN WARS, (b) THE 'WARS OF RELIGION'

As in most other spheres of human activity, so in the Art of War, the sixteenth century starts a new epoch. The military history of the immediately preceding period might be described, not inaccurately, as being shut up in a number of water-tight compartments. There had been no struggles affecting the whole of Europe simultaneously—as there had been, for example, during the Crusades in the twelfth and thirteenth centuries, or the Mohammedan inrush in the eighth, which made itself felt from Constantinople to the plains of Central France.

But in the fifteenth century we find six or seven groups of wars which had, as a rule, no connexion with each other. These were: (1) the Wars of the English and the French from Agincourt to Castillon; (2) the wars in Spain—the strife of the Kings of Castile with their neighbours of Granada, Portugal, and Aragon; (3) the wars of the Bohemian Hussites with the Germans and Hungarians; (4) the wars of the kings of Hungary with the Ottoman sultans and occasionally with their Hapsburg neighbours on the German frontier; (5) the wars of the Russians with their old masters the Tartars, whose power they had almost broken by the end of the century; (6) the complicated strife of the Italian states with each other, all waged by proxy by means of bands of condottieri; (7) the aggressive wars of the Swiss Confederates with the Hapsburgs, the lords of Milan, and later with the Duke of Burgundy; (8) the continual bickering of the Danes and Swedes.

These can all be treated as separate studies, having few and infrequent cross-relations with each other. Attempts to join up groups for international action there were—generally taking the belated form of Crusades. As I have said already, there was an attempt to crush the indomitable Hussites by the joint attack of the Germans and Hungarians—which was possible because the Emperor Sigismund was king of Hungary as well as head of the Holy Roman Empire. And there was the unhappy Crusade of Ladislas of Poland, which ended at Varna in 1444, to which came not only Poles and Hungarians, but Western Crusaders under Cardinal Cesarini.

But putting aside these belated crusading aspirations, there were very few other crises in which the nations interested in one of the eight sections of military activity which I have cited above became involved in the progress of another. Alfonso of Aragon's occupation of Naples was not a Spanish attempt to conquer Italy, but only a large specimen of condottiere warfare, practically Italian and not international. Charles the Rash was a more universally disturbing factor, since in the building up of his visionary 'middle kingdom' of Burgundy he contrived to clash with France, with the Empire, and the Swiss. But he perished, leaving behind him little more than an unexpected advertisement for the military power of the Swiss Confederates, who (despite the memories of Morgarten, Sempach, and Arbedo) had practically been an unknown element in European politics. The wars of the Middle Ages ended with the Flemish campaigns which had as their cause the beginning of the competition between Hapsburg and Valois for the Burgundian inheritance, typified by the strife for the hand of Mary of Burgundy the heiress of the widespread dominions of Charles the Rash. But Maximilian of Hapsburg did not represent Germany, but only his paternal house, and his decisive victory at Gravelines (1479) was won by a purely Burgundian army. This war was not a struggle between France and Germany, but a continuation of old contests—dating back to Roosebeke, Mons-en-Pevéle and Courtray, which turned on the ambition of successive kings of France to get possession of Flanders, and the other lands which we now call Belgium.

Everything in the way of wars is changed when we move

The Italian Wars 175

on from the fifteenth to the sixteenth century; and all the old local groups of conflict gradually grew into one single complex, in which Italy, France, Spain, Germany, the Netherlands, Hungary, and the Ottoman Empire are all involved simultaneously. Even England, so long cut off from continental campaigns, joins in, intermittently and rather ineffectively. While, at the other end of Europe, though the Sultan's main contest with Christendom is on the Danube and the Mediterranean, it is slightly affected by the expansion of the new Muscovite empire down the Volga and the Don, which impinged upon the Tartar vassals of the Porte, and once brought a Turkish army to Astrachan, where it perished from Russian frosts. About the only region of Europe in which the great wars of the first half of the sixteenth century do not fit into the general scheme of national history is Scandinavia—where the successful effort of Sweden to cut itself loose from the Union of Calmar has no clear connexion with the great struggles in the south, though Charles V once lent some mercenaries to his brother-in-law Christian of Denmark, and there were once or twice some ' Danish horse ' seen in the imperialist army in the Netherlands.

The Pan-European complications which set nine-tenths of the Continent ablaze started, of course, with the great Italian ventures of Charles VIII and Louis XII of France. These brought into the struggle not only all the powers of Italy, but Ferdinand of Aragon, interested for his kingdom of Sicily, the Emperor Maximilian, who was still suzerain in theory of Northern Italy, and not least the Swiss, who were at this moment not averse to laying hold on any convenient scraps of territory on their borders— whether Savoyard, Milanese, or German, which could be got by selling their spears to one combatant or another. It resulted that all the various forms of military efficiency which were prevalent in different regions of Western Europe were hurled into the general strife and had their temper tested, by being put into operation against hitherto untried enemies.

From France came the *gendarmerie* of the *Compagnies*

d'Ordonnance, reckoned the best heavy cavalry in Europe: from Italy the trained mercenaries of the condottiere bands, which had fought all the wars of the peninsula for the last two hundred years. The Swiss phalanx of pikemen had achieved startling successes in the recent wars with the great Duke of Burgundy. Their rivals were the German *landsknechts*, whom the Emperor had raised and trained in strict imitation of the Swiss methods. A new element in Italy were the 'genitours', the light horse of Spain, who had learned their tactics in the long wars with the Moors of Granada—with them came the Aragonese sword-and-buckler men, whose practice was equally new to Central Europe.

We may add that the problem of the use in the open field of fire-arms, small and great, was now about to become a prominent feature of war. They had been seen before, but never employed on such a scale as was to be tried in the great wars of Italy. The Spaniards, Swiss and Germans had already arquebusiers in their ranks, while the French and the Italians were still adhering to the use of the old-fashioned crossbow—and the English with (as a curious pair) the Turkish Janissaries were still armed with the very effective long-bow, which had often beaten the crossbow in the past.

There was a similarly wide divergence in the national use of the larger fire-arms. The French had, all through the earlier episodes of the great wars, a marked superiority in artillery, more especially field artillery to be used in battle. As much as fifty years back they had won the last two battles of their long struggle with the English—Formigny and Castillon—by these cannon. But they had also a predominance over their neighbours in the use of heavy siege-artillery—though not such a marked one. The Italians had cannon, but were not yet skilled in their use: Machiavelli (as every one remembers) speaks of these in his *Arte di Guerra* as unlikely to get off more than one or two salvos before a battle was joined in earnest, and as more fit to terrify than to settle the fate of a general engagement. The Germans had progressed farther in the theory

The Italian Wars 177

than the practice of the employment of artillery—there are good technical books on the subject, but German guns never seem to have decided a battle. Nor did the Swiss or the Spaniards shine in their use of field artillery. The latter had used siege artillery in their long Moorish wars, but do not seem to have been accustomed to manœuvre it in the open.

All these various national methods of warfare and of military equipment came into sudden conflict just as the fifteenth century was in its last years, starting from the great invasion of Italy by Charles VIII of France in 1494. The English long-bow and the shorter but very formidable bow of the Turkish Janissaries persisted well into the sixteenth century, though both were destined to be superseded by small fire-arms before our period had run out.

The opening of the strife was, in the first great pitched battle of the war—Fornovo—a test of the relative efficiency of the French heavy cavalry, the *Compagnies d'Ordonnance*, and the Italian heavy cavalry of condottiere bands belonging to Venice and Milan. Though somewhat outnumbered, the French achieved a complete but unfruitful victory—they rode down the Italians, who showed no staying power whatever. Both sides had some infantry, and some guns, but neither played any decisive part in the action. The guns on both sides were not moved about, and the Italian infantry only served to increase the number of casualties when its cavalry broke. An attempt to distract the French main blow by a division of Venetian light horse (*stradiots*) on the flanks had no effect—that they plundered the King's baggage-train was a negligible fact, when the main army was routed. The result of Fornovo seemed to be a reiteration of the fact that heavy cavalry was the all-important arm in battle.

But, as every one knows, this was to be almost the last great triumph of the *gendarmerie*. The French were very far from having conquered Italy—the only result of Fornovo was that Charles VIII secured himself an unmolested retreat into Piedmont. The next really important series of tactical actions are those connected with the name of the

'Great Captain'—Gonsalvo de Cordova—who taught his Spanish levies how to deal with an enemy possessed of an indubitably superior cavalry. After one initial check at Seminara (1495), which taught him his danger, for his light Spanish horse were scattered and his infantry ridden down, Gonsalvo set himself for a time to avoiding pitched battles, and adopting 'guerilla' tactics, the method of surprising detachments and cutting off convoys. But he also took to providing himself with pikemen to cover his crossbowmen and arquebusiers: the latter he multiplied as fast as he could manage, abandoning the old weapon in favour of the small fire-arms. He also adopted the system of 'digging himself in' whenever possible, i.e. of rapid field fortification, and resolved always to receive attacks in position, rather than to wage offensive battles. His first great triumph, the isolating and starving out of Montpensier's army at Atella (July 1496) was achieved without any general action, by a combination of partial attacks and careful entrenching. His second, the battle of Cerignola (August 1503) was a case of inducing a superior enemy to charge in upon a prepared position. The Duke of Nemours had taken the offensive, with the usual combination of heavy cavalry and masses of Swiss pikemen, hoping to run down the Spaniards by one determined charge. Gonsalvo had drawn up his army on the lower slopes of a vine-clad hill, had dug a ditch along his whole front, and made a bank behind it with the excavated earth. His light cavalry were thrown out far on the flanks, to worry and delay the deployment of the French, when they came upon the field. Nemours, arriving late in the afternoon, attacked headlong and without any reconnoitring of the Spanish position, sending his *gendarmerie* against the left of Gonsalvo's line, while his infantry, Swiss pikes and Gascon crossbowmen, made for the centre. He had no knowledge of the ditch in front of him, and his leading squadrons were precipitated into it; the rest had to halt, and while Nemours was riding along the front, looking in vain for a gap, he was shot by a long-range arquebus bullet. Though his guidance was now gone, his infantry on reaching the field charged the centre of the Spanish position, but entirely failed to break in. While endeavouring to cross the ditch, which completely broke their order, they were shot down in hundreds by the thick line of arquebusiers ranged on the bank above it. When it was clear that the attack was beaten off all along the front, Gonsalvo ordered his whole force to advance, putting in his cavalry—which was much inferior in numbers to the French—on one flank. The enemy having no leader, since Nemours had fallen, gave way in all directions. Most of the *gendarmerie* got off, but the beaten infantry, retreating in great disorder, were much cut up by the Spanish horse, and the whole train of artillery was captured—it had never been in action, as Nemours had scorned to wait for a preliminary bombardment.

The celebrated Italian condottiere Fabrizio Colonna, who had been with Gonsalvo's cavalry reserve that day, made the very true but sarcastic remark that it was neither the courage of the troops nor the steadfastness of the general that settled the day, but a ditch and a parapet of earth and the arquebus. But surely Gonsalvo deserves all the credit for discerning that the charge of the French horse and the impetus of the Swiss pike-column could be brought to a stand by the combination of field-entrenchment and lavish small-arm fire. Of course the enemy had been most obliging—as French feudal generals generally were. But, as we shall presently see, one French prince discovered the way of dealing with Spanish tactics—though only nine years after, on the bloody field of Ravenna.

Gonsalvo's 'crowning mercy', to use a Cromwellian phrase, was the battle of the Garigliano (29 December 1503), in which he completely destroyed the French army of Italy, both the wrecks which had escaped from Cerignola, and the heavy reinforcements which Louis XII had sent down to join them. Gonsalvo had taken position along the line of the Garigliano, then swollen by winter rains and reaching the sea by the famous marshes of Minturnae, where Marius of old took refuge in the mud. The French made several fruitless efforts to force the line of the flooded stream, but were foiled: they then went into winter quarters, seeking shelter from the inclement weather in the towns behind the river, and scattering their forces over many miles, mostly far back from the Garigliano. The Spaniard, having waited for them to settle down and disperse, made a sudden and unexpected passage of the river by a concealed bridge far up-stream, and plunged into the middle of the enemy's cantonments. The French were never able to concentrate, were beaten in detail in a number of rear-guard skirmishes, and were finally chased into the sea-girt town of Gaeta, losing all their guns and thousands of prisoners. A few days later their commander, the Marquis of Saluzzo, capitulated, on much the same terms that Junot got from Sir Hew Dalrymple at the Convention of Cintra in 1808—leave to depart by sea on evacuating Gaeta and the other forts which he was holding, with all their armament and stores. Gonsalvo had driven them completely out of the much-coveted kingdom of Naples: but this was not by any means the last of their campaigns in that region. The Garigliano was not a battle settled by superior equipment or tactical details, but a fine example of the 'victory by surprise', when the better general struck at such an unexpected point, and so rapidly that the enemy was never able to collect for a general action.

The next battle in which the Spaniards and French were the chief combatants registered a very different result—the triumph of artillery over an army which had got into a strong but cramped position, and refused to leave it for a fight in the open. Ramon de Cardona, the successor of Gonsalvo as Viceroy of Naples for Ferdinand of Aragon, was endeavouring to relieve Ravenna, then closely besieged by a French army under Gaston de Foix. Trying the scheme of action which Gonsalvo had practised at Atella in 1495, he did not attack the enemy's camp, but placed himself in a position across the French line of communications, 'dug himself in', with a river covering one flank and a marsh the other, and asked to be attacked. The French must drive him off, or be starved out in their siege

The Italian Wars 181

lines. But he himself had no good line of retreat, having the Reno river behind him.

This very rational design failed disastrously, because Cardona had failed to realize that a passive defence in a confined space could not be kept against a very superior artillery. Gaston de Foix drew his army out of the lines around Ravenna, and deployed in front of Cardona's trenches. He then proceeded to develop an intense and prolonged bombardment of the position, parts of which could be enfiladed by guns placed on the extreme southern flank of his army. The bombardment did not greatly incommode the Spanish infantry in the front line, who were well sheltered in their earthworks, but wrought terrible damage in the reserves and the cavalry, who were drawn up in the narrow ground between the trenches and the river in their rear. The position was not deep enough to allow them to be drawn back out of gunshot, and they had no cover. After standing this devastating fire for some time —Fabrizio Colonna mentions that he saw one cannon-ball kill or maim twenty-five of his men-at-arms—the Spanish commanders resolved that it would be better to charge out, and take the desperate risk of attacking superior numbers, instead of standing still to be shot down in detail. They broke out at both ends of the line, and charged the French horse, with the inevitable result that they were beaten after a severe struggle—most of the leading officers were killed or taken prisoners.

When the attack of the Spanish cavalry was obviously a failure, Gaston de Foix ordered his infantry to assail the whole of the entrenched front of Cardona's position. The attack, made in four columns mainly by German auxiliary pikemen—but there were also French crossbowmen—was a costly failure. The arquebus fire of the Spaniards held back the assault on most points—at a few the assailants got inside the lines but were ejected. This success, however, was fatal to the Spaniards, for while they were engaged in holding back the French frontal attack, Gaston's cavalry got in behind them on both flanks, in pursuit of the routed Spanish horse, and charged down the back of the lines, sweeping away reserves, and taking the men in the trenches in the rear.

By far the greater part of the Spanish infantry perished—it is on record that eleven of the twelve colonels present were killed. A few companies held together in desperation and pushed their way out of the fight through the midst of the French, though surrounded on all sides. One of these isolated bodies caught the eye of Gaston de Foix, who rashly charged it at the head of his staff alone—he was killed, as were almost all those who followed him, and the company got away in safety.

The death of this capable, if headstrong, young leader, seems to have paralysed the French directing power—they took and sacked Ravenna, but then retired from a devastated county on to Ferrara. The enemy took several months to collect even the shadow of an army: but the campaign had been absolutely resultless, save for the tactical conclusion, patent to both sides, that trenches were insufficient shelter against an overpowering artillery, though most effective against infantry and cavalry not so supported. The Spaniards by no means gave up their belief in fieldworks used in proper fashion. But it was ten years before they had the opportunity to prove at Bicocca (1522) that their confidence was not misplaced.

Meanwhile another set of lessons in the military art were being taught to the French and the Swiss. Only a year after Ravenna the Swiss won their last victory, fought on the old principle of the charge of heavy columns of pikemen, against an enemy surprised and not fully arrayed to receive an attack, for want of effective scouting. The French under La Tremouille were besieging the Duke of Milan in Novara, when news arrived that a Swiss army of relief was approaching, and that its vanguard was not far off. La Tremouille was prepared to fight, and had chosen his position on a hillside two miles east of Novara. He reached it in the evening, and encamped in no great order along the ground which he intended to hold on the following day. But the Swiss completely surprised him: instead of resting in Novara, they marched through it and

The Italian Wars

attacked before dawn, charging up against the French position in their usual three columns of pikes in echelon.

La Tremouille was taken completely unawares—the first warning of what was coming was a rush of Swiss skirmishers against his picket-line, just in front of the house where he was sleeping. He had only just time to scramble out of the back door, and the trumpets were sounding and the horsemen getting together, while the fate of the day—or rather the dawn—was being settled elsewhere. The Swiss main column had dashed into the camp of the French infantry—at the foot of the hill, who were only just getting into order when the clash came. Their guns fired one salvo into the front of the column, and were then overrun and captured : the infantry—mainly German mercenaries—still in some disorder, were overwhelmed. The cavalry, assembled too late to save the unfortunate foot, retired down the Milan road, and made a disorderly retreat to Vercelli. This was a case of the beating of a force of all arms by an inferior number of the enemy, who had no cavalry but 200 of the Duke of Milan's followers and only eight small guns. And neither this handful of horse nor the guns came into the main action. Surprise did everything—an impudent *tour de force* against a careless and improvident foe. With ordinary precautions, La Tremouille would not have been caught without any observing patrols to watch the road from Novara, nor with an army encamped haphazard instead of in its destined fighting position.

This was the last Swiss victory. Their next clash with the French showed that, when properly tackled, the pike-columns could not cope with artillery and cavalry duly supporting the infantry arm. On 15 September 1515 Francis I, newly crowned and ambitious, had resolved to renew once more the claim on the duchy of Milan which his predecessor had urged. Crossing the Alps not by any of the passes where he was expected but by the lofty Col d'Argentiere, he presented himself in front of Milan while the forces of his enemies were scattered—the Spaniards and the troops of the Pope were still some way off. There were opposite him only the Swiss mercenaries of Duke Maximilian Sforza and a few hundreds of the Duke's Lombard horse. The Swiss were at first thinking of selling their employer, and retiring to their mountains on the receipt of a large sum of French gold. Some of them had, indeed, marched off already, but the majority were taunted into fighting by the Bishop of Sion, the Pope's representative, and sallied out of Milan in their usual three pike-masses, accompanied by Sforza's few hundreds of men-at-arms. There was no question of a surprise, such as had been seen at Novara, for the French light cavalry had been watching the gates of the city only four miles off, and fell back in good order, sending accurate information of the situation to King Francis, and the battle was joined only in the afternoon in front of the French position at Marignano (13 September 1515).

Its course was settled by the fact that none of the Swiss columns succeeded in making the complete breach in any part of the French line which was essential to their victory. Their right-hand mass made some impression on the French left, and captured some guns, but did not get through. The main central column was completely checked by a form of tactics which confers some considerable credit on King Francis. It was making straight for his line of guns in the centre of his array : he caused it to be charged in flank again and again by squadrons of his *gendarmerie* ; each charge forced the column to halt, lower its pikes, and make a front of its flank, so that it could no longer advance. Meanwhile the French artillery continued to make easy shots into the thick of the phalanx, causing dreadful slaughter. All the cavalry charges were beaten off—the King says that twenty-five of them were made—but meanwhile the Swiss could not advance, or could only move a little between one assault and another. After four hours' fighting, during which the Swiss never reached the line of the French guns, both sides drew off somewhat, for night had fallen, and nothing had been settled.

When day broke the French were found to have reformed a close and orderly line of battle. The undaunted Swiss, however, came on once more : ' if they had charged fiercely overnight they charged more fiercely in the morning '. The main column suffered again terribly from the French artillery fire, but actually succeeded in closing with the King's German mercenary infantry. It was then charged in flank by the main body of the French cavalry, and brought to a stand. A qualified success on the part of one of the flank columns had no decisive result, whereupon, most unwillingly, they gave up the game, and retired in a deliberate and sullen fashion, carrying off their wounded and their few guns. Only their rear-guard was cut up in a village where it got blocked : they then marched home, leaving the Duke of Milan to capitulate a few days later.

The losses on both sides had been very heavy—probably about 5,000 or 6,000 a side, for while the Swiss had been racked by artillery, the French horse had lost many riders in their self-sacrificing charges, and their infantry had been trampled down on some points of the field. But what ought to have been conclusive proof was given that the pike-column, unsupported by an adequate provision of cavalry and guns, could not hope to beat a properly managed force of all arms. Yet one more lesson was required to show the obstinate mountaineers that the day of their system was over.

This lesson was given seven years later at Bicocca (1522), when the Swiss were no longer the enemies but the auxiliaries of the King of France. It was to prove that the steam-roller tactics of the Swiss could be beaten by the Spanish combination of sound entrenchment with concentrated fire of small arms, on ground where cavalry could not act, nor artillery be brought up close to the defensive position.

On this occasion an Imperialist army, mainly Spanish but with strong contingents of German *landsknechts* under the Italian condottiere Prosper Colonna, had taken up its ground to cover the road from the north to Milan, along which a composite army under the Marshal Lautrec, consisting of French horse, Venetian horse and foot, and Swiss pikemen, was advancing. Colonna, a master of defensive tactics, had selected as his position the walled Park of Bicocca, where a large manor-house was surrounded by ornamental gardens and a ditch, with meadows scarred by irrigation-cuts in its front, and a small running stream on its right flank, crossed by a single narrow bridge. Colonna made a formidable entrenchment out of a hollow road which ran along the north side of the park wall, by throwing up earth along the inside of the wall, so as to make a parapet, which broadened out in several places into a platform on which guns were placed. Along the rampart he arranged his Spanish arquebusiers, four deep, with German pikemen in support. The position having ample depth—unlike the one which had proved fatal to Cardona at Ravenna—the Spanish horse were placed far back, almost quite out of cannon-range from the front line.

Lautrec did not like the look of the entrenchments, and was for leaving them alone, and seeking some other line of approach to Milan, but his hand was forced by the Swiss captains. The pay of the mercenaries was much overdue, and they informed the general that they should march home, unless he consented to attack at once, and to abandon the idea of tedious manœuvring to the flank. Most unwillingly Lautrec committed himself to the venture, the Swiss undertaking to lead the van and deliver the central assault. They were to be accompanied by guns to batter the Spanish rampart; but when the pieces stuck in the marshy meadows in front of the enemy's line, and could not get forward at any pace, the Swiss captains refused to wait for the preliminary bombardment, and hurled their columns straight at the sunken ditch and the park wall. Lautrec sent a detachment of French cavalry to coast along the running water on the east side of the Spanish, and to endeavour to cross at its bridge. The rest of the army drew up in a second and third line behind the Swiss.

The assault of the pikemen, though delivered with desperate courage, was a complete failure. They advanced over the soggy meadows under destructive fire, reached the ditch and found it much deeper than they had calculated, but rank after rank jumped down and tried to scale the wall and parapet on the other side. Few reached the top, for the concentrated fire of four ranks of arquebusiers blew the head of the columns to pieces, and only a few desperate men from the rear ranks, mounting over heaps of the dead, ever reached the top of the parapet. The survivors finally turned back and retreated in a slow and sullen fashion—as at Marignano—to the ground from which they had started. They left 3,000 dead, including all their captains, in the fatal ditch. Meanwhile the French cavalry diversion against the bridge on the enemy's right rear came to nothing —some of the horsemen actually got into the Spanish camp, but were driven out again.

When the Swiss had been crushed, Prosper Colonna refused to pursue, saying that the French had still two intact lines of battle, but would now be cured of all idea of persisting, and would retreat—as indeed they did. The surviving Swiss deserted Lautrec and went home, the Venetians went off to defend their own lands, and the French retired to Cremona, and sent for help from Paris. This was the last experiment of the Swiss for carrying out their 'steam-roller' tactics—which were for the future thoroughly discredited. But though the pike could no longer be expected to work alone, there remained a use for it as a protection for the arquebus—the latter could only be trusted as a purely defensive weapon in an entrenched position inaccessible to cavalry. In the open field it might be helpless against rapidly moving cavalry, and would require the support of the long weapon, which could keep off horses.

The last of the series of great battles in the open, which illustrated the development of the military art in the Italian wars, was Pavia (24 February 1525). King Francis, invading Italy once more, had captured Milan. He then sent off about a third of his army, under the Duke of Albany, to overrun Naples, on which he still nourished pretensions. This was a most unwise detachment, for Lombardy was not yet fully conquered, and a strong Spanish garrison lay in the well-fortified town of Pavia. Francis sat down before this place, blockading it on both banks of the Ticino (28

October 1524). He attempted to breach its western front with his siege-train, but failing in this project fell back on the slow but sure method of starvation. For more than three months he lay before the place, which he surrounded with a line of circumvallation. This delay gave the Imperialists time to collect an army of relief, under Francis's rebel subject the Constable Bourbon, and Lannoy the Viceroy of Naples. The French king would probably have done well to drop the siege and to march out to drive away this 'army of succour', but instead clung to his siege-lines and allowed the enemy to encamp opposite him on the farther bank of the Vernacula stream, which covered his flank. He threw up along this watercourse a long entrenchment guarded with artillery as far as the Park of Mirabello, and defied the Imperialists to cross it. For three weeks they dared not attack him, but on the night of 23 February, hearing that his army was diminishing by desertion, and seeing that it was drawn out along the very long lines of circumvallation, they resolved to try a surprise attack. They crossed the Vernacula far up-stream, by a night march, and broke down the walls of the Park of Mirabello, at a point beyond the extreme French flank. At dawn on the 24th they came down unexpectedly into the rear of the King's lines of circumvallation, and caught him with his army strung out along many miles of blockading posts.

The surprise was complete, and Francis had to hurry up his troops from distant fronts to hold back a concentrated enemy. He himself with the larger part of his *gendarmerie* happened to be quartered in the section of his lines which was nearest to the approaching enemy, and charged straight at their rearward and left-centre, hoping to gain time for his infantry to come up and form behind him. He broke up one brigade of the Imperialist cavalry, and threw some of their columns into confusion, but three-quarters of the hostile line was intact, and three successive attacks made on it by Francis's infantry failed completely—his Swiss contingent, which arrived first, did not come up to its ancient reputation, and retreated *en masse* after a short engagement. His German mercenary *landsknechts*, who

The Italian Wars 189

arrived later, made a desperate plunge into the middle of the Imperialist infantry and were almost exterminated. Meanwhile the King was charging right and left with his *gendarmerie*, losing men every moment by the fire of the Spanish arquebusiers, who sheltered themselves in the copses and hedges of the park. The final disaster came when the native French infantry, who had been quartered in one of the remoter fronts of the circumvallation, came up in their turn, and were overwhelmed by the same corps which had already disposed of the German mercenaries. The King and the wrecks of his chivalry were left on the field alone, and were finally surrounded and crushed; Francis himself was slightly wounded, and had to surrender to a Burgundian knight, a follower of the Constable Bourbon.

Several corps of the French army never got into the main engagement: those south of the river and in the west end of the lines of circumvallation failed to join up with the main body, and left the field after some feeble skirmishing. This detachment left the field, picked up the garrison of Milan and retired to France: its commander, the Duke of Alençon, incurred much contempt—and is said to have died of a broken heart. The slaughter among the French noblesse had been terrible—only paralleled by that at Agincourt a hundred and ten years before.

From the point of view of tactics Pavia was an interesting battle. Mainly, of course, it was a victory won by surprise, for the French army never got into line, and fought irregularly, as each corps came up in succession. But one deduction made by all contemporary critics was that it raised the reputation of fire-arms—not that cannon had counted for much, but that arquebus fire is said to have been most decisive, not only in riddling the flanks of the French infantry columns when they charged, but in thinning and disabling the squadrons of the *gendarmerie*, when they got split up after their first charges. Sheltered in hedges and copses, the arquebusiers eluded the horsemen, and no corresponding force of French light infantry seems to have been sent against them. Indeed, the French had few arquebusiers, and the crossbow was ineffective.

Pavia might have ended the war if the Emperor Charles had been content to impose less onerous terms of peace upon the captured King. It was the project for dismembering France, imposed by the treaty of 1526, which goaded Francis into breaking his oath, and renewing the struggle in desperation as soon as he was released from his captivity.

General engagements became very unusual after Pavia, the will to fight for the pleasure of victory, which was predominant in the preceding years, especially among French generals, seems to have been dying out, and the risk of throwing away an army by misplaced pugnacity seems to have been felt in a way that was unknown at the beginning of the wars. If success could be achieved by manœuvre, by cutting the enemy's line of communication, or starving him out in the face of impregnable lines, or distracting him by a sudden transference of troops to an unguarded front, success was no longer considered less creditable than if it had been won in a pitched battle.

In the later campaigns when armies of first-rate strength lay opposite one another, so that a general action would have seemed inevitable to the men of the previous generation, we often find both parties drawing off, because each was loth to try the final arbitrament of war. This happened in 1553-54 when Charles and Henry II lay opposite each other for weeks in Picardy, yet parted without any decisive clash. Before one of the few pitched battles of the later wars, a French general, d'Enghien, actually sent for leave to the King at Paris before risking a general action (Cerissoles, 1544), a thing which would have been incredible twenty years before. There were three or four chances of a first-rate battle which both sides deliberately shirked, e.g. during the invasion of Provence by the Emperor in 1536, and the deadlock in Champagne before the peace of Crépy in 1544.

Cautious generals refused to put the matter to a test. Sometimes the reason for removal was starvation—an undisciplined army had eaten up the whole country-side, and could live on it no longer. Sometimes, and this is more surprising, the reason for a retreat was financial rather than strategical. When pay was many months in arrear the mercenaries, who formed the greater part of all armies, deserted the colours without scruple—and that not individually but *en masse*, marching off with their colours. This was a particularly trying habit of the Swiss, who were so much used by the French kings, from their rather unjustifiable distrust of native French infantry. But the *landsknechts* and the Italian and other bands were almost as tiresome to their employers on both sides. As far as we can make out, there must have been thousands of mercenaries who served indifferently on either side. National feeling was very low, and the armies were singularly leaky. Inspired neither by loyalty to a sovereign nor devotion to a cause (such as was to be found later in the Huguenot and Dutch wars), the mercenaries were held together at best by *esprit de corps*. They followed their captain when he changed his employer—the ' Black Bands ' of the celebrated Giovanni de Medici shifted over several times ; and the Emperor's rebels, the Duke of Bouillon and the Duke of Guelders, seem never to have found difficulty in raising German companies against their lord and master. It was hazardous to seek battle with an army whose morale was low, from arrears of pay or prolonged short commons. This was certainly a main cause of much tedious manœuvring, when a decision might have been found. A general who met with no disaster was almost as esteemed as a general who won battles—the capable Italian condottiere Prosper Colonna was given by his admiring Italian friends the nickname of ' Fabius Cunctator ', a classical reminiscence from the old Roman general who foiled Hannibal, year after year, by refusing to fight him.

The untrustworthiness of mercenary armies was, of course, one of the main causes for the gradual establishment of standing national corps all round Europe, except indeed in England, which (as we all know) had no standing army till the ' new model ' of 1645. France started in the fifteenth century with the ' Compagnies d'Ordonnance ' or *gendarmerie*, but this was purely a select cavalry corps of modest numbers. Not only the men-at-arms were gentlemen in full armour, but also their squires, or *archers* as they were rather inappropriately called. For many years men of good birth were quite content to start as ' archers ' in a company, as did the celebrated Montluc and others. But this very select cavalry of high spirit and efficiency could not compose an army. Louis XI tried to extemporize a militia-infantry called the franc-archers, liable to be called out on due occasion but not permanently embodied. This expedient failed, and after the battle of Guinegate (1479), when their weakness lost the day, King Louis turned to the expedient of hiring Swiss pikemen as the core of his infantry. He kept as many as 6,000 of them, and the system of regarding these foreign mercenaries as the base of the army continued right through our period—and as a survival (after a real army had been established) went on down to the French Revolution.

In addition to the Swiss the French kings relied in the early wars of the sixteenth century on other bands raised for the occasion only, both native French ('*aventuriers*') and German *landsknechts*, of whom the rebel princes of Germany (Guelders and Bouillon) could always collect a horde. The French native infantry were mostly crossbowmen—Gascons and Picards—the smaller fire-arms having been introduced very late in France—not on any scale, indeed, till after the battle of Pavia.

The first attempt to raise an organized force of native infantry was made by Francis I as late as 1533, when he created the so-called ' legions '—quite large corps on the analogy of the classical Roman legion, as many as 6,000 apiece. There were four legions, Picardy, Champagne, Normandy and Languedoc, composed of a mixture of pikemen and arquebusiers—whose number Francis was set on increasing. These ' legions ' went on as a permanency, and were the origin of the French standing army of foot-soldiery. ' Languedoc ' disappeared in 1562, when its commander and most of his men deserted to the Huguenots during the Wars of Religion. Normandy was disbanded in 1593, but Picardy and Champagne went on into the seventeenth century, and with diminished numbers became

The Italian Wars 193

'regiments' in the modern style, with perhaps 1,500 pikes and muskets.

The non-legionary French infantry—*aventuriers*—was a shifting mass; the King authorized captains to raise bands, took them into his pay for as long as the war went on— or more often till his finances failed—and then disbanded them. They were of very varying value—an old 'band' which had served several years under a popular and capable captain would be very effective—a new corps almost worthless for many months, and doomed to prompt leakage and desertion if the captain was a failure. All French commanders preferred Swiss or Germans—in spite of the obvious faults of these mercenaries. They even seem to have valued these aliens more than the 'legionaries'— whose behaviour was sometimes not all that could have been desired.

Quite early in the wars the French kings discovered that their *gendarmerie*, though excellent battle troops, were too heavy for some of the duties of cavalry, exploration, outpost work, and raids. To supply themselves with light cavalry they copied the Venetians in raising 'stradiots', unarmoured horse trained in the Turkish fashion for skirmishing and rapid movement. There was a considerable force of these foreigners in the French army that fought at the 'Battle of the Spurs' in 1513. Afterwards they were not so alien, and became '*chevaux légers*', taking also to the use of the pistol or short arquebus which could be fired on horseback. By the end of the wars the *chevaux légers* outnumbered the gendarmes, and were sometimes used in battle, though they could never be trusted against mailed men-at-arms, who rode them down.

Through the early period of the wars the French were as superior to their enemies in artillery as they were inferior in infantry with fire-arms. It was noted that they were the first to employ field guns drawn by horses, and capable of being moved about during a battle. Their gunners were noted for their rapidity in reloading, and their good direction of fire. Still the cases of battles won by artillery fire (e.g. Ravenna, and Marignano) were few compared with those in which the matter was settled by the cavalry or infantry. As a rule, Machiavelli's axiom that guns would only put in a few salvoes before the general battle was joined, remained true down to the end of the great wars.

The Spanish standing army which appears in the great wars of Italy by the year 1500 had nothing to do with the old feudal organization of Castile for wars in the limits of the Iberian peninsula. That had been a system for home defence—wars against the Moor or the Portuguese. But when Ferdinand and Isabella took in hand the conquest and retention of the kingdom of Naples, the end made necessary the creation of an overseas force, committed to garrisoning a conquered kingdom: for Naples under Spanish rule could never have furnished troops for its own defence—the larger half of the local nobles belonged to the old Angevin faction, and habitually joined the French whenever Charles VIII or Louis XII sent down an expedition into the South. Houses like the San Severinos and the Caraffas were persistently pro-French. Hence the expeditionary force under Gonsalvo de Cordova which Ferdinand sent to Calabria in 1495, and which the 'Great Captain' organized into a permanent force, had to be kept going even in the long intervals where French attacks had failed. Gonsalvo's original army consisted mainly of 'light horse' and miscellaneous infantry of no great repute, in which crossbowmen were mixed with arquebusiers and Aragonese 'sword and buckler men'. His first experiences showed him that he could not face the French *gendarmerie* in the open field—the consequence was that he took up a system of avoiding pitched battles and trusting to a combination of guerilla warfare, for which his light cavalry was well suited, and of entrenchment. The latter was the more important, and led to the reorganization of the infantry, who had to hold entrenchments, into corps of which arquebusiers were the more important part: the crossbow dropped out. To support the arquebusiers there were pikemen, and for some years the 'sword and buckler' infantry for close fights, who finally dropped out and were entirely replaced by pikes. The last battle in which we hear of the 'sword and buckler' infantry is Ravenna (1512), when its doings provoked the admiration of Machiavelli—who liked this reversion to ancient Roman armament. But nevertheless the pike ultimately superseded the sword entirely. It would seem to be as early as 1505 that King Ferdinand conceived the idea of concentrating bands of arquebusiers, pikemen, and buckler men into bodies of some size, containing troops with all the three sorts of weapons, which were called 'colonelcies'—the word colonel is found as early as 1508. That they must have been of moderate size, perhaps 1,000 strong, is shown by the fact that twelve colonels were present at Ravenna—of whom no less than eleven were killed that day, while the total Spanish native infantry cannot have numbered more than 10,000 men on that field.

The old infantry of Gonsalvo de Cordova was practically destroyed at Ravenna, but the new Spanish army of Italy was apparently reformed on the old lines, with the exception that the 'sword and buckler men' are no longer heard of, and that the arquebusiers are strengthened in numbers, and are evidently considered the most important arm—as would be the case naturally in an army whose fundamental tactic was entrenchment protected by concentrated fire of small arms. Bicocca (1522) was a complete testimonial to the efficiency of trench and arquebus on the defensive : while at Pavia (1525), where the fighting was in broken and wooded ground, the Spanish fire-arms are credited with the best part of the victory.

The first complete table of organization for the Spanish army of Italy which has survived is one of 1534, which gives it divided into much larger units than the colonelcies of Ravenna—these are called 'tercios', and were a little over 3,000 strong. The name tercio or 'third' seems to mean that they were each strong enough to make one of the three 'thirds' of van, main battle, and rearward, in which an army habitually drew up. There were twelve companies in the 'tercios', six of pikes, six of arquebusiers : it is notable that the men with the fire-arms had slightly better pay if they were passed as competent shots—getting an 'extra testoon' for efficiency. Perhaps the most characteristic point in this Spanish regimental organization is that the tercio had thirteen chaplains to only three surgeons —spiritual rather than bodily ailments being apparently more important.

The tercios were named from the Italian provinces where they had their depôts—Naples, Sicily, Lombardy. Under Philip II more were added—Portugal, Armada (the navy, marines), Brabant, and many more—but the individual numbers in each were somewhat cut down.

The Spanish horse was never the important arm—in particular the heavy cavalry were always beaten by the French gendarmes: the light cavalry was held much more effective for raids, and long-distance marches. When Charles V took the field in force he seems mainly to have relied on his Burgundian (i.e. Netherlandish) and German heavy cavalry. In 1536 he had 2,000 German heavy horse to 580 Spanish in pay. According to sixteenth-century ideas the Spaniards were always deficient in the mounted arm. In 1536 Charles had 5,300 horse of all nations to 67,000 foot. At the battle of Cerissoles (1544), the last pitched battle in Italy, the Spanish commander Del Guasto had only 1,000 cavalry to 18,000 infantry.

Unlike the French, whose special forte was heavy cavalry and field artillery, and the Spaniards, whose strong points were infantry with fire-arms and scientific entrenchment, both the Swiss and the German specialized on the pike-column, the 'steam roller tactics' which had proved so successful against the armies of Charles the Rash at Granson, Morat, and Nancy. As we have already seen, these tactics, under the changed military conditions of the fifteenth century, were only successful for the future when the element of surprise was used in combination with the heavy thrust of the pikes. Novara was the last victory of the Swiss, and here surprise had been happily used against an army caught encamped, and not in battle-array. The decisive failure against guns and cavalry combined was at Marignano (1515), and against entrenched infantry at Bicocca (1522). After this the spell of the invincible pike-column was broken, and the pike was only retained as a necessary supporting force for the arquebusier—who would be helpless if caught in the open without some solid protection, behind which he could take refuge.

There were only three general actions of importance during the long years of war between 1525 and 1559— Cerissoles (1544) was the last instance of a pitched battle in which each side came into the field with intent to arrive at a decision. The French hoped to win by superior cavalry strength, the Spaniards by a preponderance in veteran infantry well furnished with fire-arms. The day went in favour of d'Enghien the French general, entirely by reason of the disgraceful failure of the Spanish and Italian horse to contain even a portion of the French *gendarmerie*. When they had fled from the field, the Spaniards, though at first victorious on one wing, suffered a complete disaster, because infantry attacked by other infantry and by cavalry simultaneously, is almost bound to lose in the end. The infantry of the French centre and right immobilized the corresponding Imperialist infantry, while d'Enghien's victorious cavalry (though it suffered severely) settled the day by its charges against tired troops.

The other two battles of the end of the war were both what we may call 'victories by surprise', not victories in which the armament of one side or the other was the decisive element. At St. Quentin (1557) the Constable Montmorency was manœuvring with the object of succouring a besieged town, believing his flank to be covered by the river Somme, which had been reported to him as impassable. But while his infantry and cavalry were divided by a gap of some miles, his adversary Philibert of Savoy crossed the Somme with his whole cavalry force, on fords which had been reported almost impracticable, and left hardly watched and practically unguarded. He routed the French horse before it could get into array, and then cut up the foot which was in retreat a long way ahead of the routed horse. At Gravelines (1558) the Marshal des Thermes, raiding along the Flemish coast, kept such bad watch that the Count of Egmont marched round his inland flank unseen, and threw himself across the Marshal's road to his base at Calais. Des Thermes, caught on a march of retreat, had to form up anyhow, on sandhills, one flank to the sea, and to fight with his face toward his goal of safety. Committed to a defensive action in this uncomfortable position, he was completely surprised by the appearance in-shore of an English fleet, which opened fire on the seaward flank of his army and threw it into hopeless disorder, whereupon Egmont ordered a general charge and won an easy victory.

(b) The Wars of Religion

Though the contest between Philip II and his rebellious subjects in the Netherlands and the contest between the Catholic and the Huguenot parties in France spread over much the same series of years, and though they are generally described in common as the 'Wars of Religion', their character from the military as well as the political point of view is essentially different.

The struggle in the Low Countries was between an autocratic monarch and a great body of his subjects, which originally took a constitutional aspect, and only assumed a purely religious aspect when the King's discontented subjects in the South, who were mainly Catholics, found that they could not co-operate with their Calvinist fellow-rebels in the North, owing to a fundamental difference in creed. Holland became a Protestant Republic : Belgium —in which the large Protestant minority had been exiled or exterminated—remained in the hands of the Spanish King.

In France the struggle was not between an autocratic monarchy and subjects claiming constitutional rights. The Crown wished for peace at almost any cost, and had to face two rival factions, of which the Catholic party was almost as hateful to the opportunists of the House of Valois as the Huguenot party. Catherine de Medici and her sons patched up truce after truce and peace after peace, not because they liked the Huguenots or toleration for its own sake, but because they hated the Guises and the League. Their policy wavered in the most puzzling fashion according to the inspiration of the moment—hence such apparently contradictory freaks of violence as the massacre of St. Bartholomew on one side, and the murder of the Guise brothers at Blois on the other. Both were desperate attempts to preserve the power of the Crown, and both were as ineffectual as they were immoral. Peace only came when the nation, sick of civil war, concurred in recognizing a king who became officially a Catholic, but was able and ready to grant complete religious freedom to the Huguenot party in which he had been reared, and with which his sympathies lay.

The war in the Netherlands was continuous, the war in France can be broken up into eight separate 'periods of troubles', with uneasy pacifications brought about by the Crown dividing them. The struggle between the Catholic and the Huguenot parties was spasmodic and illogical, hopelessly unscientific from the military point of view. It was a war of raids, skirmishes, and occasional battles, though it also showed some fine specimens of sixteenth-century siege-work.

The Dutch War of Independence, on the other hand, was essentially one of sieges. The armies of the rebels could never face in the field the old Spanish disciplined infantry, tried in the wars of Italy. They were composed partly of local levies, partly of mercenaries hired from Germany, both *reiters* and *landsknechts*. The Netherlanders failed in discipline, the aliens in loyalty. The best energies of the Dutch were turned to the sea, where from the first they maintained an unbroken superiority over the Spaniards, but on land their levies were nearly always beaten. The German hirelings, on the other hand, had no enthusiasm for the cause which they were hired to support. They habitually mutinied when pay ran short, and melted away when it ceased to be forthcoming even in driblets. William of Orange once saw an army that had originally mustered over 20,000 men dwindle down to 1,800, kept together by his personal influence, after money had ceased to be forthcoming (1568). With the exception of the single casual victory on a small scale at Heiligerlee (1562), we find nothing but a roll of defeats for the insurgents—Jemingen, Gemblours, Mookerheyde, and many a smaller disaster. On the other hand, the Dutch were at their best in obstinate defence of fortified towns, held not so much by regular companies of soldiery but by burgher levies fighting for their hearths and their families. The habitual atrocities which attended a successful storm by a Spanish army, or even a surrender on terms to a Spanish general, inevitably led to very desperate defences, even beyond the limits of reasonable endurance—as e.g. during the eleven months leaguer of Leyden in 1573-74. Now the Low Countries were more thickly strewn with fortified towns than most districts of Europe : even small places had their walls, though they might not be up to the level of Renaissance engineering. But during the long war military architecture developed rapidly, and the simple enceinte-walls of the Middle Ages were strengthened with all sorts of horn-works, demi-lunes, ravelins and redans, till a siege-plan of 1580 or 1600 shows a most complicated system of defence—Ostend with its outworks held out for four long years, and the garrison finally capitulated on decent terms merely from exhaustion.

But the main strength of the Netherland fortresses of the North—those in the Walloon lands were not so blessed—lay in their water-defences. Bergen-op-Zoom and Flushing were proverbially difficult to tackle, because their ditches were fed by tidal sea-water, which no besieger could drain away or fill up. But dozens of less formidable places had great part of their fronts screened by marshes, river-channels, or canals, and could only be approached on narrow fronts, where (of course) fortification was made elaborate. Such was the case at Ypres, Ghent, Antwerp, Maestricht, Haarlem, Leyden, Dordrecht, Zutphen, Sluys, Groningen, and countless other places. When the besieger was forced to attack on a limited front, at the only accessible points, the besieged heaped line after line of defence on the menaced section, often building new works during the progress of a siege. In a country of water-defences the military engineer ended by beating the artillerist. Hence the enormous length of late sixteenth-century sieges, and the result that when a town did fall it was more frequently from the exhaustion of the garrison, starvation, and occasional surprise or treachery, than from the technical work of sapping and battering. Putting aside such exceptional happenings as surprise or treachery, an honestly defended town could protract its resistance for long months, in the hope that the approach of winter, or the operations of a relieving army might compel the enemy to abandon his trenches and depart. Parma's extraordinary success at Antwerp, after a siege of fourteen months, was due to an exceptional feat of engineering—the blocking of the broad Scheldt by an immense fortified bridge which cut off all succour from the sea. The end was worth the cost, but it took more than a year to reach. At Ostend Archduke Albert ultimately forced the Dutch to depart on not illiberal terms—but it was only after four years of effort; and 40,000 Spanish troops, or more, had died in the trenches.

In spite of the marshes and water-courses of Holland, where general actions could not be fought, and sieges were immensely difficult, it is rather surprising that the Dutch were not finally worn down in the black years that followed the murder of William the Silent, and Parma's capture of Ghent and the long-defended Antwerp. That they endured is a wonderful testimony to their toughness, for the help that they got from abroad was always disappointing: the alliance with the Valois had ended disgracefully in the 'French Fury' of 1583. The English alliance with the parsimonious and tricky Queen Elizabeth, which ought to have been decisive, only staved off disaster without bringing victory. The best help which England gave was non-governmental—the continuous supply of good fighting men like Francis and Horace Vere, Morgan, and their companions, whose regiments were the flower of the army of the States—far better trusted than German hirelings or even the native levies of the land.

Of course the United Provinces might have been overpowered in the end, by mere brute force of numbers and money, if their master had not been distracted by the external troubles which came inevitably from the worldwide extension of his empire. If he had never been forced to turn his attention to other affairs, and had not been worried by the problems raised by Elizabeth of England, Henry of Navarre, the Turkish sultan, and the Morisco rebels at home; if there had been no need to think about the Ocean and the Indies, he might have concentrated a force that the Netherland rebels could not have faced.

The most potent of distracting problems was undoubtedly the condition of France, to which he was lured away to send his best general and his best troops from the Low Countries, at the critical moment in 1588–89, when his great Armada-scheme against England had just come to a disastrous end. To keep France from falling into the hands of a Huguenot king seemed at the moment more important than renewed attempts to crush the Dutch. It matters not whether Philip had made up his mind to support a dummy-king nominated by the League, or whether he entertained serious designs of placing the French crown on his own head or that of his daughter. In any case he transferred the main pressure of war from the Dutch frontier to northern France, and left his Netherland possessions exposed to the inroads of the first real general of mark whom the rebels had ever produced—Maurice of Nassau, the fortunate son of that most unfortunate commander William the Silent—who never won a battle in all his long military life.

While Alexander of Parma was relieving Paris and campaigning in Normandy with the flower of the old Spanish tercios, the long-despised Dutch army at last took the offensive under the guidance of a young general who was at once a skilled artillerist and engineer, a resourceful mover of troops in the field, and the patron of a new school of drill and tactics. The capture of Breda by Maurice in 1590, by surprise and stratagem, started a long series of successful offensive enterprises by the Dutch armies which had no parallel in the earlier years of the war. He went

The 'Wars of Religion' 203

on capturing town after town, while Alexander of Parma, being tangled up in the French War, was forced to leave the King's lands in the Netherlands under-garrisoned, and finally died, a worn-out man, at Arras in December 1592.

Without detracting from the obstinate endurance displayed by the rebels through the first twenty years of the war, it must be said that they were saved from subjection by two dominating facts. The first was the topography of the northern half of the Netherlands; the different fate of the Belgian half may be ascribed, not unfairly, to its inferior capacity for defence. Belgium is for the most part a rolling country of hill and dale, destitute, save along the Flemish coast, of the flat marsh areas and interminable waterways which preserved Holland. The second governing fact was the personal character of Philip II, whose minute and mistaken orders frustrated all the plans of his generals, imposed on them a policy which they knew to be ruinous, and distracted them at critical moments into enterprises against which they made vain protests. He viewed even the most loyal of them with unnecessary suspicion and jealousy. He threw away all the advantages which he possessed from having armies infinitely superior to those of the rebels, and generals of merit, to whom they opposed for a whole generation no single commander of capacity. Alva, Alexander of Parma, even Requescens and John of Austria were able to deal with the enemy in the field much as they pleased—it was only in sieges that the troubles began. William of Orange was no more of a general than Philip II himself; his campaigns are a record of disappointment, though as an administrator and propagandist he was of the first rank. His warlike kinsmen of the House of Nassau were a gallant but unlucky race—four of them fell in lost battles for a cause that seemed almost lost. It was reserved for the next generation to produce commanders of real capacity, Maurice and Frederic Henry, men of military talent such as their father never possessed.

Philip just survived long enough to hear of the first considerable Dutch victory in the open field—Tournhout (1597)—not a decisive one by any means, but a clear indication that the old military superiority of the Spanish hosts had passed away. Maurice of Nassau had routed a force of all arms on an open heath by a brilliant display of cavalry tactics. He won the day by attacking an army caught upon the march by a smashing blow with his horse alone—his infantry never reached the field till all was over. It is curious to note that in the last years of the War of Independence the Dutch cuirassiers, under Maurice's training, won a complete superiority over the Spanish lancers and 'herreruelos' or light horse. In the last great battle of the war, Nieuport (1600), it was the marked ascendancy of Maurice's troopers over their adversaries—who broke again and again—that settled the day, no less than the tough defensive power of Horace Vere's English foot regiments.

After the death of Philip II in 1598 it may be said that the last ten years of the War of Independence were spent in wasted efforts on both sides. Maurice of Nassau and the Dutch could see that there was no chance of winning the Catholic counties and duchies of the Southern Netherlands into a union with the Protestant North. Any such possibility had vanished when Alexander of Parma recovered Ghent and Antwerp, and the rebel faction in the south migrated or was exterminated. On the other hand, Philip, on his death-bed, had resigned himself to the idea that Holland was unconquerable, and left Belgium away from the Spanish Crown, giving it to his daughter Isabella Clara Eugenia, and her husband, the Austrian Archduke Albert. He apparently thought that the seven United Provinces of the North might consent to acknowledge some sort of sovereignty under Isabella, though it was hopeless to get them to recognize a Spanish king. With the experience of the last forty years before them, the Dutch refused any such negotiation, and the war went on.

Even when the French problem was disentangled from Spanish policy by the Peace of Vervins (1598) and Philip III could withdraw the armies that had so long been wasted in fights with Henry of Navarre, the Dutch remained unconquerable. After ten years of unnecessary strife a

The 'Wars of Religion' 205

truce in 1607 and a peace in 1609 split the old Burgundian heritage of the Netherlands into two separate states, a Protestant republic in the north under hereditary Stadtholders of the House of Nassau, a Catholic state in the south, which might have become a kingdom of Belgium, if only Albert and Isabella had been blessed with offspring, but which fell back into the unhappy condition of a Spanish province after the death of Isabella in 1633. The final settlement of the very anomalous boundaries between the two halves of the Low Countries was not to be reached for many a year. As to union, it was impossible. After Waterloo Great Britain tried to undo the work of 1609 and to create a single kingdom of the Netherlands, under the House of Nassau. But the Belgian revolution of 1830 proved the experiment impossible. Disunion to-day is the logical consequence of the atrocious perseverance of Philip II four centuries back ; by the ruthless use of sword and stake he tore the once united provinces into two irreconcilable communities.

The Wars of Religion in France, which for over thirty years synchronized with the Wars of Religion in the Low Countries, and were from time to time closely connected with them, display from the military point of view the most curious and interesting contrast with the struggle farther to the north.

Odd as it may seem, their nearest analogy is not to the Dutch War of Independence, but to the English Civil War of 1642–46. The Huguenot armies were like those of Charles I ; their strength lay in masses of chivalrous horsemen, valiant but undisciplined, backed by a wholly inadequate provision of infantry. The Catholic armies were distinctly inferior in the mounted arm, but had behind them the machinery of government (as had the Parliamentary armies of the English Civil War), the power of taxation, the support of the all-important capital city of the realm. They could use the convenient appeal to loyalty in a way that was impossible to the English Parliamentarians, since till 1589 the French Crown was technically contending with rebels. When the Two Houses at Westminster pretended to be fighting for the King, it was obviously an odious piece of hypocrisy. The French Catholic armies from 1562 to 1589 could be conveniently royalist, though their leaders were aware that Catherine de Medici, Charles IX and Henry III hated them with good reason, and longed for peace, even peace with heretics.

Nothing is more curious than the way in which the Huguenot party in France, which seemed helpless and insignificant in the days of Francis I and Henry II, merely contributing a certain amount of martyrs to the intermittent fires, suddenly flares up as a great fighting power in 1562. The armies that fought at Dreux or Jarnac were not, of course, entirely composed of dogmatic Calvinists, any more than the English ' New Model ' of 1645 was entirely composed of fanatical Independents with a tendency to 'levelling' or 'Fifth Monarchy' views. There was a strong nucleus of convinced Protestants in the Huguenot party, men like Coligny and La Noue, but they had strange comrades in the battle line. They met not only simple souls to whom the condition of the Church was repulsive—with its evil-living cardinals and pluralistic bishops and idle monks, and plain men like the Duke of Bouillon, who observed that he did not know much about the Bible, but could not stand the sight of decent *bourgeois* being sent to the stake because they had views of their own as to the mode of the presence of Christ in the sacramental wafer. There were much more doubtful elements in a Huguenot squadron of horse—discontented young soldiers from the wars of Italy in search of adventure, gentlemen with old family quarrels against a nearest neighbour of Catholic tendencies, broken men with a grievance against the Government, like that Sieur de Baubigny, who shot his old oppressor, the captive Marshal St. André, in cold blood, after the battle of Dreux ; or mere reckless swashbucklers like the cruel Baron des Adrets.

Even the leaders of the Huguenot cause did not always inspire confidence in their more sober followers. For many years the typical man of the party was the Admiral Coligny, who could be trusted as a truly religious man, austere, and a patriot—though a patriot generally in arms against his king. But his predecessor had been the genial dashing Louis of Condé, whose morals were those of a cavalry colonel rather than a Puritan, and his successor was that strange being Henry of Navarre. The Huguenot who was to become a king had little Protestant about him save a genuine dislike for the Catholic Church to which he was in the end to submit himself. Chivalrous in a way, but with a cynical outlook on mankind and womankind, entirely self-centred, though capable of generosity and self-denial when circumstances demanded, a jovial companion of a careless good humour, he was about as different a figure from Cromwell, Gustavus Adolphus, or William the Silent as could well be conceived. Yet for many years he led the Huguenot party, and was adored by those of his followers who knew him as the recklessly brave cavalry officer and the merry companion in adversity, without suspecting the depths of wiliness and selfishness that lay behind his frank and careless exterior.

A Huguenot army was always a rather amateur assembly of fighting men. Its commander could never be quite certain whether he could count 1,500 or 3,000 cavaliers behind him on a battle morning, if bad news had been coming in from the west or the south, to draw off local contingents to the protection of their own firesides, or if some powerful lord had quarrelled with another. The record was much like that of the Royalist army of Montrose in the next century, or the Highland gatherings of Charles Edward in 1745–46. And the remedy for French flightiness that was experimented upon—the hiring of solid squadrons of German *reiters*—was tried and found wanting. Like their contemporaries in the Dutch Wars, they looked for regular pay; and they seldom got it; for the Huguenot war-chest was always depleted and often empty. When they had been unpaid for a few weeks the *reiters* went home *en masse*, and left their general with a scanty following of 'die-hards', the genuine enthusiasts who stuck to the cause of 'the Religion'.

The Catholics had at their disposition much more solid

stuff, not merely the levies of their own half of the *noblesse*, who were similar material to the Huguenot cavalry, but the remnant of the old national army, the *compagnies d'ordonnance* of horse, and the old foot-regiments which had not been disbanded after the Peace of Cateau Cambrésis—Picardy, Champagne, Piedmont—with an inevitable Swiss contingent of steady pikemen. For all through the wars the Cantons continued to supply the troops that were due under the old 'Perpetual Peace' made with Francis I. Having the Government machinery of the greater part of the realm at their disposition, the Catholic party could raise taxes to pay their Swiss. Moreover, Philip of Spain was from the first ready to lend his veteran infantry from the Low Countries—there were 3,000 Spanish troops at Dreux, the earliest battle of the wars (1562). Later he supplied whole armies under Alexander of Parma, when the cause of the old Faith seemed to be flagging in the days of the 'League'.

The help which the Huguenots got from the parsimonious Queen of England was much more intermittent and ineffective. Elizabeth could never forget the way in which she had been tricked at the Peace of Amboise in 1563, when the Huguenots, granted toleration by the French Crown, turned against their ally, and marched along with the Catholics to evict the English garrison of Havre. Yet Elizabeth saw that it was very much to her interest that France should not fall into the hands of the Catholic party, the tools of Spain, and continued to supply the Protestant faction with men and money from time to time. She was well aware that Henry of Navarre was not to be trusted, but it was essential to keep strife alive across the Channel, lest the Spanish interest should dominate the whole of Western Europe.

Another analogy might be drawn between the French Wars of Religion and the English struggle between King and Parliament in 1642–46. In both the chief campaign might be going on between the main armies, but local wars were proceeding at the same time, which were singularly unconnected with the central strife. And it was almost

The 'Wars of Religion' 209

impossible to get the local armies of the West and North in England, and the West and South in France, to quit their bickering, and draw in for the conclusive struggle in the centre. The provincial commanders wanted to make an end of their neighbours of the opposite faction, in order to have their own hearths and homes safe. It was difficult to lure them away from their own districts, and when they were occasionally drawn into connexion with the main stress of the war, they were always liable to melt away in order to cope with some local danger of their own. Hence both in England and in France we can write narratives of side-campaigns in remote corners of the realm which seem to have no connexion with the main issue. Civil war went on in Shropshire or Yorkshire, in Provence or Gascony, in a most independent fashion. The brilliant campaigns of Lesdiguiéres in Provence and Dauphiné, or of Montrose in the Highlands have no direct influence on the main decision of the wars. At most they immobilized part of the enemy's potential strength, and prevented it from being utilized elsewhere. All that Montrose's astounding victories accomplished was that, after much delay, part of the Scottish army in England had to be distracted against him.

Sieges, though much less prominent in the French than in the Netherland Wars of Religion, were far more important in history than the sieges of the English civil strife. Looking at the art of war in general during those centuries, we are surprised at the lack of long and important leaguers in the English campaigns of 1642-46. This, no doubt, was largely owing to the fact that military architecture had languished in England since the reign of Henry VIII, and that few towns had more than their medieval enceinte walls, sometimes supplemented in a hasty way by lines of earthworks. Important places like Bristol changed hands rapidly, for want of sufficient modern improvements, when an army furnished with artillery came against them. And the longer sieges were generally protracted owing to the inefficient equipment of the attacking party rather than to the competence of the fortification of the beleaguered place.

There is nothing in the English wars to correspond to the long resistance of the all-important La Rochelle—where (as in other French ports) there had been good sixteenth-century improvements made, before the Huguenots took in hand supplementary outworks and redoubts. We gather that in some cases extemporized earthworks were added to old walls—which was called 'fortification à la Huguenotte'—and proved not ineffective, as at Montauban and elsewhere. Havre was a modern fortress, built by Henry II with the latest sixteenth-century designs, when he planned to make it the main defence of the Seine estuary, as a substitute for the old-fashioned Harfleur and Honfleur. And the fortresses of the northern and Alpine frontiers had been brought up to date during the later years of the long struggle with the Hapsburg power of Charles V. Undoubtedly France in 1560–90 contained many more defensible places than did England in 1642–46. But it was exceptional to find strongholds so well served with water-protection as were the towns of Holland; La Rochelle is an almost unique instance. And this, no doubt, accounts for the fact that sieges in the French 'Wars of Religion' play a not unimportant part, but did not constitute the main turning-points of the long strife, as did the sieges of the Netherlands. When they do occur, we find that, as in Holland, the best service was done by burgher companies defending their homes from the horrors of a sack, which sometimes approached in atrocity those which were habitually seen in the Netherlands when a Spanish army got into a long-beleaguered town.

In nearly all the pitched battles of the French wars we find the cavalry the preponderating arm, but this did not mean that the Huguenots, whose horsemen were their main strength, did not suffer defeat after defeat for want of a sufficient infantry backing. A fine example may be seen at Dreux, where the squadrons of Condé and Coligny cut up more than half the Catholic army, but, having dispersed themselves in pursuit and become exhausted, were driven off the field by Guise with the intact wing of the Catholic army, because their inadequate infantry force

The 'Wars of Religion' 211

could not hold up the enemy till the cavalry was once more collected and in order. At St. Denis Condé practically fought Montmorency with his horse alone, engaging only a few hundred arquebusiers, and had to draw off when his desperate charges came to an end. At Jarnac Condé—always a most rash commander—allowed himself to be brought to action when his infantry were on the march some miles away, and was beaten and killed in their absence. At Moncontour the cavalry on both sides used itself up in the early stages of the fight, and when the big battalions of the Catholic infantry came on the scene the Huguenot infantry, much inferior in number, was crushed and mostly cut to pieces. The horsemen, on the other hand, got together, and left the field without any excessive loss : but the foot-soldiery had perished wholesale. In the later years of the war Henry of Navarre shone entirely as a brilliant cavalry leader, not as a great strategist. When he came into collision with Alexander of Parma and the old Spanish infantry he never succeeded in dealing with them in a satisfactory fashion. But at Ivry, as at Fontaine Française, he showed what might be done against a less competent adversary by skilful and furious cavalry charges.

We leave the sixteenth century with cavalry still in the ascendant—as, indeed, it was to be during the greater part of the succeeding age. Infantry never came to its own till the invention of the bayonet put an end to the clumsy division of every unit into pikemen and musketeers—and enabled every musketeer to become his own pikeman.

CHAPTER XII

THE OCCULT IN THE SIXTEENTH CENTURY

WIZARDS and witches, spirits good and evil, incantations and forecasts, curses and spells, have been known in all ages and in almost all lands. They are not peculiar to any race or civilization or religious system. Not only were they as familiar to classic antiquity as to the Middle Ages, but the explorers of the sixteenth century found them well established among the Black Men of Africa and the Red Men of America. To deal with the Occult by one method or another is a common human impulse, as familiar to the lowest as to the highest type of intelligence. Folklore is full of it in every region of the world. If I have ventured to make a special note of the working of this tendency in the sixteenth century, it is because there was a specially complicated development of its phenomena in the century when the old ideas clashed with the new, when the most primitive conceptions of the preternatural survived alongside with the appearance of the most modern scepticisms, when the boundary between magic and science had not yet been drawn, when psychology could not be disentangled from religion, nor astrology from astronomy, nor chemistry from alchemy. Few disbelieved in witches, but it required a clever inquisitor to distinguish a 'white witch', who might be tolerated, from a 'black witch' who ought to be burnt. And how could one certainly differentiate between a prophesying mystic, who might be inspired, and another utterer of strange sayings who might be suffering from diabolical possession? Charlatans there certainly were, who deceived from malice aforethought, but self-deceivers were probably still more numerous. And many, no doubt, like the typical modern medium, started with a genuine belief in their own revelations, but when the phenomena refused to materialize, replaced them with conscious trickery to save their reputation, or earn their patron's gold. The net result of a study of the theories and practice of the men of the sixteenth century is very puzzling. The most diverse general conclusions might be drawn from a study of details—probably all general conclusions would be inaccurate, and (as I have already said in another place) we can only catalogue individual happenings, and must not pontificate in any cut-and-dried conclusions.

The oddest thing about the dealings of the sixteenth century with the occult is to note the contradictions between theory and practice. There were very few indeed who would have denied the existence of sorcery in various forms, or would have shrunk from authorizing its suppression by fire or rope, but there were a great many persons of importance who, while denouncing it in general terms, were quite ready to utilize it for their private ends. And these were not only obvious tyrants, criminals or degenerates, but princes and magnates of ordinary respectability. While commonplace wizards and witches were being burned wholesale, a certain number of more distinguished practitioners of the same arts enjoyed considerable court-influence. It was always open to critics to accuse their enemies of utilizing occult arts—such an accusation was not without effect even in the seventeenth century, when 'the Galigai' was indicted for exercising unholy domination over the regent Mary de Medici, in France, and dealing with the celebrated Dr. Forman was one of the most damaging insinuations made against the murderous Countess of Somerset in England.

Dealing with wizards or witches in high circles had not been unknown in earlier ages, though it was specially prominent in the sixteenth century. The idea was quite well known—as far back as the eighth century King Grimoald of Lombardy had been much plagued, according to Paulus Diaconus, by a wizard who spied out his plots in the form of a blue-bottle fly, while King Duffus of Scotland in the tenth century, according to Boece, had been afflicted by witches, who worked on him by the familiar method of melting down his image in wax—of which procedure this is the first example that I can recall. Macbeth's dealings with the Weird Sisters, about eighty years after the Duffus story, have a curious peculiarity—they were not (as one might have expected) emissaries of Satan—who would certainly have appeared in the legend if it had been written in the later Middle Ages, but sibyls, 'fates' or 'norns' from some primitive mythology. Shakespeare, following the legend carefully, does not make them 'raise the devil' in their incantations, but some powerful Spirit of the Waste—whom he oddly enough calls Hecate—a purely classical goddess of the infernal world.

All through medieval history similar tales crop up at not very frequent intervals. One or two Byzantine emperors are accused of having dabbled with magic. Robert of Artois was accused in 1332 of having suborned a witch named Divion, to kill his aunt and niece by sorcery, and then to enchant King Philip VI. The woman was burned—but he escaped overseas, to lay the foundations of the 'Hundred Years War'. Joan of Navarre, the widow of Henry IV, is found accused in the Rolls of Parliament of 1419 of having compassed the death of her stepson Henry V 'in the most high and horrible manner that can be conceived', i.e. by incantations made on her behalf by Roger Colles of Salisbury, and was shut up for two years in Pevensey Castle on the charge. A better-remembered case is that of Eleanor Duchess of Gloucester in 1441, who with an astrologer named Bolingbroke, and Margery Jourdain 'The Witch of the Eye', had not only presumed to inquire of the stars concerning the life of the young King Henry VI, but had actually, in proper necromantic style, melted a waxen image of him over a slow fire. If he had died her husband, the 'Good Duke Humphrey', would have come to the throne. The astrologer was hanged, the witch burned, and the Duchess banished to solitary confinement for life in the Isle of Man. She may very possibly have been guilty, as she was an ambitious and unscrupulous

The Occult in the Sixteenth Century 215

woman, but her trial was certainly exploited to the uttermost by Gloucester's political enemies.

In the black business of the trial of Joan of Arc, the prosecution tried to drag sorcery into the indictment. Not only were the maid's visions of saints, St. Michael, St. Catherine, and the rest, alleged to be either imposture or perhaps diabolical apparitions, but some play was made with matters which seem to be pure local folk-lore. Joan was said to have frequented an ancient oak-tree with a spring below it, which was known as the Fairies' tree of Bourlemont. She was said to have been seen dancing around it, and hanging garlands of flowers upon its branches. No doubt she did, in company with other village girls—trees and streams honoured by the fairies were common all over Christendom in the fifteenth century, and long after. But the fairies are distinctly not diabolical, as we shall have to note later on, when dealing with them. They were not children of the devil, but feckless creatures who belonged to quite a different scheme of superstition— whimsical and occasionally mischievous, but not destructive to the scheme of salvation. However, Joan's judges thought it worth while to add this petty accusation to the more weighty matters of her charge. It is distressing to find Shakespeare, in *Henry VI*, part I, turning Joan into a commonplace witch attended by fiends—in consonance with the most crude and vulgar English versions of her story. Let us hope that he was not personally responsible for those scenes in that patchwork play, which makes such havoc of dates and events.

I must diverge here for a moment to say that I have not any belief in a theory of medieval witchcraft which has been put about of late with great ingenuity. It is to the effect that the whole system was not primarily malignant nor destructive, but was a mysterious survival of a prehistoric nature-cult, connected with ritual intended to produce fertility. To use the words of a competent exponent of this view :

Underlying the Christian religion was a cult practised by many classes of the community, chiefly however by the most ignorant, or those in thinly inhabited regions. It can be traced back to pre-Christian times, and appears to be the ancient religion of Western Europe. A god, in human or animal form, was worshipped with well-defined rites : the organization was highly developed, and the ritual analogous to that of many ancient religions. The deity of the cult was incarnate in a man, woman, or animal, the animal form being apparently earlier than the human. On certain fixed festivals—May Eve, Midsummer Night, and November Eve (All Souls' Day) the votaries met to practise rites which were supposed to promote the fertility of animals, and less frequently of crops. The religious rites varied according to circumstances or the requirements of a people. They were orgiastic, and in late examples may have degenerated into a Bacchanalian revel. The most important feature was the adoration of a fertility god, who was worshipped with ceremonies of disgusting and indecent reverence, after which the assembly indulged in feasting and dances ending in hysterical orgies. The central figure of the revel was always a person more or less disguised, sometimes in semi-bestial shape, who represented the fertility-god, but was really the 'Grand Master' or high priest of the cult, taken to represent the supernatural being, and worshipped as such.

Many confessions of witches under torture, or of hysterical people suffering under auto-suggestion, can be alleged to support this theory or parts of it. But the general survey of medieval witchcraft seems to prove that it was almost invariably malignant and destructive, and that the idea that it centred in a propitiatory worship of the powers of fertility seldom or never emerges. If we investigate the confessions of the unfortunate wizards and witches, we find that they were, or said that they were, conscious that they had sold themselves to the Devil in most cases, or at least to spirits who had no place in the orthodox scheme of the supernatural. And in the large majority of cases they had sought power to harm enemies, or to win financial profit, with no thought of benevolence at large, or the cult of a benevolent nature-power.

As to the notion that the witch-fraternity were descendants of the worshippers of a primitive pre-Christian deity common to all prehistoric Europe, it must be remembered that the rites and ceremonies which they were supposed to practise are not particularly European, but found all over the world. In India, among the most out-of-the-way hill tribes,

The Occult in the Sixteenth Century

fertility festivals accompanied with human sacrifice in many cases were, and are still, known. And the North American Indians, who certainly can have had no truck with the European orgies, had similar legends and practices, as those who remember the story of Mondamin the slain and revived corn-god will remember.

If we are to look for pre-Christian survivals in fifteenth-century superstition, it is much safer to bear in mind the Fairies, who are certainly personified spirits of the wild and waste and the terrors of the night, freakish rather than universally malevolent. The organization of witch-societies, of which so many sixteenth- and seventeenth-century stories are full, is only found in certain regions—notably Scotland and South France; in England the tales of 'covines' and clubs, such as the Lancashire witches of the time of James I, are rare—though there are some stories from the North-country (where perhaps Scottish influence was felt) and one from Somerset. Normally the English witch or wizard operated alone, or only with the help of some near relative (daughter, wife or husband) as accomplice. And stories of 'Sabbaths' or great meetings of sorcerers are rather exceptional.

Wizardry, as I said before, is found at intervals all through the Middle Ages, but it is clear that its phenomena thicken up, and quite certainly the whole of Europe gets more packed with sorcery, as we draw near to the sixteenth century. In the days of Edward IV the miserable Clarence made some pretence that his wife and infant child had been bewitched rather than merely poisoned. In retaliation his royal brother employed the same insinuation of dark and unholy machinations. For Burdett and Stacey, Clarence's tools and confidants, were undoubtedly executed for conspiring against the King by sorcery as well as by more practical methods. Only two years after Clarence's death James III of Scotland seems in 1480 to have been making a careful study of his English contemporary's method in fratricide. His brother, John Earl of Mar, was accused of compassing treason with the aid of a whole band of occultists. While he himself was put to death secretly, no less than three warlocks and twelve witches were burnt at Edinburgh as his accomplices. Better remembered is the astounding accusation made by Richard III against his brother's widow, Queen Elizabeth Woodville and his mistress Jane Shore—strangely bracketed together—of having worked by sorcery against his health as well as his political rights.

The absurdity of many accusations of witchcraft does not disprove the fact that there were unscrupulous persons who actually meddled with it, for the most crude and selfish ends. The infamous Marshal of France, Gilles de Retz, kept three sorcerers—of whom the chief was an Italian—sold himself formally to the devil, and propitiated his master by human sacrifices, generally of young children. He had been promised in return wealth, power, and perpetual youth. There can be no doubt of the atrocities for which he was burned at Nantes in 1440.

Several of the more cowardly and treacherous of the Italian tyrants, who lived in constant fear of a well-deserved assassination, used to keep a domestic sorcerer, just as they would keep a domestic poisoner—sometimes the two functions could be discharged by the same person, for black magic always tends to run over the edge of scientific murder. And most tyrants tended to be superstitious—it was only the most capable and hard-hearted of them who despised the supernatural, and sought no aid from the servants of a devil whom they did not believe to exist. Oddly enough James III of Scotland, whom we have just had occasion to mention, was a perfect type of the degenerate fifteenth-century tyrant—he ought to have been born at Milan, not at Stirling from the fierce line of the Stuarts. He was superstitious, repulsively cowardly, cruel by fits and starts, a patron of art and music, a shirker of ceremony no less than of war, given to low-born favourites, and accused of every form of sexual vice. We think of Galeazzo Maria Sforza, or Filippo Maria Visconti as his spiritual kinsmen, instead of his stirring ancestors James I and II. And his son and grandson James IV and V reverted to the old adventurous type of the family. Was the reversion of

The Occult in the Sixteenth Century 219

James VI to timidity and superstition an example of Mendelian principles?

Renaissance influences, which might perhaps have been expected to have worked in the direction of scepticism with regard to sorcery—as they often did with regard to accepted religion and ordinary morality—seem at first to have strengthened rather than weakened the already prevailing trend of public opinion concerning the occult. For a few who doubted about magic—as about everything else in the way of orthodox belief—there seem to have been many who took up ideas from classical antiquity, and mixed them with ideas from primitive folk-lore. We find in the sixteenth-century stories that might have come out of Tacitus or Plutarch—and probably the persons concerned in them had actually been delving into classical authors. The accusation of 'majestas', high treason against the emperor, so often detailed by Tacitus, had as one of its most typical developments the charge of working against the imperial health by incantations, or by the less obvious method of consulting witches or 'mathematici' (occult calculators often in the astrological line) concerning the dates at which the sovereign might die. To fix a year or day for the Emperor's death was (when malcontents or conspirators were concerned) very near to contriving his decease, for the wish is father to the deed. The conception of conspiracy by astrological or other occult means went on right through the Roman Empire, into Christian days.

One of the last and most curious cases occurs in the time of Valens (364–83) when (as Ammianus Marcellinus relates at some length) a group of rather important courtiers were executed for inquiring about the unpopular Emperor's decease not by astrology but by 'table turning' in quite the nineteenth-century style. They had a round disk inscribed about its edge with the twenty-four letters of the alphabet : this was placed on a table of consecrated wood, and above it was hung a ring suspended on a linen thread. When the inquirers had said their spell, and asked who was to be the successor of Valens, the ring commenced to swing about, and touched in succession the letters THEOD

—on the edge of the disk. The company at once exclaimed that it must mean the prefect Theodorus, a most likely candidate for the succession of an invalid emperor who was childless. Unfortunately the matter got whispered about, whereupon the jealous Emperor put Theodorus to death—though there was no proof that he knew anything about the spiritualistic meeting—whose organizers shared the same fate. But the ring was right, for when Valens fell shortly afterwards at the battle of Adrianople, the virtuous Theodosius was his successor. Astrology, however, was much more popular than table-turning for these disloyal inquirers.

It is most interesting to find in the reign of Henry VIII several trials that immediately recall the old Roman habit of counting treason as implied by occult inquiry into the King's destined death. The first is that of the famous Edward Duke of Buckingham, whose fate Shakespeare has immortalized. One of the most damning clauses in his indictment is that he had got Nicholas Hopkins, a Carthusian friar of Hinton Priory, to cast the King's horoscope, and had got the answer that Henry should have no male issue, and that after him he (Buckingham) should wear the crown. Hopkins was hung when Buckingham was beheaded. Later in the reign Walter Lord Hungerford, who had no claim to the throne, but was a feudal tyrant in his own region, suffered for the same charge in 1541. He was apparently a Catholic malcontent, and kept a chaplain who not only called the King a heretic, but endeavoured to read his fate in the stars.

Henry VIII was a profound believer in the existence, if not in the efficiency, of sorcery practised to his own detriment. That at the time of the fall of his unfortunate second wife, Anne Boleyn, he seriously explained that the lady had practised witchcraft against him [1] may pass perhaps as the mere spite of a disillusioned husband. But it was undoubtedly conviction, and not hypocrisy, that caused him to get his parliament to pass the wide-spreading Statute against Witchcraft of 1541, which imposed the penalty of

[1] *Letters and Papers*, X, 199.

The Occult in the Sixteenth Century

death without benefit of clergy, on all convicted of practising invocations to destroy any man's person or goods, of making images of men, angels, devils or beasts, of founding prophecies on augury from beasts or fowls, of discovering by spells things lost or stolen, and—this is a curious addition against alchemists—of practising inventions to find gold or silver. In 1562 this astounding Act, which was little employed after Henry's death, was re-enacted in a much less horrible form, which subjected persons guilty of anything below murder to a mere year's imprisonment and four exposures in the pillory—only repeated and persistent use of sorcery making wizards or witches liable to a trial for felony. As a matter of fact there seem to have been in Elizabeth's reign comparatively few prosecutions for witchcraft—a great contrast with what happened in the reign of her successor, who was absolutely obsessed with the fear of sorcerers.

A certain amount of influence in the direction of common sense was undoubtedly exercised by the very notable book of Reginald Scott, *The Discovery of Witchcraft*. The author, a Kentish squire, commanded a company in the army raised to resist the Armada, was for some time a member of Parliament, and was a strenuous opponent of superstition of all sorts, somewhat inspired by the fact that as a Protestant he was under the impression that the Roman Church was at the bottom of all tales of the miraculous, whether saints, devils, or wizards were concerned. He took the very bold line that, so far as his experience went, witchcraft had only two sources—deliberate charlatanism, and mental delusion. He had come into touch with malicious people who tried to scare their neighbours for their own profit. 'One knave in a white sheet has cozened and abused a thousand, when Robin Goodfellow kept such a coil in the country; some never feared the devil but on a dark night.' Other impostors sold drugs and charms, to be applied to doubtful purposes. The name of witches was applied to those who were really but poisoners, soothsayers, and cozeners. There was nothing supernatural, but only fraud, in those who pretended to sell sovereign remedies and love-potions to fools. 'Robin Goodfellow was but a cozening merchant, and no devil indeed.' As to those who said that they were bewitched, they were either spiteful folks who wished to further a horrible charge upon a neighbour whom they disliked, or else persons distraught, who had visions and illusions, real enough to them but with no foundation of fact. Any one with a diseased mind might, from wantonness or unconscious prejudice, attribute his or her imagined sufferings to some unlucky resident in the same village—probably to an eccentric individual with no friends.

Scott had been much interested in such questions, apparently because he had seen a case of witch-condemnation on what he considered most absurd evidence—perhaps the trial at St. Osyth's in Essex in 1582, which led to several executions. Applying himself to research, he had frequented charlatans and found out some of their tricks—he even gives diagrams in his book to show how some apparently miraculous exhibitions of legerdemain were managed—one much resembles a modern feat of Maskelyne and Cooke ! The vulgar, he says, would indubitably have ascribed it to sorcery. Fortune-tellers had, on being cross-questioned, confessed to him the vanity of their science, which consisted in guessing what an inquirer wanted, and giving vague promises of an encouraging sort. He had several times suborned likely persons to make acquaintance with witches, and offer them bribes for an introduction to their 'familiar' demons—but to no effect : only fraud was discovered. Scott gives a supplementary excursus on what he himself believed about spirits and devils. He was of opinion that Satan and his crew were a reality, but worked by mental temptation to make unscrupulous people commit crimes : God would not permit him to do miracles, or to enable wicked men and women to do them. The idea was repulsive that an honest and worthy man could be afflicted by supernatural methods with the permission of the Deity. But of course an enemy might poison him with drugs got from some cozener—but that was not sorcery, only crime. He had come to the conclusion that Satan and his crew were incorporeal, and only worked by suggestion on the minds of the wicked. In that way men might be said to

The Occult in the Sixteenth Century 223

be inspired by a devil—who put into their brain ingenious and horrible ideas, when they were already contemplating sin. But wizards and witches who offered to enable these dupes to blast the crops, or to brew love-potions were only impostors. He relates some absurd stories of frauds that had come under his notice. A long chapter goes into the various classes of devils with strange names, each in charge of some vice—lechery, revenge, gluttony, wrath, covetousness, &c.

The only parts of the book in which Scott shows that he was still a man of the sixteenth century, are some curious chapters in which he allows that strange qualities may attach to some precious stones, and to certain beasts or other creatures. He says that he had seen what he calls ' natural magic ' in such things as the magnet, and the perspective glass—i.e. the telescope, and would not speculate as to how far such inventions might progress—e.g. the compass and the power of gunpowder would have been deemed diabolical inventions in an earlier age—but are really ' natural magic '. Alchemy he had investigated, and concluded to be a fraudulent practice of charlatans exploiting greedy princes or nobles.

This is altogether an extraordinary book for 1584. It had considerable influence, mainly on the educated classes, as might be expected. But not only did it provoke abuse from the ignorant, but many who professed to be scholars and specialists wrote angry replies, accusing the sceptic of being more of an unbeliever than a Protestant. When James the First came to the throne, and got the Act of 1603 passed by his parliament, he ordered the *Discovery of Witchcraft* to be burned by the common hangman! Scott certainly failed to destroy the superstition that he hated, but probably he had some part in bringing about the noticeable diminution of witch-trials which marked Elizabeth's reign. They did not entirely cease—there had been enough to provoke his indignation—probably (as I mentioned before) the St. Osyth hangings of 1582 may have brought about his book of 1584. Of the later trials for witchcraft in Elizabeth's long reign the most notorious was that of three unfortunate cottagers named Samuels at Worboys in 1593—they were the victims of the superstitious cruelty of two families of the local squirearchy, Cromwells and Throgmortons—who accumulated against them a mass of evidence from malicious children, who declared that they had been tormented by evil spirits with grotesque names set on them by Dame Samuels. They were hanged at the Huntingdon assizes of 1593 after a regular trial before the Justice of Assize. It may be some small defence for the working of English law in Elizabeth's time to remember that there are several cases in which persons accused of witchcraft were merely put in the pillory as impostors and charlatans, or acquitted as victims of local slander. That the Queen herself was no witch-hunter seems to be proved by the fact that, when plagued with toothache in 1578, she had private application made to Dr. Dee the well-known astrologer and spiritualist as to remedies, and once visited him to see spirits in his famous *specula* or magic mirror. Dee, a most extraordinary mixture of pretentiousness and simplicity, revelled for years in alleged intercourse with spirits, which might have cost him his life under a less broadminded (or free-thinking) sovereign than Elizabeth. He had a reputation abroad no less than in England, and received gifts from the eccentric Emperor Rudolf II, who was a great patron of astrologers.

All through the sixteenth century there was a controversy as to whether dealing with spirits meant dealing with the Devil, the 'prince of the powers of the air', or whether the world was full of non-diabolical spirits—occasionally benevolent, occasionally freakish and irrational, over whom a wizard might get control without mortal sin, and utilize their knowledge. These spirits were of the most diverse sort—some pure folk-lore creatures going back even to pre-Christian beliefs, such as fairies, brownies, cobolds, Jack-o'-lanterns, pixies, pucks (or pookahs in Ireland) or kelpies or nixies. Of these many were obviously mere personifications of the terrors of the night or of the waste, to which all human beings outside or inside Christendom were (or perhaps one should say *are*) liable. Reginald

Scott was quite certain of this. The kelpie who drowns travellers at a perilous ford, or the Jack-o'-lantern who leads him into dangerous morasses, or the cobold who haunts mines and causes explosions, are mere reflections of the danger which man suspects in the dark or in unknown surroundings. Pucks and pixies are the less malevolent spirits, gifted mainly with a misplaced sense of humour, which leads them to foolish practical jokes on poor mortals—Shakespeare has immortalized the type in the *Midsummer Night's Dream*. Strange as it may appear, the belief in these tricksy spirits long survived Shakespeare in remote corners of the land. You may perhaps hardly believe me when I say that only fifty years ago, in the 1880's of Queen Victoria's time, I met an old man in Cornwall who assured me that he had been pixie-led. On a foggy night he had been lured out of his lonely cottage by cries of help! and murder! in a neighbouring path, and having sallied forth with a cudgel was drawn some distance in the fog by the sounds, which suddenly ceased. Whereupon, trying to regain his domicile, he found himself completely lost, and wandered for two hours over a moorside perfectly familiar to him, without being able to find his own house. When the fog ceased and the moon came out, he was within a hundred yards of his starting-point, and his foot-tracks next day proved that he had been walking in something like a circle. He solemnly declared to me that only pixies could have misguided him in this nocturnal ramble. I may add that he was a total abstainer, and a prominent member of a Baptist congregation. This was a fine example of the way in which the 'terror of the night' can take a supernatural explanation even in modern times.

Fairies, a very primitive folk, are (I suppose) partly survivals from the pre-Christian creatures of the air, the forest and the waste—what the Greeks and Romans might have called nymphs and fauns, partly conceptions hatched in the simple brain to explain phenomena of a puzzling sort—'fairy rings', noises of the night, and illusions of the sight. The curious thing about them is the very definite cycle of folk-lore which grew up about them, their habits and their organization in a fairy realm with kings and queens. The *Romance of Thomas of Ercildoun*, the Border laird, and the Fairy queen, who was but a beautiful show, and hideous within, is but one among many illustrative tales which might be gathered together. Were the fairies malicious—stealers of changelings and so forth—or merely freakish? Fairy gifts sometimes melted away or turned to leaves and stones. Yet the goodwill of the fairies might take a human favourite through many dangers or difficulties. And that odd drudge-fairy the brownie did good turns to the housewife or the dairymaid without any thought of reward. The belief in fairies was dying out in the sixteenth century—but was to linger on long after its close. Already in the late fourteenth century Chaucer was complaining ' that now can no man see no elves mo ' though in days past

> The Elf queen and her jolly company
> Danced full oft in many a greene mead.

But Chaucer was quite wrong, it is clear, for Bishop Corbet of Oxford was writing about 1628 that fairies were common objects of the country-side down to the Reformation.

> Witness those rings and roundelays of theirs which yet remain,
> Were footed in Queen Mary's days on many a grassy plain.
> But since of late Elizabeth, and later James came in
> They never dance on any heath, as when the time hath bin.
> By which we note the fairies were of the Old Profession—
> Their songs perchance Ave Marys—their dances were procession!
> But now alas they all are dead—or gone beyond the seas.

While we may detect a temporary slackening of the repression of witchcraft and the general crusade of authority against the occult in the England of the later sixteenth century, this tendency was purely local and quite unparalleled by anything that was going on in other countries. Even in Scotland, which one would have expected to be more influenced by English psychology than other countries, the urge toward witch-hunting increased rather than diminished as the century went on. And in continental Europe, as in Scotland, the attempt to discover

The Occult in the Sixteenth Century 227

and suppress supposed unholy dealings with the nether world went on in full force far into the seventeenth century.

Not only were the Stuarts personally vigorous witch-hunters, but in the long intervals of minority which fell between one sovereign and another, the regencies which held power were equally active. And—what at first sight seems surprising—the transference of authority from the Catholics to the Calvinists made no difference in the attitude of the State towards the occult. If anything, the reformers were more busy against the warlock than their predecessors of the old religion. The last Stuart who reigned over an indisputably Catholic country, James V, was the nephew and younger contemporary of Henry VIII, whose habit of connecting treasonable intent with occult practices he seems to have copied with accuracy.

The great case was that of 1537 : what the Clarences and Courtenays were to Henry VIII, the House of Douglas was to his nephew. Its head, the Earl of Angus, was in exile in England, but his many relations and adherents were scattered over all Scotland. Having lost his French bride Madaleine, the daughter of Francis I, only seven weeks after she had landed at Leith, King James declared that she had been done to death by witchcraft, though it was notorious that she had been in bad health even before she quitted France. He arrested Janet Douglas, the dowager lady Glamys—the sister of Angus—her young son, the actual Lord Glamys, her second husband, Sir Archibald Campbell—a son of the Earl of Argyle—John Lyon, a kinsman, an apothecary and a friar, under charges of having wrought by witchcraft and poison, not only against the deceased Queen but against James V himself, as well as having kept up constant secret communication with the banished Angus—which was no doubt the real root of the matter. The unfortunate lady was burned at the stake—she was the person of highest rank who was ever executed as a witch. Her second husband escaped the fires by breaking his neck over the crags of Edinburgh Castle : he tried to descend from his prison by too short a rope. John Lyon was hanged—the young Lord Glamys was respited, but imprisoned for as long as King James lived. Accusations of sorcery were freely employed in political trials even before the witch-hunter-in-chief, James VI, assumed control over his realm. The Regent Murray, often conspired against before he was actually murdered, had Sir Walter Stuart, the Lyon King-at-Arms, executed for conspiring against him by witchcraft in 1588. He has a bad record as a burner—having been personally present at three separate holocausts at Edinburgh, St. Andrews, and Dundee in 1569. But these were apparently of persons of humble degree—the usual victims of superstition, not political conspirators.

The main cause of the dreadful tightening up of witch-hunting in the sixteenth century seems to have been the gradual acceptance in most countries—in England (as it chanced) latest of all, and not till the influence of James VI and I became decisive—of the theory that dealings with the supernatural were direct dealings with the Devil. As long as fortune-tellers, astrologers, vendors of charms and amulets, &c., were able to plead that they were helped by spirits of the air, 'elementals', fairies, &c., who were not emissaries of Satan, the prejudice against them was not so fatal. But when popular superstition came to the conclusion that all spirits were devils in disguise, the certainty of dreadful punishment became much greater, and there was little tolerance for any one who dabbled in the occult—whether he or she was a charlatan or (as was sometimes the case) a self-deluded believer in his or her revelations. It is curious to find that this view as to the diabolical origin of sorcery was in no wise conditioned by the fact that the country in which a hunt for witches was raised belonged to the Catholic or the Protestant half of Europe. The phenomena and the persecution was the same in Spain, Italy or France as in Scotland, Sweden, or Germany. Reading a detailed account of some proceedings at Fontarabia in Biscay, I found exactly the same accusations of 'overlooking' children, causing death among cattle, and injuring the goods of neighbours, that one finds in many Scottish trials. Very big holocausts of nests of wizards and witches are common to Sweden and Italy. The elaborate tales of organizations of circles or 'covines' of devil-worshippers, at which Satan himself was occasionally present, are to be found in France and in Scotland, with much the same disgusting and orgiastic details. A cynical observation which I once noted to the effect that the Scots, having got rid of the saints, had only the devils left, is quite without foundation. Thirty years before Luther nailed up his theses at Wittenberg, Pope Innocent VIII was issuing a bull in 1489 to bid his inquisitors deal with the numbers of both sexes 'who have intercourse with the infernal fiends, blight the marriage bed, blast the crops on the ground, and wither the grapes of the vineyard'. Hence a general witch-hunt in Northern Italy, in which more than 100 sorcerers were burnt in Piedmont only, and many more in the duchy of Milan. Such outbursts were common all through the century—in 1524 1,000 persons are said to have been burnt in the diocese of Como alone. In another profoundly Catholic country, Lorraine, the home of the Guises, the procurator general Nicolas Rémi sent, as he boasts in his *Demonalatria*, more than 800 wizards and witches to the stake during his sixteen years of office. The rites and ceremonies, witches' sabbaths, orgies, 'black masses', &c., which he attributes to them are much the same as those which were described by the Scottish victims of James VI, when they had been sufficiently racked and tortured.

There was a very crucial trial in Scotland in 1576, when James was only a child of ten, and therefore not responsible for what happened, which seems to me to mark the moment at which the public mind had come to the conclusion that all dealing with the occult, in which no direct intercourse with devils was confessed, was sorcery and worthy of death. This was the curious case of Elizabeth Dunlop, a cottager who dealt in the recovery of lost goods, the healing of diseases, and the selling of simples. She did not deny her trade, but professed that all her knowledge was derived from a spirit, one Thomas Reid who dwelt in fairyland, to which he had been snatched away after the battle of

Pinkie, thirty years back. He could, and did, resolve any hard problem which she might put to him, and she could always summon him by calling his name thrice. Although all her activities seem to have been directed to harmless or even laudable ends, and no mention of devils occurred either in the prosecution or the defence, she was condemned to death and burnt. The most damaging thing that she acknowledged was that her 'familiar' had once advised her to deny the faith that she took at the font, and come with him to Fairyland, to which (as she said) she gave a prompt refusal. The judges evidently considered that Tom Reid was a devil—like other 'familiars', and perhaps a more effective one than Bessie Dunlop would allow.

In other late sixteenth-century cases in which the fairies were implicated, the intentions of those who dealt with them were not so harmless as those of Bessie Dunlop. In the complicated Fowlis trial of 1590 the witches shot with 'elf arrows' at the images of those whom their suborners wished to harm, and brewed possets of poisonous stuff on recipes from Elfland. Undoubtedly here we have a mere instance of charlatanism, practised for gain by unscrupulous persons who traded on the superstition of the would-be murderers who paid them. The ends of justice were probably not defeated in this instance—the only surprise is that by 1590 malevolent purpose, usually attributed to the Fiend, was endeavoured to be shuffled off on to the comparatively innocuous fairies.

If we endeavour to get to the bottom of the widespread belief in malignant sorcery all over Europe, we must probably allow for several very different causes. And we shall find ourselves following the lines of that admirable person, Reginald Scott.

The first is the actual existence of charlatans, who practised evil arts for gain. They ranged from village witches, who would sell abortives to girls in trouble, or even poisons to persons who wanted to get rid of an unwanted relative, up to high-class conjurers who practised legerdemain, and used elaborate paraphernalia—skeletons, pentacles, fumigation—like the man who raised the devil for Benvenuto

Cellini—not entirely to the satisfaction of that very slippery artist—in the awe-inspiring circle of the Roman Colosseum. Such charlatans would be capable of doubling the part of sorcerer with that of astrologer, alchemist, or professional poisoner. They often were implicated in the shady side of politics.

Secondly, there would be a class of persons who practised sorcery not for mere gain, but for revenge, or hatred of enemies—sometimes from a general misanthropy developed from a hard life. Such malignant persons often believed in their own spells—had (as they believed) sold themselves to the Devil by drawing up some formal bond, or carrying out some unholy ceremony, which they conceived to be really operative in the way of selling their souls. If their evil wishing seemed to be corroborated by actual harm happening to an enemy—even after long months—they were convinced of their own power.

Thirdly, we have to allow for persons actually mentally diseased, cases in modern times for the lunatic asylum rather than the stake. They saw visions, went on impossible journeys, committed atrocities, indulged in orgies, all in pure imagination. There are many cases when a witch, who alleged herself to have been in some distant place on some evil errand, was demonstrated by credible witnesses to have been at home in a state of somnolence or apparent trance. Sorcery-hunters (unfortunately for these poor lunatics) were content to assert that a witch might send her soul or her semblance to work evil elsewhere, while her body remained torpid, so that evidence as to the position of the body did not prevent the accused from having been guilty of the sins of which she accused herself.

While some persons indicted for sorcery were actually insane from the first, many more were driven mad by the long and continuous tortures to which they were subjected, and after losing control of themselves gave wild replies to any allegations of crime which were made to them. When released from the torture, they often declared that they had no memory of having made these confessions, which were sometimes very curious and circumstantial. But the prosecuting authorities persisted in believing that such retractations were merely attempts to escape from conviction, and appear to have held that the more shocking a story appeared, the more likely was it to be true. The disciples of the Devil were capable of anything.

So much for the wizards and witches : I think that they all sort themselves into one of these four classes—the conscious charlatans, the malignant persons who believed that they had power to harm their enemies, the sheer lunatics, and the victims of torture, who made wild confessions when they had lost their self-control. It is obvious that an individual might belong to two of these classes, e.g. a charlatan under torture might own to crimes of which he was wholly innocent, though he was certainly a designing scoundrel. Or a malignant person under torture might allow that his or her evil intentions had been much more effective than was actually the case. And the mentally diseased individual might, with or without torture, run off into implicating in his or her revelations any one whom he or she looked upon with envy or dislike : the mania of imaginary persecution by neighbours or relatives is one of the most common forms of delusion. Again the person quite wrongly accused of sorcery without any grounds, might under the pressure of the rack or the thumbscrews, assume a character of the malignant sort, and, if forced to name accomplices, would probably designate any one against whom a grudge was felt.

It is a curious fact that a very large proportion of the evidence against witches, other than that which they gave against themselves under torture, came from children or very young persons under sixteen years of age. The judicious Reginald Scott ascribed this to the fact that children were often scared by nurses or injudicious parents with stories of bogies : ' in our childhood our mother's maids have so terrified us with tales of an ugly devil with horns on his head and fire in his mouth, that we started and were afraid when we heard one cry Boh ! ' Imaginative children would take any ugly or angry old man or woman for an evil-intentioned witch or wizard, and would romance to their elders as to the sights they had seen, or the words that had been uttered against them by the village outcast. But in some cases there seems a strong suggestion that malicious children repaid a curse or a box on the ears by inventing lying tales of marvels against the person who had offended them. Another probable cause of delations is the mere wish to attract attention to themselves by a strange story, which some children still display—and no doubt the young people of the sixteenth century were as liable to this foible as the children of to-day—a tale about the unpopular neighbour would be sure to attract sympathetic notice. Experience of modern times points to another source of delusion. A misplaced sense of humour often leads the young to silly practical jokes : cases of strange noises, displacement of furniture, breakage of crockery, and such-like phenomena have been often ascribed to 'poltergeists'—tricky and malevolent spirits—by the members of a simple household. There are numerous instances of these tiresome happenings in the witch-trials.

They continue to occur right down to this day, and when minutely investigated can generally be traced to some mischievous young person—sometimes a half-witted boy or girl—who delights in startling his or her elders. I remember two 'poltergeist' hauntings in my own day, which were discovered to be mere sleight of hand practised by boys or girls to puzzle the family or the neighbours. Sir Walter Scott quotes three eighteenth-century cases of the kind, where the imposition was detected. An almost equally certain case is that of the disturbances which worried the Wesley household in the youth of John and Samuel—any one reading the story with modern parallels before him cannot doubt that some of the young Wesleys were playing practical jokes of a rather malicious sort on a credulous father, and the rest of the family. Unfortunately such tricks in the sixteenth or seventeenth century sometimes led to accusations of witchcraft against persons in whose neighbourhood these unaccountable freaks of mischief occurred —though there was nothing supernatural at the bottom of the incidents, but only a very misplaced sense of humour.

There was thus a certain solid basis of fact underlying the widespread belief in sorcery which obsessed the average man in the sixteenth century. There were unscrupulous persons, from kings down to cottagers, who were desirous of injuring people whom they disliked by magic arts, and they could without great difficulty find designing charlatans who were prepared for their own profit to undertake evil practices, which ranged from 'raising the devil' down to providing 'dopes' or infectious ointments, or charms and amulets bringing ill luck, which were to be foisted upon some victim. The sorcerer's fee depended on the gullibility of the client who sought him out with evil purpose, and was very high when a sufficiently credulous and malignant inquirer came to hand. But I have come upon one delightful case, from north of the Tweed, where the warlock declared that the only effective method was to raise the Devil himself: but his client, after inquiring into the cost, remarked that the sum asked was much too great—and dropped the whole business.

It being granted that there existed wizards and witches, and persons small and great who were prepared to buy their services, a natural result was that when any person of some importance died suddenly, from causes other than some obvious disease, such as the plague or smallpox, and when it was known that they had enemies of an unscrupulous disposition, public opinion believed that sorcery had been used to kill them, or if not sorcery then poison. Sudden deaths which in these days would be put down by the physician to ptomaine poisoning, botulism, or appendicitis, would in 1500 have been ascribed to the successful machinations of criminals. What seems an obvious case of ptomaine poisoning was the sudden death of Lady Margaret Drummond, perhaps the secret wife of James IV of Scotland—perhaps only his mistress—who with her two sisters Euphemia and Sibylla died suddenly in acute agony a few hours after partaking of a meal together. Scottish public opinion held that they had been bewitched or poisoned from jealousy by another lady who had enjoyed the King's favour. Tainted food seems a more likely explanation of the common

The Occult in the Sixteenth Century 235

fate of the three ladies (1503). No one was tried or punished. An equally unconvincing story is that the Dauphin Francis, the eldest son of Francis I of France, had been poisoned in a draught of water given to him when heated at tennis-play, which had been handled by an Italian gentleman named Montecuculi, who was supposed to have been the agent of the Dauphin's famous sister-in-law Catherine de Medici, or perhaps of the Emperor Charles V. The unfortunate courtier was hung, drawn, and quartered—undoubtedly the Dauphin's death was due to natural causes (1537). A still wilder tale is that of Jeanne d'Albret, Queen of Navarre, who was alleged to have been poisoned by wearing a pair of gloves given her by Catherine de Medici (1572)—of which there is no evidence of any worth.

It is probable that several of the poison-murders attributed to Pope Alexander VI and his son Caesar Borgia were cases of common disease—but on the principle of 'cui prodest' the Pope was credited with the death of any one whose departure was profitable to him. That real poisoning, however, did sometimes occur is quite certain—Eric King of Sweden was undoubtedly made away with by mercury placed in his pea-soup, in 1577. He had been deposed and imprisoned, but revolts in his name breaking out, the Swedish privy council formally ordered—the document has been preserved—that he must be poisoned, or if he refused to take food, stifled or smothered. The pea-soup sufficed. Incidentally we may mention that Eric had, in his time, dabbled in astrology, imbibed a great fear of magical practices on the part of his brothers and his courtiers, and had put to death several persons of note for dealing with wizards. Sweden was as obsessed with fear of the occult as Scotland.

James I had been reared in an atmosphere of sorcery. The regents who had charge of his youth, from the Earl of Murray onward, had all been witch-burners, and he himself had gone through so many unpleasant adventures of kidnapping and treachery that his natural timidity had been enhanced by very reasonable fears of a sudden end.

Two of those who had exercised malign influence over his youth had been particularly notorious dabblers in the occult, the disreputable James Stuart Earl of Arran, and his own illegitimate cousin Francis Stuart Earl of Bothwell,[1] nephew of the more famous Bothwell who married Mary Queen of Scots. It was in the interest of the latter that the most elaborate of all alleged sorcery-plots was (as the King believed) set going, in the attempt of a 'covine' of some forty wizards and witches to wreck his ship, when he was bringing back from Norway his newly-married bride Anne of Denmark. Bothwell, fleeing from Scotland some time after, died at Naples much involved in stories of necromantic practices. But, indeed, an enormous proportion of the Scottish nobility of this period are accused of keeping domestic sorcerers—as, for example, the Earl of Huntly, who was killed at the battle of Corrichie (1563); Archibald Earl of Argyle, whose favourite witch urged him into unlucky battle against the Earl of Errol in 1594; Margaret Countess of Athol (1566); and the Earl of Gowrie, whose mysterious attempt to kidnap the King in 1600 has led to countless unsatisfactory explanations. Indeed, in so many trials of this period does advice from sorcerers turn up, that one is almost driven to believe that a family witch or wizard was as essential a part of a great Scottish household as a family astrologer is to that of an Indian rajah.

James believed every story of witchcraft that was brought to him, and he got a steady support from the majority of Scottish ministers, who are found prominent in most cases of witch-hunting, and showed considerable ingenuity in demolishing common-sense objections as to the impossibility or improbability of the charges that were brought against persons accused of sorcery. When we read of the details of some trials, in which it was solemnly held that baptizing a cat and casting it into the sea would infallibly produce a storm, or that anointing the cast-off linen of an intended victim with the venom of a crushed toad would bring

---

[1] The son of John Stuart, bastard son of James V, and of Jane Hepburn, sister of the infamous earl, who inherited her brother's title and estates.

The Occult in the Sixteenth Century 237

sickness on the late owner, or that by crying 'horse and hattock' to a broomstick a witch could cause it to carry her many miles through the air, we are filled with acute disappointment. The methods are so far more trivial than the very impressive old tricks of melting an image of an enemy in wax over a fire fed with dead men's bones : or of distilling liquor from the corpse of an unbaptized infant—which are at least gruesome and repulsive. But many witch-devices are simply trivial and silly—one can but wonder how any magistrate could have listened to the description of them, and then pronounce the awful condemnation to the stake.

The accession of James I to the English throne marks a distinct recrudescence of witch-hunting in England—it had been comparatively slack in the long reign of Elizabeth. It is started by the dreadful Statute 1 James I, which gives a far broader scope for persecution than Elizabeth's statute of 1562, for whereas malignant intent was required to be proved in the latter, the statute of James makes any practice of witchcraft, even when for beneficent ends, criminal. . The result was to be seen in trials of large groups of persons accused of associated action—a thing not much known in England before : the most notable was that of the famous 'Lancashire Witches' in 1613, which resulted in ten executions, beside one death in prison. These trials went on at a steady rate, though never so numerous as the contemporary Scottish cases. Their 'peak' in statistical figures occurs during the years 1646–49, when all that side of England which was in the hands of the Parliamentary party was full of witch-trials, largely the work of that malicious impostor Matthew Hopkins, who assumed the title of 'Witchfinder General', and went through the Eastern Counties trying suspected persons with his 'pricking', or test by the needle for Satan's marks. Persons designated by him as showing these marks were in many cases sent by the magistrates to the assizes to be tried and hanged. The House of Commons, then entirely in the hands of the Presbyterians, made itself partly responsible for all that happened—having sent down a commission of investigation in 1645, which reported that sorcery was prevalent in the Eastern Counties, and permitted Hopkins to continue his tours of inquiry. Oddly enough the mania died down when the Independents came into power under Cromwell—that sect being averse to what occasionally had taken the form of religious persecution when the Presbyterians had been addicted to it. This is one of the more unexpected results of the ascendancy of Cromwell, and is a little difficult to explain, but quite indubitable. The same effect was seen in Scotland after the Protector had conquered it—witch-hunting, very vigorous north of Tweed during the early years of the Civil War, dies down for several years during the rule of Monk and the Major-Generals after 1651, to revive again fiercely after 1660.

It is curious to find that the period when James I was inspiring the hunt after sorcerers in Scotland and England coincides with the most widespread and sanguinary inquisitory proceedings in France. The Councillor Pierre de Lancre and the President Espagnel of the Parliament of Bordeaux ravaged Southern Gascony and Bearn in 1609 with peculiar ferocity, and succeeded in extracting not only the usual confessions from tortured peasants, but very widespread acknowledgment of lycanthropy and cannibalism. More disgusting details as to the alleged ceremonies at 'Sabbaths' can be got from De Lancre's boastful account of his doings, than even from Rémi's stories from Lorraine, or King James's *Demonologia*. It is interesting to find that while in Great Britain the devil almost invariably appeared in the shape of a black man, or a large black cat or dog, when he wished to be adored, he was greatly addicted under the Pyrenees to taking the shape of a black goat or ram—which gave more opportunity for the display of horns —a thing rare on this side of the Channel. De Lancre sometimes burnt forty witches at a time, and his average monthly total of executions must have exceeded Rémi's, though his commission lasted for a much shorter period of years.

It is notable to find that while the executions for witchcraft in England died out with the last Stuarts, and

The Occult in the Sixteenth Century 239

while in France Louis XIV issued an *arrêt* against prosecutions in 1672, the custom went on much longer in Scotland, where a witch was burned by the sheriff-depute of Sutherland in 1722—well into the Hanoverian period—and in Spain there were cases right down to the end of the eighteenth century and the eve of the French Revolution.

But we have now strayed far beyond the sixteenth century. Though incredulity began to appear in our period, as witness the book of Reginald Scott, the gradual cessation of prosecution for sorcery belongs to the later seventeenth century, with which we are not concerned. And the first punishment of persons concerned in lawless and cruel witch-hunting appears in the reign of George II. The mild form which crusading against the votaries of the Occult takes to-day, is the prosecution for 'obtaining money under false pretences' of sibyls who, with more or less parade of mystery, tell fortunes for half a crown. The sixteenth century is a long way off.

INDEX

Adrian VI, Pope, 68–9 ; excommunicates Christian II of Denmark, 113
Alexander VI, Pope, his calamitous papacy, 16, 24–5, 31, 33, 65 ; uncertainty of crimes attributed to him, 235
Alexandria, commercial importance of, in fifteenth century, 158
Algiers, expedition of Charles V against, 167
Alva, Fernando, Duke of, his tyranny in the Netherlands, 92, 95
America, importance of the discovery of, 5, 45, 47, 91
Ammianus, his curious tale of 'table-turning', 219
Anabaptists, the, 86, 135
Antwerp, Parma's siege of, 201
Armada, the Spanish, 96, 202
Artillery, early superiority of the French in, 176, 193 ; successful employment of by the Turks, 157–8, 163–4
Artists, position of, in the Middle Ages, 52 ; and in the Renaissance, 53
Arundel, Thomas, Archbishop, his persecution of Lollards, 137
Asia and Europe, early clashes between, 142
Atella, siege of, 178
Avignon, the Popes at, 21–2

Ballad Poetry, English, 56
Barbarossa (Khaireddin), Barbary pirate, 166–7
Bartholomew, St., Massacre of, 133, 199 ; commemorated in the Vatican, 67, 76
Bayard, the Chevalier, 55, 106

Bajazet II, Sultan, negative results of his reign, 154–5
Belgrade, sieges of, 153, 162
Benvenuto Cellini, 130 ; his dealings with devils, 230–1
Beza, Theodore, at Orleans, 49
Bicocca, battle of, 185–6
Bogesund, battle of, 112
Boleyn, Anne, Queen, her fate, 102, 109 ; accused of witchcraft, 220
Borromeo, Carlo, St., his reforming work, 75 ; his miracles, 48, 141
Bosnia, apostasy to Mohammedanism, in, 153
Bothwell, Francis, Earl of, wizard, 236
Bouillon, Robert, Duke of, rebel to Charles V, 84, 191–2
Bourbon, Charles, the Constable, wins battle of Pavia, 188–9
Brill, the 'Beggars' at, 95
Brownists, the, persecuted by Elizabeth, 135
Bruno, Giordano, burnt at Rome, 40
Buckingham, Edward, Duke of, executed by Henry VIII, 101 ; his dealings with astrologers, 220
Buda, captured by the Turks, 164
Burgundy, strife for the inheritance of, 174
Burleigh, William Cecil, Lord, his opportunist policy, 134, 138

Cadiz, English sack of, 96
Caesar-worship, the futility of, 7–8
Calvin, John, 40, 56
Cambray, League of, 155
Caraffa family, the, 72 ; oppressed by Pius IV, 74

Cardona, Ramon de, Spanish general at Ravenna, 180-2
Carlyle, Thomas, on 'Heroes', 62
Catharine of Aragon, Queen, 108
Catherine de Medici, Queen of France, her troubles and policy, 133-4; her dealings with the Huguenots, 198-9, 206
Cerignola, battle of, Gonsalvo de Cordova's triumph at, 178-9
Cerissoles, battle of, 197
Cervantes, Miguel, his literary work, 58-9
Charlemagne, the Emperor, 18, 25
Charles V, Emperor, his early career, 81-2; his African Wars, 82-3; his long struggle with France, 83-4; his abdication, 85; his religious policy, 86-7
Charles VIII of France, and Crusading ideas, 13, 64; his triumph at Fornovo, 177; Italian campaign of, 177-8
Charles the Rash of Burgundy, his wars, 174
Chaucer, Geoffrey, on relics, 49
Christian II, King of Denmark, his atrocities, 112, 113; his dealings with religion, 113; expelled and imprisoned, 114
Clarence, George, Duke of, prosecuted for witchcraft, 217
Clement VI, Pope, election of, starts the 'Great Schism', 21
Clement VII, Pope, his dealings with the Reformation, and with Charles V, 70; and with Henry VIII of England, 102
Clement VIII, Pope, annexes Ferrara, 78; receives Henry of Navarre into communion, 79
Cognac, League of, 72, 86
Coligny, Gaspard, Huguenot chief, 206-7
Colonna, Fabrizio, condottiere general, 179, 181
Colonna, Prosper, condottiere general, wins battle of Bicocca, 185; his reputation, 191
Comines, Philip de, his outlook on history, 33

'Conciliar Movement', the, 22-4
Condé, Louis, Prince of, 207
Conquistadors, the, 45
Constantinople, taken by the Crusaders, 14; taken by Mahomet II, 152
Convocation, dealings of Henry VIII with, 102-3
Copernicus, Nicolas, destroys the geocentric theory, 42; his works proscribed, 74
Corbet, Richard, Bishop of Oxford, on Fairies, 226
Cordova, Gonsalvo de, Spanish General, his successful campaigns in Italy, 178-80
Cranmer, Thomas, Archbishop, 109, 138
Cromwell, Thomas, his character and fate, 101, 131-2; his vandalism in destruction, 49
Crusades, the, 11-14, 15, 31
Cumming, Dr., his political prophecies, 6

Dabek, battle of, 157
Dante, political views of, 25
Demonologia, King James I's book on Witchcraft, 238
Denis, St., battle of, 211
Denmark, wars of, with Sweden, 111, 112
Diaz, Bartholomew, rounds the Cape of Good Hope, 159
Discovery of Witchcraft, Reginald Scott's, 221, 223; burned by James I, 223
Dreux, battle of, 206, 210
Drummond, the Lady Margaret and her sisters, supposed murder of, by witchcraft, 234-5
Duffus, King of Scotland, destroyed by witches, 213, 214
Dunlop, Bessie, her trial for witchcraft, 229-30
Dürer, Albert, and the Dance of Death, 37
Dutch War of Independence, the, 198-205

Earthly Paradise, the situation of, 43

Index 243

Edward IV and his period, 34-5; uses accusations of witchcraft, 217

Egmont, Larmoral de, victorious at Gravelines, 198; executed by Alva, 95

El Dorado, 45

Elizabeth, Queen, excommunicated by Pius V, 75; her unscrupulous opportunism, 134; her dealings with religious problems, 135; her alliance with the Dutch, 201; and with the Huguenots, 208; her legislation concerning witchcraft, 221, 224; her dealings with Dr. Dee, 224

Elizabeth Woodville, Queen, 36; accused of sorcery, 218

Erasmus, his activities, 32, 54

Ercildoun, Thomas of, and the Fairy Queen, 226

Eric, King of Sweden, persecutes wizards, 235; poisoned in prison, 235

Eugenius IV, Pope, his contest with the Councils, 23

Exploration, importance of, in fifteenth and sixteenth centuries, 43-5

Fairies, the, their origin, 217; their character, 225, 227

Ferdinand of Aragon, his Italian Wars, 175, 178, 180

Ferdinand I, Emperor, his religious policy, 90, 131; his wars with Sultan Soliman, 164-5, 168-9

Fire-arms, importance of, growing, 176, 178, 181, 184

Foix, Gaston de, French General at Ravenna, 180-2

Fornovo, battle of, 177

Fowlis family, witchcraft in the, 230

Franc-archers, French infantry, their failure in the field, 192

Francis I of France, his alliance with the Sultan, 64; his successful tactics at Marignano, 184; defeated at Pavia, 107-9

Francis, dauphin of France, his death attributed to poisoning, 39, 235

Frederic I, of Denmark, his religious troubles, 131

Frederic II, Emperor, his struggle with the Papacy, 27-30

Frederic III, Emperor, his disastrous reign, 30

Gama, Vasco da, opens the sea-route to India, 159

Gardiner, Stephen, Bishop, last clerical Chancellor, 5

Garigliano, battle of the, Gonsalvo de Cordova's tactics at, 179-80

Gendarmerie, the French *compagnies d'ordonnance*, embodied by Charles VIII, 192; their efficiency, 193

Genghis Khan, conquests of, 142

Geocentric theory, the, 39, 40; disproved by Copernicus, 74

Geography, limits of medieval, 40-7

Glamys, Janet, Lady, burned for witchcraft, 227

Gloucester, Eleanor, Duchess of, prosecuted for witchcraft, 214

'Golden Age', the, 3, 5

Gravelines, battle of, 197-8

'Great Schism', the, 18-21

Gregory XIII, Pope, his reformed calendar, 76; his policy, 76-7

Grimoald, King of Lombardy, and the wizard, 213

Guelders, Charles, Duke of, 84, 191

Gustavus Vasa, king of Sweden, his early adventures, 115; crowned king of Sweden, 117; his character, 118; his dealings with the Swedish Church, 118-19; at Diet of Westeräs, 120-2; conforms to Lutheranism, 123; his political troubles, 125-6

Hapsburg, origins of the House of, 27, 29; and *see* under names of sovereigns

Havre, military importance of, 210

Heaven, medieval conceptions of, 44

244 The Sixteenth Century

Heiligerlee, battle of, 200
Hell, medieval conceptions of, 43-4
Henry V, of England, his dream of a Crusade, 13
Henry VII, of England, a Renaissance king, 53
Henry VIII, his character, 99 ; his ruthlessness, 101 ; his plunder of the monasteries, 102 ; 'the King's Religion', 102, 107 ; his futile wars, 104, 106 ; his debasement of the coinage, 107 ; his dealings with Convocation, 108 ; his wasted energies, 109-10 ; his legislation against witchcraft, 220-1
Henry IV of France, 68, 199 ; his character, 207 ; his military talent, 211
Henry, the Navigator, of Portugal, his explorations, 43, 159
Hereford *Mappa Mundi*, the, 42-3
Hesiod, and the Series of Ages, 6
Historical perspective, origins of, 4
Hobbes, Thomas, and the Natural Man, 60-1
Hopkins, Matthew, the 'witchfinder general', 237
Hopkins, Nicholas, astrologer, executed, 39, 220
Howard, Queen, Catherine, her fate, 109
Huguenots, the French, their strength and weakness, 205-7
Hungary, the buffer-state against the Turks, 29, 146, 150 ; ruin of, 161-3
Hungerford, Walter, Lord, dabbles in witchcraft, 220
Huss, John, burnt at Constance, 29, 33
Hussite Wars, the, 15, 29, 32

Index Librorum Prohibitorum, the, 73
India, the sea-route to, ruins Venice, 159
Infantry, the French, 192-3 ; the Spanish, 194-5 ; the English, 106 ; the Swiss, 182
Innocent VIII, Pope, legislates against witchcraft, 229

Inquisition, the Roman, 73
Isabella, daughter of Philip II, sovereign of the Netherlands, 204-5
Italy, decadent state of in the late sixteenth century, 66-7 ; witchcraft in, 227

James I (and VI), his zeal against witchcraft, 223, 235 ; his supposed persecution by witches, 236 ; his legislation against them, 237 ; burns Reginald Scott's book, 223
James III, king of Scotland, prosecutes witches, 217-18
James IV, of Scotland, excommunicated, 20
James V, of Scotland, persecutes wizards and witches, 227
Janissaries, the, their military capacity, 148 ; its decay, 171
Jeanne d'Albret, queen of Navarre, her death attributed to poisoning, 39, 235
Jesuits, the, their activities, 45 ; encouraged by Paul III, 79 ; persecuted by Queen Elizabeth, 135
Joan of Arc, her martyrdom, 33 ; prosecuted for witchcraft, 215
Joan of Navarre, queen of Henry IV, prosecuted for witchcraft, 214
John of Austria, Don, Governor of the Netherlands, 96 ; wins battle of Lepanto, 170
John Cantacuzenus, Emperor, calls the Turks into Europe, 146
John XXIII, Pope, election and deposition of, 21-3
Julian the Apostate, Emperor, 5
Julius II, Pope, 18 ; his political designs, 65
Julius III, Pope, his policy, 71

Kossovo, battle of, ends the Serbian kingdom, 147

Lainez, James, Superior of the Jesuits, 79
Lancashire witches, the, 217, 237

Index   245

Lancre, Pierre de, burns witches in Gascony, 238
La Noue, François, his ideas of a Crusade, 13 ; deprecates alliance with the Turk, 64
La Rochelle, sieges of, 210
Laurentius a Valla, and the Donation of Constantine, 32
Laymen, supersede clergy in official posts, 50-1
League of Nations, the, its difficulties, 17
Legions, the old French, 192-3 ; in the Huguenot wars, 208
Leo X, Pope, his policy, 65, 70
Lepanto, battle of, 167-70
Leyden, siege of, 200
Lollards, the, their influence in England, 137
Lopez, Dr., his plot against Queen Elizabeth, 39, 135
Louis I, the Great, king of Hungary, overruns the Balkan Peninsula, 146
Louis II, king of Hungary, slain at Mohacs, 162
Louis XI, of France, his character, 33
Luther, Martin, 65, 138, 144

Macbeth and the witches, 214
Machiavelli, Niccolo, 55, 57
Mahomet II, Sultan, his successful wars, 150-1 ; takes Constantinople, 151 ; conquers the Balkan Peninsula, 153 ; raids Italy, 154
'Majestas' in ancient Rome, 219
Mar, John, Earl of, executed for sorcery, 217
Margaret of Parma, Regent of the Netherlands, 94-5
Marignano, battle of, 183-4
Marlowe, Christopher, his dramas, 59
Martin V, Pope, stops Conciliar reform, 22, 32
' Maundeville ', Sir John, his apocryphal travels, 47
Maurice of Nassau, his generalship, 202, 204
Maximilian I, Emperor, 80, 174-5

Medici, Giovanni dei, his ' Black Bands ', 191
Melville, Sir James, his autobiography, 55
Mexico, the Conquisadors in, 45, 89, 91
Miracles, medieval conception of, 47
Mohammedan Invasions, the, 11, 29 ; and *see* Turks
Moncontour, battle of, 211
Montmorency, Anne, the Constable, defeated at St. Quentin, 197-8 ; at Dreux, 210 ; killed at St. Denis, 211
More, Sir Thomas, 34 ; a historian, 54 ; his martyrdom under Henry VIII, 101, 138
Murad I, Sultan, the wars of, 146-7 ; Murad II, Sultan, his wars, 150-1
Murray, James, Earl of, Regent of Scotland, a witch-burner, 228

Nassau, the House of, 203-4
Nemours, Louis, Duke of, killed at Cerignola, 179
Nicopolis, battle of, 13, 156
Nieuport, battle of, 204
Northumberland, John Dudley, Duke of, his career and ambitions, 122
North-west Passage, the, 47
Notitia Dignitatum, the, 9
Novara, battle of, 182
Nuremberg Chronicle, the, and the End of the World, 36-7

Oldcastle, Sir John, his disputation with Archbishop Arundel, 137
Opportunists of the sixteenth century, varieties of, 128-33
Orchan, Turkish ruler, his organization of the Ottomans, 148
Orosius, his conception of history, 4, 9, 10
Ostend, long siege of, 200-1
Osyth, St., witch trials at, 222
Otranto, sacked by the Turks, 154

Paganism, the decay of, 7-9

246 The Sixteenth Century

Palaeologi, weakness of the Emperors of that House, 144–6
Paleario, Antonio, burnt at Rome, 73
Papacy, the, the theory of, 16–18; its conflict with the Holy Roman Empire, 16; attempted reform of, 18–25; *see also* under names of popes
Parliamentarianism, modern unpopularity of, 61
Parma, Alexander, Duke of, 201, 203, 204, 208, 211
Paston Letters, the, 34
Paul III, Pope, his policy, 70–1
Paul IV, Pope, his political importance, 71–3
Pavia, battle of, 187–9
Pessimism in historical thought, 5–6
Petersen, Olaf, first Protestant archbishop of Upsala, 123
Philibert of Savoy, wins battle of St. Quentin, 197
Philip II of Spain, his policy, 89, 90; resources of his empire, 91–2; his dealings with the Netherlands, 93–5; his disasters, 91–6
'Philosophy of History', the, a misconception, 2
'Pilgrimage of Grace', the, 103
Pius II, his Crusading schemes, 15–24
Pius IV, Pope, and the Council of Trent, 74
Pius V, Pope, his policy, 75
Pixies, malicious fairies, their habits, 225
Political prophecy, the futility of, 2
Polo, Marco, his travels, 43, 47
'Poltergeists', stories of, 233
Portugal, early commercial importance of, 91, 159, 160
Prevesa, naval battle of, 155
Purgatory, St. Patrick's, 43

Quadra, Bishop, ambassador of Philip II, 52

Ravenna, battle of, 180–2
Relics, medieval veneration for, 49

Rémi, Nicolas, persecutes witches in Lorraine, 229, 238
Renaissance, the, a dissolvent not a reconstructive movement in morals, 138–41
Retz, Gilles de, Marshal, his practice of witchcraft, 218
Richard of Cornwall, elected emperor, 26
Richard III and his character, 35–6; persecutes witchcraft, 218
Ridanieh, battle of, 158
Ridolfi Plot, the, 75
'Rising in the North' the, 94
Robert of Artois, employs witches, 214
'Robin Goodfellow', malevolent fairy, 221–2
Robinson, John, Bishop of Bristol, last English clerical ambassador, 51
Rousseau, Jean Jacques, his social theories, 61

'Sabbaths' of witches, 215–16
Saint-worship, Protestant hatred of, 48
St. Quentin, battle of, 197
Scanderbeg (John Castriot), his struggles against the Turks, 148, 152
Schmalkaldic League, dealings of French kings with, 64, 84
Scholastic Philosophy, the, 38–9
Scotland, witchcraft in, 213, 214, 217, 227, 229, 235, 236
Scott, Reginald, his *Discovery of Witchcraft*, 221, 223
Selim II, Sultan, his conquest of Armenia, Syria and Egypt, 156–8
Seminara, battle of, 178
Septima Aetas Mundi, the, 6
Serbs, dominant in Balkan Peninsula in the fourteenth century, 145; crushed by the Turks, 147
Servetus, Michael, executed at Geneva, 40
Shakespeare, William, his dramas, 57, 59–60
Sigismund, Emperor, his ambitions, 28–9

Index

Sin and Grace, the conception of, 10
Sixtus V, Pope, his policy, 77
Slaghoek, Dietrich, unscrupulous minister of Christian II, 113
Soliman, Turkish Sultan, takes Rhodes, 160; invades Hungary, 161; takes Belgrade, 162; wins battle of Mohacs and conquers Hungary, 163; besieges Vienna, 165; leagued with France, 166, 169; his Persian wars, 167-9; becomes master of Tunis and Algiers, 167-8; his later wars with the Hapsburgs, 168-70
Speier, Diet of, 86
Spurs, battle of the, 106
Stephen Dushan, king of Serbia, his career, 145
Stillington, Bishop Robert, his political intrigues, 36
Stradiots, Light Cavalry, used by the Venetians, 177; and by the French, 193
Sture, Niels, impostor, 120
Sture, Steno II, last Administrator of Sweden, 112
Surrey, Thomas Howard, Earl of, executed by Henry VIII, 103
Sweden, introduction of Protestantism into, 119, 125; *see also* under Gustavus I
Swiss, the, rise of military power of the, 174; their territorial ambitions, 175; triumph of the, 182-3; checked by French tactics, 182; and by Spanish tactics, 184; in the Huguenot Wars, 208
Szigeth, siege of, 170

Tartar invasion of the thirteenth century, 143
Tchaldiran, battle of, 157
Telemachus, St., his martyrdom, 8
Thermes, des, Paul, French Marshal, defeated at Gravelines, 198
Timar system, the Turkish military feudalism, 149-50; its decay, 171-2

Toleration, religious, slow growth of, 136-7
Torregiano, Pietro, employed by Henry VII, 53
Touman Bey, last Mameluke Sultan of Egypt, 157
Tournhout, battle of, 203-4
Trent, Council of, 71-3
Trolle, Gustavus, Archbishop, his complicity in crimes of Christian II, 112-13, 116
Tunis, expedition of Charles V against, 167
Turks, the Ottoman, their first landing in Europe, 146-8; *see* under names of Sultans

Urban VI, Pope, election of, 21

Valens, the Emperor, prosecutes 'table turners', 219
Varna, battle of, 13, 156
Venice, selfish policy of, 15; her mercantile ambition, 144; her neglect of the Turkish danger, 151-2; her wars with Mahomet II, 153; and with Bajazet II, 155; her commercial monopoly injured by Selim II, 158; and by the Portuguese discovery of the sea route to India, 159
Villon, François, his literary position, 59
Vinci, Leonardo da, 53

Wells, Mr. H. G., his conceptions of history, 4
Wesley family, the, and their Poltergeist, 233
Westerås, the Diet of, foundation of Swedish Protestantism, 120-2
William of Orange, his ineffective campaigns, 199-203
Witchcraft, world-wide belief in, 211-13
Wolsey, Thomas, Cardinal, his foibles and fate, 51, 103, 108
Worboys, witch-trials at, 224
Wycliffite Movement, the, 32

Xavier, St. Francis, his missionary work, 46

For Product Safety Concerns and Information please contact our EU
representative GPSR@taylorandfrancis.com
Taylor & Francis Verlag GmbH, Kaufingerstraße 24, 80331 München, Germany

www.ingramcontent.com/pod-product-compliance
Lightning Source LLC
Chambersburg PA
CBHW070723020526
44116CB00031B/1402